1543

Nicolaus Copernicus publishes his work on the orbital movements of heavenly bodies, arguing that the Earth moved around the Sun.

1555

The Peace of Augsburg officially recognises the Protestant religion in Germany.

1558

In Spain, Philip II takes a hard line on religious dissent, persecuting thousands of Lutherans, Jews and Moriscos, the descendants of the Moors.

1567

The Duke of Alba becomes governor of the Spanish Netherlands. His brutality pushes the Dutch into a war of liberation.

1545

The discovery of silver in Bolivia stimulates a new wave of immigration.

1562

The English privateer John Hawkins makes his first speculative voyage to the Caribbean.

1550

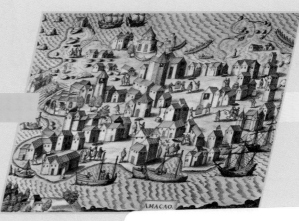

c.1550

Kalala Ilunga takes power in the Luba Empire and greatly extends the Central African territory under its control.

1552-6

Tsar Ivan IV, 'the Terrible', opens the way for Russian expansion into Siberia by conquering the eastern khanates of Kazan and Astrakhan.

1557

The Chinese government grants Portugal a lease on the island of Macao as a trading base in return for tribute payments.

67

n fleet aro de Mendaña reaches the Solomon Islands.

EUROPE

1571
The European victory at the naval Battle of Lepanto prevents Ottoman mastery over the Mediterranean.

1572
On the eve of St Bartholomew's Day, Catholics launch a massacre of Huguenot Protestants in Paris.

E
b
jo

AMERICA

1577
Francis Drake passes thr
Magellan Strait to attack
on the Pacific coast of S
He sails on to make the
circumnavigation c

1570

AFRICA

1570
Portuguese troops are sent to aid Diego I of Kongo when his invasion – encouraged by the Portuguese – of Ndongo territory to the south of his kingdom backfires.

1578
Sultan al-Mansur defeats a Portuguese invasion force at the Battle of the Three Kings. Under his rule Morocco experiences a golden age.

15
The Po
Fort Jes
(in wha
to guar
African p
Ottoman

ASIA

1569–70

Emperor Akbar embarks on the construction of a new Mughal capital at Fatehpur Sikri.

1573
Oda Nobunaga deposes the last Ashikaga shogun of Japan.

Sha
on
cap
emp
an ir
build

OCEANIA

DISCOVERY AND RELIGIOUS CRISIS

1492 – 1648

PUBLISHED BY THE READER'S DIGEST ASSOCIATION LIMITED
LONDON • NEW YORK • SYDNEY • MONTREAL

A whole new world On his first westard voyage, Columbus's last port of call was Hispaniola ('Little Spain', below), the second-largest island in the Caribbean, which today is split between the Dominican Republic and Haiti. He built the first, unsuccessful, European settlement there. Later, his brother Bartolomé founded Santo Domingo, now the capital of the Dominican Republic and the oldest European city in the Americas.

EUROPE

Renaissance popes – Rome's secular rulers

The Holy See was plunged into crisis by a most unspiritual lust for power and pleasure demonstrated by a succession of popes. Only vigorous reform could stop the rot.

Spiritually, the Roman Catholic Curia was at a low point at the start of the 16th century. Excess reigned within the Vatican's precincts as a succession of popes enjoyed lives of unbridled extravagance, abandoning the traditional Christian virtues of altruism and self-denial. In the view of the papacy's many critics, Rome had become the Sodom and Gomorrah of the age. The nadir was reached when the immensely rich Spaniard Rodrigo Borgia ascended the papal throne in 1492 as Alexander VI.

An imposing and adept figure in international affairs, Alexander brokered the 1494 Treaty of Tordesillas, which divided the uncharted lands of the non-Christian world into Spanish and Portuguese spheres of influence. Yet his abilities were eclipsed by the worldliness of his conduct and his ruthless pursuit of his own family's interests. Despite his supposedly spiritual office, he maintained an extensive network of concubines: his favourite, Vanozza Catanei, bore him four children, upon whom the 'celibate' Catholic pope lavished high posts and honours. The eldest of the four, Cesare Borgia, was archbishop of Valencia at the age of 16 and a cardinal the following year. Said to be the handsomest man in Italy, the young Cesare shared Alexander's taste for sexual adventure, and there were even accusations of incest when Alexander's daughter Lucrezia bore an illegitimate child: both Alexander and Cesare were rumoured to be the father.

The two Borgias did more than swell the Church's growing reputation for corruption: they alienated the college of cardinals, opposed long-overdue Church reforms, and emptied the Vatican's coffers to fund their lavish lifestyle. They also fought a series of wars in pursuit of their own political ambitions, creating a climate of fear across northern Italy. Alexander died in 1503, officially of malaria, but it was claimed that he had, in fact, been poisoned by one of his many enemies.

Great patrons of the arts

For the next 18 years Italians occupied the papal throne, notably Pope Julius II and Leo X. Both men were unscrupulous power brokers, but at least they devoted their considerable energies to restoring the authority of the Holy See.

At the time, popes were active patrons of the arts, bringing leading Renaissance artists to Rome to undertake important commissions. In 1506 Julius II laid the foundation stone of the new Basilica of St Peter, built to designs drawn up by the great architect Bramante. Michelangelo was commissioned to create the Sistine Chapel frescoes, and the painter Raphael

A prince of self-interest
Pope Alexander VI showed little concern for the spiritual well-being of the faithful. A worldly and ambitious man, he set about filling high ecclesiastical offices with his own relatives and had few scruples in doing away with his adversaries.

St Peter's Basilica in Rome was a tangible manifestation of the wealth and magnificence of the Renaissance papacy.

Habsburg triumph
Pope Clement VII and Emperor Charles V in Bologna in 1530, at the coronation of the Habsburg monarch as Holy Roman Emperor and king of Italy by the pope. Charles had been crowned emperor in Aachen a decade before, and just three years earlier his armies had captured and sacked Rome, bringing Italy under his control.

decorated the walls of the Pope's private chambers. Julius also began one of the greatest collections of classical antiquities in the Vatican Museum.

As pope until 1513, Julius championed Rome's political interests and put the Borgias to flight. He also brought large parts of northern Italy, including Milan, under papal control, thus curtailing the ambitions of Louis XII of France to win control of the region. Julius's successor, Leo X, was a son of Lorenzo de' Medici, Duke of Florence. Leo consolidated Julius's achievements, but like his father he was a generous – perhaps too generous – patron of the arts. When he died, in 1521, he left behind a mountain of debt.

Both Julius and Leo maintained good relations with the Holy Roman Emperor of the day – Maximilian I until 1519, then

Charles V. Yet despite this, a strong sense of indignance and resistance was growing towards the Church in reaction to the extravagance of its leaders. Across Europe the faithful were paying for letters of indulgence – documents issued in the Church's name that promised individuals absolution for their sins in return for cash payments. The money raised in this way financed the lavish lifestyle of the Renaissance popes. It was in Leo's time that the German reformer Martin Luther posted his famous 95 Theses on the church door at Wittenberg, marking the start of the Protestant Reformation.

The sack of Rome

The next pope was Adrian VI, who hailed originally from Utrecht and had been associated with Charles V since 1507, when he became tutor to the seven-year-old future emperor. The last non-Italian pope until the 20th century, Adrian died in 1523, to be replaced by Clement VII, another Medici and cousin to Leo X.

Clement's 11-year tenure was a disaster. Francis I of France and Emperor Charles V were then vying for supremacy in northern Italy, and by trying to play the two off against each other, Clement angered both. Charles defeated the French in Italy, then in 1527 up to 20,000 of his troops – many of them mercenaries who had not been paid for months – sacked Rome. Estimates of civilians killed in the destruction range up to 30,000; what is known is that some 45,000 Romans were either killed or forced to flee. Clement took refuge in the Castel Sant'Angelo, a fortress by the River Tiber, and watched helplessly as the mob ran riot.

The Church fights back

When Clement died in 1534, Rome lay in ruins, the Papal States were bankrupt, and the Catholic faith was in crisis. The new pope, Paul III, set about recalling

the Church to its spiritual mission. The Counter-Reformation had begun, and Luther's 95 Theses were a prime target. Paul insisted on doctrinal orthodoxy and in 1542 he reorganised the Inquisition, which had lain dormant in the later medieval period, making it an instrument to fight Protestantism. Those who challenged the Church's teachings were hunted down and tortured or condemned to death; apostates were shown no mercy.

Another important milestone in Paul's papacy was the establishment in 1540 of the Jesuit order, dedicated to reversing the tide of the Reformation and reviving piety among the Catholic population at large. In 1545, he convened the Council of Trent to establish the exact tenets of Catholic orthodoxy. Paul died in 1549 with the Council's work unfinished, but the reforms he had set in motion continued under his successors.

Paul IV (pope 1555–9) set up the Index of Forbidden Books to ban works considered detrimental to the faith, and confined Rome's Jews to a ghetto. In 1555 he protested vehemently against the Peace of Augsburg, which recognised the Lutheran religion in those central European states whose rulers had opted for Protestantism. For all the inherent intolerance in such measures, however, the Counter-Reformation retained its momentum and succeeded in reversing the moral decline that had been undermining the Catholic Church.

Selling forgiveness
The Renaissance popes financed the extravagant splendour of their lives in Rome partly through the trade in indulgences – documents promising absolution in return for cash. Priests would charge 12 ducats for remission of the sins of adultery, whoring or sodomy, and 9 ducats for absolution of theft and lying. Surprisingly, a murderer only had to raise 8 ducats in order to wipe the slate clean.

Masterpiece in marble
The sculptor Michelangelo created his magnificent *David* (left) in Florence, where he grew up, but much of his career was spent in Rome, working for the papacy. His most famous commission was the Sistine Chapel, where he completed the ceiling in 1512 and the wall painting of *The Last Judgment* a quarter of a century later. In 1547 he was appointed architect of St Peter's Basilica, and was responsible for designing the dome that crowns the building.

The struggle for supremacy in Europe

Rival claims to lands in Italy led the Habsburg emperors and the French kings to fight a series of wars in the early 16th century. Through a combination of military might and successful marriage alliances, the Habsburgs finally prevailed, but at a terrible cost in lives and money wasted.

A show of unity
Confronted with the threat from the Ottoman Empire, Pope Paul III succeeded in brokering the Peace of Nice in 1538 between the French King Francis I (left, below) and the Habsburg Emperor Charles V (right).

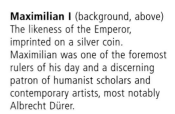

Renaissance Italy was both wealthy and politically divided, which made its lands a natural target for the two great powers struggling for supremacy in western Europe at the time – France and the Holy Roman Empire. By 1538, when Holy Roman Emperor Charles V and France's King Francis I signed the Peace of Nice, troops from all corners of Europe had been battling one another on Italian ground for more than 40 years. The Nice agreement brought Italy some respite from the clashes that had laid waste to cities and entire regions, but it was only a temporary truce: intended to last ten years, it was broken in less than five.

Beginnings of conflict

The accession of Maximilian I to the imperial throne in 1493 had marked a significant turning point. Unlike his father, Frederick III, Maximilian had an active, even ambitious, foreign policy. The desire to safeguard the Habsburgs' ancestral homelands in central Europe was fundamental to his plans, as was the aim to extend his lands eastward through the acquisition of Hungary and Bohemia.

Maximilian's first major foreign-policy initiative as Holy Roman Emperor was an attempt to end the long-running hostility that existed between the Habsburg emperors and France. In the Treaty of Senlis, signed on May 22, 1493, he agreed to cede the Duchy of Burgundy to King Charles VIII of France. In return, he wanted French recognition of his own claims to the regions of Franche Comté (the Burgundian lands west of the River Saône), Lorraine, Luxembourg and the Netherlands – lands located for the most part on France's northeastern border, which he had inherited on the death of his wife, Maria of Burgundy.

Maximilian thought the treaty would bring lasting peace between the two countries, but instead its main effect was to transfer the focus of rivalry between the Habsburgs and France from central Europe to Italy. The constant state of strife that existed there at the end of the 15th century offered the two neighbouring great powers an open invitation to intervene. The result was constantly shifting alliances both with and between the city-states and principalities of the region. Over the next 40 years, whenever one power looked like winning a dominant position on the peninsula, the other players would coalesce in temporary leagues with the guiding aim of frustrating the victorious ruler's ambitions.

The city of Milan, which controlled the Alpine passes to the north, was the spark that ignited the conflict. 'Italy belongs to me' was a claim frequently made by Maximilian and, to add weight to it, in 1494 he married Bianca Maria of Milan's ruling Sforza family. His principal interest in the match lay in the huge revenues collected by the Sforzas: Bianca Maria was said to be the wealthiest bride in Christendom. In addition, Maximilian hoped that her uncle Ludovico, Milan's ruler, would fight off any attempted French invasion of Italy and give him easy access to Rome and the Mediterranean.

Unfortunately for Maximilian, the opposite happened. Convinced that Milan was under threat from Naples, Ludovico turned for help to the French king, who had long-standing claims on the southern kingdom. Charles responded by launching a full-scale invasion of Italy in late 1494.

Initially, the incursion was hugely effective. Within months Charles's troops had overrun the entire peninsula, expelling the Medici from Florence and inflicting defeat on the forces of the central Papal States before entering Naples itself in February 1495. But the very success of the army was its undoing. Faced with

Maximilian I (background, above) The likeness of the Emperor, imprinted on a silver coin. Maximilian was one of the foremost rulers of his day and a discerning patron of humanist scholars and contemporary artists, most notably Albrecht Dürer.

Renaissance artistry The goldsmith Benvenuto Cellini crafted this exquisite saltcellar in the Late Renaissance style for Francis I of France.

the prospect of French dominance on the peninsula, Pope Alexander VI joined forces with Maximilian, the Spanish royal house, Venice and Milan. Together, this Holy League (so called because of its papal connections) forced Charles to abandon Naples and retreat northwards.

The Spanish marriages

Internal tensions soon broke up the Holy League, but it had brought together the Habsburgs and the rulers of Spain, who now concluded a double marriage alliance that was the most momentous dynastic

---

BACKGROUND

A plague of mercenaries

The large armies of mercenaries that ravaged Europe in the 16th century were first raised by Emperor Maximilian. These hired soldiers of fortune fought with pikes and swords, and their fleetness of foot and disciplined tactics made them superior to the ponderous medieval armies of mounted knights.

At first, the mercenaries fought mainly for the Habsburg emperors, but soon they began to play a growing part in the fighting forces of all European rulers. The damage they inflicted increased with every new conflict. Because they

often went unpaid for long periods, they frequently supported themselves on campaign by robbing or begging, and they became feared pillagers. They also had difficulty adapting to civilian life at the cessation of hostilities.

Their reputation was such that mercenaries were often accused and arrested for crimes they had not committed. Punishments were severe. If found guilty of stealing, they risked having their eyes put out and their hands cut off, or they might be sold into captivity as galley slaves.

Hired to kill
A mercenary soldier dispatches a defeated enemy during the Battle of Pavia

union of the period: Juan and Joanna, the son and daughter of Ferdinand and Isabella of Spain, married Maximilian's offspring Margaret and Philip. Within a few years (and after several unexpected deaths), the Spanish crown fell to Joanna and her husband Philip, putting Spain and much of central Europe in Habsburg hands and creating a power bloc that was to dominate the Continent for the next 150 years. In this marital coup, Maximilian

was following the guiding principle of the Habsburg dynasty for generations to come: 'Let others fight their wars; you, O fortunate Austria, will marry instead.'

The Spanish alliance had little impact on the situation in Italy. In 1498 Louis XII came to the throne determined to revive France's claims. In 1499 he captured Milan, robbing Maximilian of his wealthiest ally. By 1501 the French were in Rome once more, intent on pressing their claims to Naples. Italy was again in danger of falling into French hands.

At the time, Maximilian was distracted by financial problems and troubles with the German imperial princes. He responded to the French threat by forging a fresh round of alliances and arranging new marriages. In the Peace of Blois, signed in 1504, he finally agreed to cede Milan to France. Yet the treaty also included a clause promising Claudia, the French king's daughter and heir, in marriage to Maximilian's own grandson, Charles – a match that would have brought almost all of western Europe into Habsburg hands. In the event, the peace did not last: just a few months after the treaty had been ratified, Louis revoked it.

War against Venice

When Maximilian's son Philip died suddenly at Burgos in Spain in 1506, his wife – who has gone down in history as Joanna the Mad – was incapable of ruling. Control over Spain reverted to Philip's ageing father-in-law, Ferdinand of Aragon. Meanwhile, the Habsburg-controlled Netherlands were threatened from all sides. Maximilian recovered from the double blow, however, and kept his plans afloat until his six-year-old grandson, the future Emperor Charles V, came of age.

In 1508, Maximilian set off to attend a much-delayed investiture as Holy Roman Emperor, only to find his progress blocked at Trento, north of Venice, by Venetian forces. Forced to proclaim himself emperor elect, he sought vengeance by helping to organise a new alliance, the

League of Cambrai, which brought the combined forces of the Emperor, the Pope, Louis XII of France and Ferdinand of Aragon down on the Venetians.

Shifting alliances

Despite suffering severe defeats, Venice survived. The other allied powers came to the view that France, rather than Venice, represented the greater threat to their own position on the peninsula. By 1512 the allies, now also bolstered by Henry VIII of England, had joined the Venetians to counter French power. The armies of this new Holy League, also backed by troops from the Swiss Confederation, managed to drive the French back over the Alps.

In January 1515, Francis I acceded to the French throne and immediately set his sights on recapturing Milan. Allied now with England and Venice against the Holy league, he won the Battle of Marignano and regained Lombardy. When a peace was agreed in 1516, France retained control of Milan, but in return, gave up its claims to Naples.

The empire of Charles V

By now Maximilian was old and tired, and his remaining ambitions focused on his grandson Charles. The death of Ferdinand of Aragon in 1516 finally brought the young man, now aged 16, to the Spanish throne. Maximilian's greatest wish was to see him also established as his own successor as king of Germany. For that he needed the support of the imperial electors. At the Diet of Augsburg in 1518, Maximilian expended huge sums in bribes to win their votes for Charles. Maximilian died on January 12, 1519, and some months later Charles was duly chosen as German king and future emperor.

Maximilian bequeathed a huge empire to Charles V. His domain stretched from the ancestral lands of Austria through the Franche Comté, Naples, Sicily and Spain to the extensive new territories that Spain had recently conquered in the New World. The end product of generations of dynastic marriages, Charles's realm made little political sense. It was scattered across much of western Europe and beyond, and the interests of its diverse parts were difficult to reconcile. Charles would struggle manfully with his inheritance for the next 37 years.

Along with much other political baggage, he inherited the ongoing

Lost harvests
The frequent fighting in northern Italy often prevented Italian peasants from gathering in the year's harvest, resulting in widespread hardship and famine. This illustration shows August from a 16th-century Book of Hours.

Imperial vessel
A model of Charles V's flagship, made from gilded brass decorated with enamelwork and embossed reliefs.

Habsburg feud with France. The conflict in Italy, briefly halted in 1516, was soon renewed. The war that broke out in 1522 culminated in a decisive victory for Charles's forces at the Battle of Pavia in 1525. Francis himself was taken captive in

The female touch

In the new war that followed there was no decisive victor. The Italian people were the losers, their lands devastated once more. The low point of the fighting came in 1527, when mercenary troops in Charles's employ, who had gone unpaid for months, fell upon Rome and mercilessly sacked the city. When peace finally came, in 1529, it was negotiated by two women – Charles's aunt Margaret of Austria and Francis's mother Louise of Savoie. The monarchs themselves flatly refused to sit down together.

The resulting treaty was signed at Cambrai, on the French border, and put the seal on Charles's military successes. Francis once more renounced his Italian claims, and in return regained recognition of French sovereignty over the Duchy of Burgundy. In the wake of the treaty Charles was duly crowned by the Pope as Holy Roman Emperor and King of Italy.

The sack of Rome
On May 6, 1527, German and Spanish mercenaries in the service of Emperor Charles V inflicted terrible devastation on the Holy City, shown here in a copperplate engraving by Matthäus Merian. Protestant critics of the Church regarded the pillaging as a divine judgment on the immorality that they saw as rife there.

the battle, and in the ensuing Treaty of Madrid in 1526 he was not only forced to renounce all his claims in Italy but to give up the Duchy of Burgundy as well.

Francis never had any intention of abiding by the settlement. As soon as he was released he rejected the terms of the treaty, claiming that his oath had been given under duress. And by that time the fickle balance of power was working in his favour, for Charles's triumph had alarmed the other European powers. That same year they came together in the League of Cognac, which united France with Milan, Florence, Genoa, the papacy and Henry VIII's England in opposition to Charles's rule in Italy.

To safeguard his position in Italy, from 1530 onwards Charles kept a standing army in Naples, an unusual move but a prudent one, for war broke out again in 1535. This time it was sparked by the death of Francesco Sforza, who had been given control of Milan by the Treaty of Cambrai. The French at once renewed their claims to the Duchy of Milan, while lending covert support to a threatened Ottoman attack on southern Italy. Calm was finally restored with the Peace of Nice in 1538, which reaffirmed the terms agreed at Cambrai, leaving both Milan and Florence under Habsburg control.

Rival claims to Burgundy

Yet the rivalry between Charles and Francis continued. It flared up again at the investiture of Charles's son Philip as ruler of Milan in 1542. In the renewed war, the now open alliance between Francis and the Ottoman ruler, Suleiman the Magnificent, ended in an allied French and Turkish fleet sacking Nice, at that time ruled by the counts of Savoy. Charles tried to win his rival round by offering generous peace terms. He agreed to renounce his claim to Burgundy entirely and offered a Habsburg princess in marriage to Francis's second son, the Duke of Orleans – a plan that failed when the duke suddenly died.

The abdication of Charles V

Both Francis I and Henry VIII of England died in the winter of 1547. This left Charles V free to deal with the discord that the Protestant Reformation was causing in Germany. His attempts to impose Catholicism across the imperial lands eventually failed.

Henry II, the new French king, took advantage of Charles's problems in any way he could. He offered financial help to the Protestant imperial princes in exchange for their support for his attempts to regain control of Naples and Milan. He sought their backing for his own future candidacy for the position of Holy Roman Emperor. He also threatened to invade the Habsburg Netherlands and concluded a pact with the Pope against the Emperor.

Afflicted by gout, worn and scarred by decades of conflict, Charles decided to abdicate. In Brussels, on October 25, 1555, his son Philip took control of the Netherlands and Burgundy; he became King Philip II of Spain three months later, on January 16, 1556. Charles abdicated as emperor later that year and died in 1558.

Peace at last

Philip II eventually beat Henry II's armies at St Quentin in 1557 and Gravelines in 1558. In the Treaty of Cateau-Cambrésis, signed in 1559, Henry acknowledged the Habsburg claims in Italy and the Franche Comté that had so long divided the two powers. The houses were reconciled by Philip's marriage to Henry's eldest daughter, Elisabeth of Valois. Henry died shortly after, and France became engulfed in its own religious wars between Catholics and Protestant Huguenots. The old rivalries faded and Spanish-Habsburg dominance in Europe was confirmed for the next hundred years.

Château of Chambord
A masterpiece of Renaissance architecture, situated on the River Loire, Chambord is by far the largest and most imposing of the Loire châteaux. It was built on the direction of Francis I in a heavily wooded region rich in game. Francis consulted the foremost architects of the age, including the multi-talented Leonardo da Vinci.

The Peasants' War in Germany

Trouble had long been brewing in southern Germany. When the Peasants' War broke out in 1525, the uprising was put down with great brutality and bloodshed.

The final straw
At the height of the harvest in 1524, the peasants of Stühlingen, near the Swiss border in southern Germany, were expected to interrupt their labours to pick strawberries and flowers for the local countess. This demand proved to be the straw that broke the camel's back, sparking a full-scale revolt against the authorities that spread across much of the surrounding region. This contemporary woodcut shows peasants on the march.

In the summer of 1493, peasants from the villages around Schlettstadt (now Sélestat in Alsace) began meeting secretly to discuss their grievances, which they blamed on senior Church clergy, the nobility and the entire German ruling establishment. They rallied under the banner of the Bundschuh ('Laced Boot'), taking the name from the heavy, long-laced boots that they commonly wore. Their demands included the dispossession of usurers and cancellation of all debts; the abolition of unjust existing taxes and the right to vet new ones; a reduction in priests' incomes; and an end to the ecclesiastic and princely control of the court system, to be replaced by locally elected court officials.

The general discontent could be felt across large swathes of central and southern Germany as the 15th century drew to a close. Tenant farmers and farm labourers were subject to the authority of landlords drawn from the aristocracy, the Church or the municipalities. They lived in a state of serfdom, often deeply in debt, made worse by repeated failed harvests and by spiralling taxation imposed by their political masters. They felt that the legal system was heavily weighted against them and were outraged by the constant threat of excommunication held over them.

First signs of trouble

In 1493, the Bundschuh rebels decided to seize control of Schlettstadt after harvest had been gathered in. They planned to use the town as their base for a more widespread armed uprising. But word got out and several had their fingers cut off as punishment, while those who fled lost lands and property.

Nine years later, peasants from Untergrombach, in the Rhine Valley near modern Karlsruhe, revived the demands of the Bundschuh conspirators. They too found themselves in open revolt against their landlords as a result of high credit repayments and failed harvests. They planned rebellion under the leadership of Joss Fritz, a local farmer's son.

Their basic aims were encapsulated in the slogans 'Freedom' and 'Divine Justice', and they won the support of some Reformation theologians, notably Thomas Müntzer and Christoph Schappeler. They demanded that everyone should have the right to hunt, fish, graze their animals on common land and exploit the forests, which were now the private domain of the princes. By appealing to divine justice, they highlighted the gulf between the system of Roman law recently introduced to Germany and the tenets of Holy Scripture.

Like the Schlettstadt rebellion, the Untergrombach conspiracy was betrayed by one of its own members. However, most of its members, including Joss Fritz, managed to escape. Ten years later, Fritz tried to foment another uprising, this time near Freiburg-im-Breisgau in southern Baden. Proclaiming the same radical reform programme as before, Fritz gathered around him a

Visionary preacher
Thomas Müntzer preached a doctrine of social equality and communal ownership of property.

Improvised weapons
Armed with pitchforks, flails and scythes, the peasants were no match for the landowner's heavily armed mercenaries.

group of discontented peasants, serfs and vagabonds, creating an underground network that eventually covered all of Baden as well as Alsace as far as the Rems Valley, east of modern Stuttgart. This rebellion, too, came to nothing. Many of the plotters were captured and executed, although once again Joss Fritz escaped.

Unrest spreads

The unrest swelled once more in the Rems Valley in 1514. This new peasants' alliance called itself the Poor Konrad movement, taking its name from a pun (in the Swabian dialect, the saying 'A poor man is bereft of hope' contained the words '*koan Rat*', which sounded like the name Konrad). The movement's 5000 members directed their anger against the Duke of Württemberg, who had imposed a new tax that sparked uprisings in towns and villages across the region. Eventually, the Duke suppressed the revolt, and many of the leaders were hung or jailed, although the rebels did succeed in winning a number of concessions from their master. But despite the

Signed and sealed
In 1512, many of Germany's dukedoms, princedoms and other feudal authorities banded together in the Swabian League to confront the threat posed by the disaffected peasantry. This document officially set the seal on the alliance.

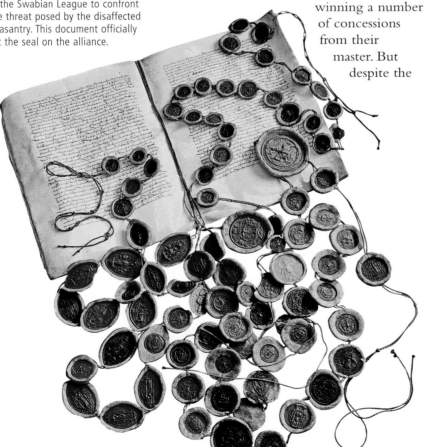

groundswell of discontent, the peasants' lot did not improve over the next decade, and soon matters got out of hand again.

In 1524, encouraged by the success of the Reformation and with the support of the Protestant theologian Christoph Schappeler, the peasants of Memmingen in Upper Swabia renewed the demands of the Bundschuh and Poor Konrad uprisings in a precise list of demands that became known as the 12 Articles. Rebel bands were soon springing up with the aim of disappropriating the wealth of the nobility and the Church. But the peasants lacked leadership, strategy and discipline, and the rebellion degenerated into orgies of pillaging and slaughter. In a pitched battle against the landowners, around 1000 peasants lost their lives, while the other side sustained no losses at all. In the Tauber Valley in Franconia the authorities moved swiftly against the uprising and some 6000 peasants met a violent death.

A swift and bloody end

In Thuringia the Protestant theologian Thomas Müntzer lent his active support to the rebel cause. At the Battle of Frankenhausen, in 1525, he led an army of some 8000 peasants against the 5000 soldiers of the elector of Saxony, and suffered a crushing defeat. An uprising in the Palatinate was put down with equal brutality and some 5000 peasant rebels were killed. Müntzer himself was captured, horribly tortured and executed.

All of the various local uprisings that collectively became known as the Peasants' War turned out to be quite easily dealth with by the authorities, and within a few months the landowners and their armies had re-established the status quo. But the toll on the peasants was heavy: more than 100,000 had lost their lives. To add insult to injury, all of their struggles had been to no avail, for when peace was finally restored the political disenfranchisement of the peasants remained just as complete as it had been before the troubles started.

Poland's aristocratic republic

The last rulers of the Jagiellonian dynasty in Poland presided over a golden age of art and culture, and saw political power passing from the monarchy to the landed nobility.

In 1505, in the city of Radom 160km (100 miles) northeast of the royal capital of Krakow, Poland's King Alexander I and representatives of the senate and the chamber of deputies of its parliament, the Sejm, put their signatures to the *Nihil novi* ('Nothing new') constitution. By this constitution the king was prohibited from taking any future decisions without the express consent of parliament, and so the Polish aristocratic republic was born.

By the time the constitution was passed, the aristocracy had already been the real rulers of the country for more than a century. In the annual state assemblies they were able to override the will of the king and passed many resolutions on their own authority. They owed their strength partly to sheer weight of numbers, for there was an unusually large number of aristocrats in Poland: over 10 per cent of the population claimed noble birth, compared to just 3 per cent in most other European countries. By granting generous privileges to the nobles over the years, the Polish kings had themselves helped to strengthen the nobles' position, increasing aristocratic self-confidence to the point where they established the right to elect future monarchs. The Sejm devoted a great deal of its time and effort to defending and extending any rights that had been granted to the nobility in the past.

A major European player

The dilution of royal power did not prevent Poland's 16th-century kings from exerting authority on the international stage. When Sigismund I of the ruling Jagiellonian dynasty was elected king at the imperial diet in Piotrkow, on December 8, 1506, he immediately set about turning Poland into a nation that all Europe would look to with respect.

Although Sigismund's military campaigns in the east against the rulers of Lithuania and Moscow were initially unsuccessful, his policies in the west developed more promisingly. Sigismund was soon able to conclude an agreement

Patron of the arts
The Renaissance came into bloom in Poland under Sigismund I, who reigned from 1506 to 1548.

Castle on the Wawel
The Polish kings transferred their court to Warsaw early in the 17th century, but the old capital of Krakow continued to be the place where monarchs were crowned and buried right up to the First Partition of Poland in 1772. Throughout that time Krakow's royal castle on Wawel Hill remained a favourite residence of the country's rulers.

Tapestry king
In just under 20 years, Sigismund II Augustus of Poland ordered nearly 350 tapestries and wall-hangings from the Flemish master-weavers of Brussels. His acquisitions not only graced the palace in Krakow (background), but also went with the king in his baggage train to adorn the walls of whatever castle he was staying in as he travelled around his realm. Over a third of Sigismund's tapestries – many depicting biblical scenes and landscapes – are still housed at Wawel Castle today, forming an outstanding collection of north European Renaissance art.

with his powerful neighbour, the Habsburg Holy Roman Emperor. At a royal diet held in 1515, Sigismund renounced his claim to the Hungarian throne, ceding complete authority in the Danube region to the Habsburgs. In return, Emperor Maximilian I agreed to end his support for the grand dukes of Moscow and swear peace and friendship with Poland.

The removal of the Habsburg threat left Poland with only one immediate local rival – Prussia, established three centuries earlier by the Teutonic Knights on the southern shores of the Baltic Sea. The Grand Master of the order, Albrecht von Hohenzollern, was Sigismund's nephew, but family ties did not stop him from conducting an unsuccessful war against Poland from 1519 to 1521. After confidential discussions with the German religious reformer Martin Luther, Albrecht bowed to Polish sovereignty, and in the Treaty of Krakow of 1525 he accepted the now-secular Duchy of Prussia as a fiefdom of the Polish crown.

Bona – an Italian princess

Meanwhile, important events had been taking place at the royal court in Krakow. Sigismund's second marriage, to a princess from the renowned and wealthy Sforza family of Milan, proved to be an inspired match. In April 1518, Princess Bona ceremoniousy entered Krakow accompanied by a retinue of 300 people. She and her entourage brought the Italian Renaissance to Wawel Castle, the residence of the Polish kings.

The new queen displayed mastery of both the political and cultural stage. With an eye to territorial expansion, she sought to consolidate the Polish realm and even offered the ancestral lands owned by her family in Italy in exchange for the Duchy of Silesia. Her high-handed manner angered the Polish aristocracy, and her enormous wealth, steadily accumulating in the banks of Venice and Genoa, caused envy. Yet Bona and her husband remained undaunted by the intrigues against her, instead directing their energies toward strengthening diplomatic ties with France in the west and the Ottoman Empire to the southeast.

At the same time, the Italian princess, long schooled in the humanist tradition, helped to embed the Renaissance firmly in the fabric of Polish life. She and her husband spent large sums on restoring Wawel Castle, summoning leading artists of the day to Krakow to carry out the redecoration and furnishing of the building. The royal collections of paintings, goldwork, jewellery and classical antiquities were among the most famous in Europe. The creativity the pair fostered encouraged Polish artists, scientists and writers to develop their talents to the full.

A new view of the heavens

The most significant figure of the Polish Renaissance was the astronomer Nicolaus Copernicus, who began his academic career at the University of Krakow. Having steeped himself in the works of the ancients, he soon began to develop his own revolutionary view of astronomy, which put the Sun, rather than the Earth, at the centre of the visible universe, overturning theories on the movement of the planets that had been held for millennia. Copernicus's findings were too much for the Catholic Church to bear. His work *De revolutionibus orbium coelestium* ('On the Motions of the Heavenly Bodies'), which appeared shortly before his death in 1543, was placed on the papacy's Index of banned books in 1611.

A royal love match

A son, the future Sigismund II Augustus, was born to the royal couple in Krakow in 1520. Bona had great plans for him, entrusting his education to Italian scholars. With her husband's support but against the will of the aristocracy, she had the young Sigismund elected and crowned co-ruler with his father when he was just 10 years old.

In 1543 Bona arranged a marriage for Sigismund to Elisabeth of Habsburg. But the young man was already in love. When Elisabeth died two years later, he transferred his affections to the true love of his life, Barbara Radziwill, daughter of a powerful Lithuanian magnate, and married her in secret in 1547. The following year, Sigismund came to the throne on the death of his father, and in 1550, despite fierce opposition from his mother and the nobility, he had Barbara crowned queen. But Barbara died childless the next year, allegedly poisoned on Bona's orders.

Sigismund later married again, this time to his first wife's sister in a renewed dynastic alliance with the Habsburg family. But this match, too, proved childless, and the issue of the succession loomed large in the latter part of his reign.

For almost 200 years Poland had been linked with Lithuania in a union of the crowns, because both nations were ruled by the same kings of the Jagiellonian line. The lack of a direct heir raised the prospect that a monarch who was not a Jagiellon might accede to the Polish throne, ending the union and disrupting relations between the two close neighbours. Sigismund's answer was to propose a full political union between the two nations, which pleased both sides.

Union with Lithuania

Accordingly, in 1569, the enlarged Sejm enacted the Union of Lublin, formally uniting Poland and Lithuania. The treaty regulating the alliance stipulated that both

A revolutionary view
The Polish astronomer Nicolaus Copernicus (below) confounded the medieval world by opposing the view that the Earth was at the centre of the universe, and proposing instead a heliocentric theory. In the Copernican universe (left), the Earth revolved around its own axis each day and around the Sun once a year. The other heavenly bodies also orbited the Sun, with the exception of the Moon, which circled the Earth.

nations should have a single ruler and parliament while maintaining separate armies, administrations and financial systems. Joined together as an 'indivisible and inseparable whole', Poland and Lithuania were officially proclaimed 'The Aristocratic Republic of the Two Nations'. The duchies of Livonia and Courland on the Baltic coast were also incorporated into the new state.

The abolition of customs tariffs quickly stimulated an economic boom, and at the same time, the unity that this strengthened alliance demonstrated to the outside world proved an invaluable deterrent to the ambitions of the neighbouring Grand Duchy of Moscow. The diverse realm created at Lublin was a major power. It had a combined population of almost 8 million people that contained a variety of national minorities professing many different faiths. This forced Sigismund to address the vexed question of religious

When Sigismund II died, still childless, in 1572, he bequeathed all his treasures, including a library of some 4000 books, to his three sisters with the proviso that, when they died, the legacy should pass to the nation. His own death spelt the end for the Jagiellonian dynasty.

At first the Sejm elected a French prince, Henry of the house of Valois, as their next king, but Henry abandoned the Polish throne when the unexpected death of his brother brought him the French crown. The assembled nobles' next choice was the Hungarian Stephen Bathory, the prince of Transylvania, who became king of Poland in 1575. This new ruler strengthened his position by marrying Sigismund's sister Anna, even though she was by then over 50 years old.

Once firmly entrenched in power, Stephen set about defending Poland's eastern frontiers against attack by Russia's Tsar, Ivan the Terrible. By 1582 he had succeeded in imposing a peace treaty on Moscow by which Poland gained Livonia and Polotsk. To finance his campaigns, Stephen drew on the revenues of the famous salt mines at Wieliczka near Krakow, which had long been the property of the crown and provided a major source of income for the court.

The start of a long decline

On Stephen's death in 1586, the Sejm offered the throne to a member of the Swedish ruling house of Vasa. Sigismund III proved a bad choice. He put his own dynastic interests in Sweden above the welfare of his adopted country, and his ambitions involved Poland in intermittent war for almost three decades, ending in the loss of Livonia to the Swedish king, Gustavus Adolphus. The defeat fatally weakened Poland, which entered a long decline. Worsened by faction-fighting among the aristocracy, its troubles would culminate in the late 18th century in a series of partitions that temporarily wiped Poland off the map, dividing its lands between acquisitive neighbouring powers.

Source of royal wealth
The revenue from the 'white gold' extracted from salt mines at Wieliczka in southern Poland had been in the hands of the Polish crown since medieval times. The mines provided the country's rulers with a third of their income.

policy. In general he supported the principle of freedom of worship, ensuring that while sectarian wars raged elsewhere across the Continent, Poland remained a safe haven for persecuted people of all confessions, be they Catholic, Protestant, Orthodox Christian or Jew.

England under the Tudors and Stuarts

The Tudors, especially Elizabeth I, were prominent among the crowned heads of Europe. Yet it took only two Stuart kings to bring England's monarchy to the point of collapse.

The first Tudor king, Henry VII, died in 1509 at the age of 50, racked by consumption. He left behind a stable and prosperous realm, very different to the one he had inherited 24 years earlier. Henry had seized power by force, defeating his predecessor, Richard III, at the Battle of Bosworth Field and putting an end to the 30-year-long Wars of the Roses. He had ruled wisely and peacefully, building up the royal finances so that he would never have to be beholden to the barons in parliament for his revenues.

The second Tudor king, Henry VIII, was not yet 18 when he inherited the throne. The young ruler – who gloried in the titles of King of England, King of France (where he had no real authority) and Lord of Ireland – was greeted with great optimism, but he was destined to evoke fascination and terror in equal measure. Henry was an egotistical despot, an opportunist, a *bon viveur* and a womaniser, and towards the end of his life – after a reign of 38 years – a glutton.

The search for an heir

Henry had been on the throne for just 40 days when he married Catherine of Aragon, the widow of his elder brother Arthur, after a special dispensation from the Pope. His father had promoted the match, which linked the English throne with the rising power of Spain, intending it to lay the foundations for a grand alliance between England, Spain and the royal houses of Habsburg and Burgundy.

For the union to produce the hoped-for dynastic benefits, the couple had to produce a male heir as quickly as possible. When Catherine announced that she was pregnant, joy was unconfined. However, the daughter she bore was stillborn. In 1511 she bore a son, who died seven weeks later. In all Catherine endured six pregnancies, from which only the future Queen Mary I, born in 1516, survived.

The handsome, energetic young king had a string of mistresses and at first he maintained these relationships discreetly. This situation changed in 1527 when he fell in love with Anne Boleyn, a 20-year-old lady-in-waiting, and began to woo her openly. By then, Henry had given up any hope that Catherine, now 43, could give him his male heir. To complicate matters for Henry, Anne would only submit to his advances if he made her his wife.

Conflict with Rome

Accordingly, after 17 years of marriage, Henry decided to divorce Catherine and marry Anne. To justify this action, he argued that the marriage had

Regal gaze (background)
The face of Henry VIII, as portrayed by the court painter Hans Holbein the Younger.

Much-married monarch
Having inherited a secure throne and a well-stocked treasury from his father, Henry VIII squandered much of his legacy on extravagant living and unprofitable wars. Nowhere was his prodigality more evident than in his private life. He famously had six wives: one died in childbirth, two were executed and two more divorced; the last, Catherine Parr, survived him. The engravings below depict the first two, Catherine of Aragon (right) and Anne Boleyn.

No exceptions
Henry VIII brooked no opposition to his plans to break with Rome. When Sir Thomas More, his long-serving advisor, refused to swear an oath acknowledging Henry's position as head of the newly established Church of England, the King had him beheaded. More went to the block on July 6, 1535, two weeks after Cardinal John Fisher, the bishop of Rochester and chancellor of Cambridge University. This coloured engraving of More's execution was made in 1584.

never been valid, despite the Vatican's dispensation, as it contravened the Biblical injunction against marrying your brother's widow. He appealed to the current pope, Clement VII, to rule on the matter, and a protracted legal tug-of-war ensued. Catherine, who disputed the divorce, solicited the help of her nephew, who happened to be the Holy Roman Emperor, Charles V. And as the papacy was in thrall to Charles, whose troops had recently sacked Rome, Clement let the process drag on.

The 'king's great matter', as the divorce became known, drove a wedge between Henry and the papacy, forcing Henry to side with the Protestant reformers who were challenging the Church's authority in Germany. After six years spent waiting for a resolution, he lost patience. In a final break with Rome, he refused to recognise

the Pope's authority, appointing himself head of a newly established Church of England. In that capacity he handed over the question of the divorce to his primate, the archbishop of Canterbury, Thomas Cranmer. Unsurprisingly, Cranmer decided in Henry's favour, declaring his marriage to Catherine invalid. Henry and Anne were married in January 1533; eight months later Anne bore him a child, although to Henry's disappointment this turned out to be another daughter. In time, she would become Elizabeth I.

In December 1533 the Privy Council passed an ordinance demoting the Pope to the status of Bishop of Rome, on a par with other foreign prelates. Almost against his will, the King who earlier in his reign had been given the title of Defender of the Faith for his loyalty to the papacy, had cut the thousand-year-old link between the English Church and the Vatican.

England's Reformation

Henry and his ministers now enacted a flurry of legislation repealing the old Catholic ecclesiastical laws. The new measures obliged the King's subjects to swear allegiance to the crown and to accept the Act of Supremacy, by which the King was named protector and supreme head of the Church and clergy of England. To refuse was treason. Henry did not shrink from applying this test to the highest in the land. When his Lord Chancellor and long-serving advisor Thomas More refused to swear, he was imprisoned then executed.

The King's next targets were England's monasteries, considered bastions of loyalty to the papacy. The smaller houses were dissolved in 1536 and the larger ones three years later, their extensive lands being apportioned to the crown or to loyal members of the aristocracy.

Marital misfortunes

Meanwhile, Henry was still waiting for the longed-for male heir. In 1536 Anne Boleyn gave birth to a son, but the infant was stillborn. By that time the King was already losing interest and had his eye instead on another lady-in-waiting, Jane Seymour. This time, however, he did not waste time on the legalities of a divorce. Witnesses were found to accuse Anne of adultery; her own brother was one of the men named. She was arrested and incarcerated in the Tower of London, where she languished for a month while Henry, wanting to exclude her daughter Elizabeth from the succession, had their marriage declared invalid. Anne was beheaded on May 19, 1536, and the king married Jane Seymour 11 days later. The following year the new queen gave birth to a son, Edward, but did not survive the labour.

Henry married three more times. His betrothal to Anne of Cleves, a princess from the duchy of Cleves in present-day Germany, was rapidly terminated by mutual agreement after the diplomatic advantages that the match had promised failed to materialise. As soon as he was free, Henry took 20-year-old Catherine Howard as his fifth wife, but within two years she was accused of adultery and dealt the same fate as Anne Boleyn. The king's sixth and final wife, Catherine Parr, outlived him.

Rivalry and war

In the latter stages of Henry's reign England's long-simmering rivalry with France was renewed, and with it came tensions with the French king's northern ally, James V of Scotland. Relations with the Scots deteriorated through the 1530s and broke into open warfare in 1542. The conflict was resolved on the marshes of Solway Moss, near Carlisle, where a force of fewer than 3000 English troops routed 18,000 Scots. The English lost only seven men in the battle and took 1200 prisoners. James suffered a nervous collapse after the defeat and died soon after, leaving the Scottish crown in the hands of his new-born daughter, Mary Stuart, who was just six days old.

By that time Henry's mental and physical health was deteriorating fast. In his later years, an ulcerated leg that would not heal caused him constant pain. No longer able to exercise as he had done when young, he grew immensely fat. Although he remained mentally sharp, he

A travelling queen
Queen Elizabeth I enjoyed meeting her subjects. She travelled around the country several times a year, and frequently stopped to address a few words to the waiting crowds. She never once left England.

Buzzing metropolis
An historical panorama shows London and the Tower in 1588. At the time, the city had some 100,000 inhabitants and the River Thames was the most important transport artery in the country.

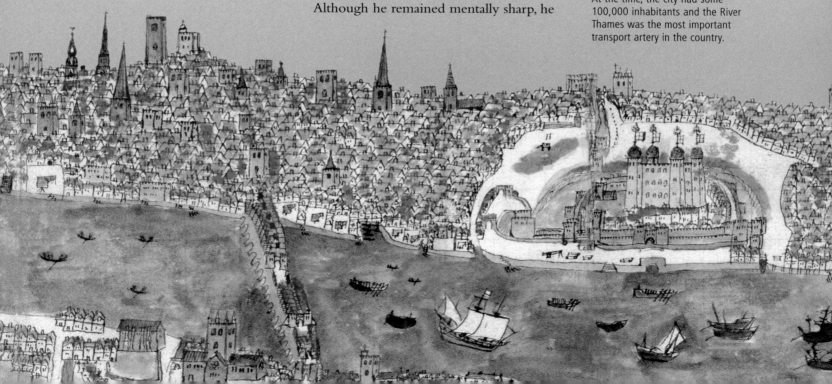

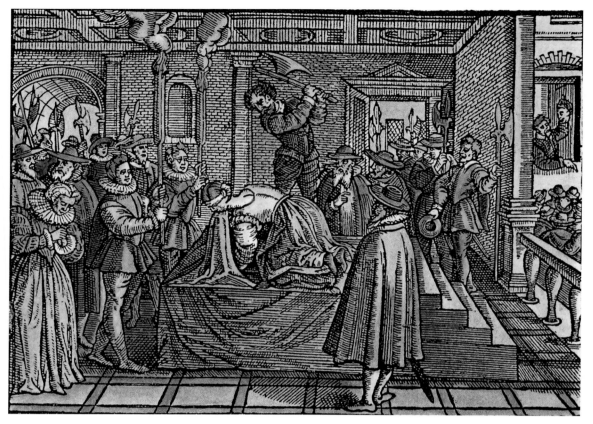

A queen beheaded
The execution of Mary, Queen of Scots, in Fotheringay Castle in 1587, shown here in a woodcut made in 1589. It was her supposed ambition to occupy the English throne that led Mary to the block. Beset with personal misgivings and pangs of conscience, Elizabeth only gave the order for Mary's execution after coming under intense pressure from her advisors.

English art
A nightcap dating from the early 17th century, embroidered with metallic threads on fine silk and decorated with vine, grape, rose and strawberry motifs.

became increasingly paranoid in his judgments, seeing plots all around him. When he finally died, in the winter of 1547, there was little left to suggest the strong and handsome Renaissance monarch who had so raised his people's hopes nearly four decades earlier.

Henry was succeeded by the 10-year-old Edward, a staunch Protestant but a sickly child who died six years later without ever attaining his majority. The throne then passed to Edward's half-sister Mary, the daughter of Henry's marriage to Catherine of Aragon. Mary and her husband, Philip II of Spain, attempted to revoke the Reformation and bring England back into the Catholic fold. They launched a wave of religious persecution, now against Protestants, that sent some 300 people to the stake. Yet Mary also went to an early grave, childless and embittered after ruling for just five years. Her death cleared the way for the accession of Elizabeth, the offspring of Henry's marriage to Anne Boleyn. Elizabeth's 45-year reign helped to shape a nation.

The Virgin Queen

Elizabeth I came to the throne in 1558, aged 25. The realm she inherited was riven by religious unrest, and costly wars with France and Scotland had depleted the nation's coffers. Skirmishes with the two old enemies continued in the early years of her reign, while a simmering conflict with Spain, over her support for the Protestants, threatened to erupt into a full-blown war.

Elizabeth's advisors regarded the search for a husband for the Queen as a matter of vital national concern. An heir was needed, and England's future, both political and religious, might depend on her choice of partner. There was no shortage of suitors. Elizabeth showed little enthusiasm for the diplomatic match favoured by her advisers with the Duke of Alençon, brother of France's Charles IX. On the other hand, her own favourite, the ambitious Earl of Leicester, was already married. Elizabeth played for time and, year by year, augmented her own position. Her reticence in matrimonial matters actually played to the nation's advantage. Philip of Spain, for instance, raged against England for having once more broken its ties with the Catholic Church; yet he could hardly go to war while Elizabeth continued to dangle the possibility that she might one day marry a Spanish prince. So the Queen flirted with many but gave herself to none. While the world waited, England enjoyed a time of peace that ushered in growing prosperity and a blossoming of culture.

The growing rift with Spain

As Elizabeth's reign progressed, however, issues arose that could not be solved even by the most astute personal diplomacy. The conflict with Spain intensified as a result of English support for the Protestant rebels in the Netherlands, fighting for independence from Spanish rule. Spain retaliated by lending tacit support to the Catholic Mary Stuart, another great-granddaughter of the first Tudor king, Henry VII. Mary had taken refuge in England after being driven from her own realm north of the border. Unwittingly, she now became a source of hope for all who sought the restoration of papal power in England.

Another provocation to the Spanish was England's growing involvement in maritime adventures, which not only threatened Spain's immense wealth from her colonial empire but also challenged her global supremacy. Seafarers like Francis Drake and Walter Raleigh vied with one another in exploring far-off lands. When the opportunity presented, they were also happy to raid the great Spanish bullion fleets that transported silver across the Atlantic Ocean from South and Central America.

Matters came to a head in 1587. Even though Mary, Queen of Scots, had been confined in various castles ever since her arrival in England 20 years before, her name had been linked with a series of conspiracies by Elizabeth's vigilant supporters. For a long time Elizabeth avoided ordering Mary's execution, repelled by the thought of sanctioning the killing of a queen who was also her own relative. She finally gave way following the discovery of a fresh plot implicating her cousin, and Mary was beheaded.

The Spanish Armada

For the Spanish king, Mary's death was the final straw. Philip resolved to send a great fleet northwards to ferry an invasion force from the Spanish Netherlands across to England. Before this Armada could set sail, Elizabeth sanctioned a daring raid on the harbour at Cadiz, where many of the Spanish ships were gathering. Her commander, Francis Drake, succeeded in destroying the bulk of the vessels assembled there. Undaunted, Philip set about rebuilding his forces, and a year later, in 1588, a Spanish fleet of 130 ships set sail for England.

England's safety lay first and foremost in the hands of her naval commanders, Drake and Sir Francis Howard. The two realised that they would have to intercept the Spanish fleet before it could make the planned rendezvous with the Spanish army in the Netherlands. The Spaniards were superior in numbers to their English opponents, but their floating wooden castles, crammed to the gunwales with

Founding charter (background)
In 1559, Queen Elizabeth granted the English East India Company its foundation charter. The company's coat of arms, made of painted and gilded wood, formerly hung above the chairman's seat at East India House in London.

An unsuccessful invasion
Seen here in a 16th-century painting, the English fleet's triumphant yet lucky victory over the Spanish Armada marked the beginning of the age of British naval supremacy.

Elizabethan theatre

The Elizabethan Age was an era of enormous creativity in all of the arts, but none more so than the theatre, which saw the blossoming of the talents of William Shakespeare, Ben Jonson, Christopher Marlowe and Thomas Kyd. The vivid dramas they produced had action-filled plots, brilliant wordplay and recognisable characters, and they attracted a wide audience.

The burgeoning number of theatres created many new opportunities for actors looking to the stage to earn a full-time living. The most gifted performers of the day – among them Richard Burbage, Edward Alleyn and Richard Tarlton – all came from the middle classes.

A stage for genius
William Shakespeare (1564–1616) came to London in his twenties to embark on a career as an actor and playwright. *Henry V*, *Hamlet* and *Othello* were all first staged at the Globe (below).

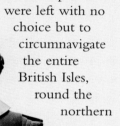

soldiers, horses and artillery pieces, were far less manoeuvrable than the narrow-beamed English ships. The English harried them all the way up the Channel, but failed to sink a single enemy ship.

When the Spaniards dropped anchor off Calais, the English took a different tack. They set fire to eight unmanned vessels laden with barrels of tar, brushwood and gunpowder and steered them downwind toward the Spanish anchorage. The fireships spread terror in the Spanish fleet, causing the sailors to cut their anchors and head for open water. Pursued by the English and driven by a strong westerly gale, the Spanish fleet was swept away from the English coast and into the North Sea. The vessels became separated, and their individual captains were left with no choice but to circumnavigate the entire British Isles, round the northern tip of Scotland, before heading back to Spain. Storms took a terrible toll – many ships were wrecked on the rocky Irish coast. Only half of the Spanish ships made it back home, and no Spanish soldier set foot on English soil. England's victory marked the high point of Elizabeth's reign and bolstered her international standing.

From Tudors to Stuarts

Elizabeth presided over an unsettled society. The upheavals set in motion by the break with Rome had disrupted traditional social patterns, leaving some old families who refused to abandon Catholicism cut off from the ruling establishment. The changes created opportunities for others. Ambitious members of the lower gentry and the upper echelons of the mercantile class could reach high levels in government and enjoy great prestige. A new breed of merchant adventurer took advantage of fresh opportunities opened up by English mariners in foreign lands. Of particular interest was the American coast, where the future colony of Virginia was named in honour of the virgin queen. This social mobility and prosperity created a cultural upsurge – the Elizabethan Age.

When Elizabeth died, at the age of 69 in 1603, the Tudor dynasty died with her. Even so, she left her realm far more stable and powerful than it had been when she ascended the throne. Ironically, she was succeeded by the Protestant son of her old rival Mary, Queen of Scots, who was already ruling Scotland as James VI. By becoming James I of England, he linked the two nations in a union of crowns that survives to this day.

The first of the Stuart dynasty, James kept England at peace and weathered the threat of the Gunpowder Plot. Internally, his reign was touched by corruption scandals and his relations with parliament were sometimes uncomfortable, but there was little sign of the gathering storm that was to engulf the country in the reign of his son and successor, Charles I.

The Gunpowder Plot
When James I tightened the existing restrictions on Catholics on coming to power in England, a group of extremists resolved to blow up parliament, along with the King and Queen and their eldest son, on November 5, 1605. The plot was betrayed and one of the conspirators, Guy Fawkes, was seized in the basement of the parliament building before he had a chance to ignite the 20 or more barrels of gunpowder that had been stockpiled there. The conspirators were all put to death. Their fame spread well beyond England: these illustrations are from a German pamphlet of the time.

The road to civil war

Charles I came to power in 1625 convinced of his absolute prerogative to rule thanks to the 'divine right of kings'. A conscientious but limited man, he soon ran into financial problems that embroiled him in ever-worsening confrontations with parliament. From 1629 he tried to get round his difficulties by governing without parliamentary consent, and for the next 11 years he ruled autocratically with the help of his advisors.

In the long run, however, Charles could not rule without parliament's revenue-raising powers. In 1640, needing funds to fight a war in Scotland, he finally gave way and called parliament once more, only to dissolve the assembly after just 22 days when it refused to accede to his wishes. When a fresh parliament was summoned shortly afterward, the positions of the two sides became yet more entrenched, with the result that soon the country at large was divided into two irreconcilable groups: royalists and parliamentarians.

The last chance of compromise was lost in 1642 when the King made a clumsy and unsuccessful attempt to arrest five of his leading opponents within the chamber of the House of Commons. London was now a parliamentarian stronghold, and Charles was forced to leave. In August of that year, he raised the standard of battle against what he considered to be disloyal subjects. The nation which just 50 years before had been so tightly bound in loyalty to Elizabeth suddenly found itself plunged into all the horrors of civil war. No more successful militarily than politically, Charles was eventually defeated, and over the next seven years would lose first his kingdom and then his head.

A writer's toolkit
Writing boxes like this one, made of walnut and oak lined with painted leather, were popular in England and the rest of Europe up to the 18th century.

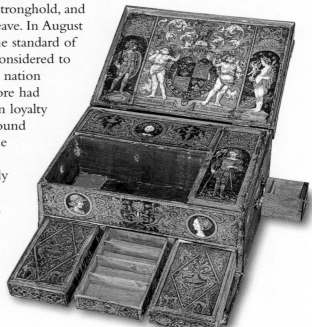

The Reformation in Germany

Martin Luther's *95 Theses* destroyed the unity of the Christian Church and unleashed a conflict that divided Germany's ruling princes.

Propaganda war
Invented in the preceding century, the printing press came into its own in the Reformation as a means of disseminating both pro and anti-papal propaganda. This pamphlet illustration depicts the Catholic Church as a monstrous hybrid, part ass, part dragon, part whore.

Durch Herrn Philippum Melanthon.

In 1517, Martin Luther sparked off a revolution that would eventually split Europe. 'It is vain', he stated, 'to hope for salvation on the basis of a letter of indulgence, even if the commissioner for indulgences or the Pope himself have staked their souls on it.' The letters of indulgence of which he was so critical were documents, sold with permission of the pope, that promised people remission of their sins in exchange for cash. Critics saw these indulgences as an outrageous distortion of the Church's moral mission, and in Luther these critics had found their spokesman.

In many ways Luther made an unlikely revolutionary. A profoundly religious man, he had become a monk in 1505 and was ordained two years later. In 1512 he gained a doctorate in theology at Erfurt and was appointed professor of theology at the University of Wittenberg, preaching regularly at the city's Castle Church.

By then, however, Luther was already deeply disillusioned by the condition of the Church. He had been shocked by the worldliness he encountered on a visit to Rome and was appalled by the shameless traffic in indulgences, which were being touted in Germany by a Dominican monk, Johann Tetzel. Luther was particularly upset that many of his fellow-citizens in Wittenberg preferred to travel to Brandenburg to purchase letters of indulgence than seek forgiveness for their sins in their own home church.

The *95 Theses*

Stung into action, Luther drew up a scathing critique of Church practices and beliefs, which he titled the *95 Theses*. He sent the document to Bishop Albrecht of Magdeburg and Mainz on October 31, 1517, and also dispatched it to Bishop Hieronymus of Brandenburg, hoping to stimulate debate on the issues.

His message soon reached a wider audience. One reason for this was a common discontent with a Church increasingly regarded as corrupt. Another factor was new technology, for Germany was experiencing a printing revolution, and the new presses were soon busy turning out pamphlets both supporting and disputing Luther's ideas.

The issues raised by Luther in *The 95 Theses* went well beyond the sale of indulgences. A growing number of scholars enthusiastically subscribed to his critique, including Philipp Melanchthon, a brilliant young professor of Greek at Wittenberg, who pledged his support in 1518. Some of the rulers of the many statelets into which Germany was then divided also showed interest, one of the first being Landgrave Philip of Hesse. Before long, the talk was of *reformatio* – a Latin word meaning 'renewal'. Since the Council of Constance at the start of the 15th century, the term had been applied to the demand for ecclesiastical reform. The Reformation was getting under way.

Excommunication

The Catholic authorities regarded Luther with hostility, and by 1518 he was under investigation for heresy by the Roman Curia. Luther refused to back down and issued new pamphlets, including his famous *On the Freedom of the Christian Man*. In 1520 he was threatened with excommunication if he did not recant. To the delight of his supporters, he publicly burned the papal bull that contained the warning. In response, Pope Leo X carried out his threat, excommunicating Luther on January 3, 1521.

The Diet of Worms

By now passions were enflamed all across Germany. The princes were deeply divided, and in an attempt to bridge the growing split, Emperor Charles V summoned Luther to attend an imperial diet (a gathering of princes and other notables) at Worms on the River Rhine so his views could be discussed publicly.

At the diet the Emperor twice asked Luther to recant his teachings, to no avail. He then proclaimed an imperial anathema on the dissident preacher, publicly outlawing him. In this desperate situation, Elector Frederick the Wise of Saxony extended a helping hand. On May 4, 1521, he spirited Luther away to the remote Wartburg Castle, near the town of Eisenach in Thuringia, and offered him refuge there under the pseudonym 'Junker Jörg' (Squire George).

For a time Luther remained in hiding, devoting himself to translating the Bible into German to make it accessible to ordinary people. However, the demand for reform had taken on a life of its own. Radical ideas surfaced that went well beyond anything that Luther himself was prepared to countenance. When the church at

Voices for reform

A double portrait, by the German artist Lucas Cranach the Elder, shows the reformers Martin Luther (left) and Philipp Melanchthon holding copies of their writings. Melanchthon urged Luther to prepare a German translation of the Bible, so that ordinary people with no Latin would be able to understand the divine word. In 1521 he published a pioneering work of his own – the first comprehensive summary of the teachings of the Reformation.

Rival currency

The Protestant princes of the Schmalkaldic League operated their own mint in the German city of Goslar from 1541 onward. This coin depicts Elector Johann Friedrich of Saxony.

Luther's protector
Frederick the Wise, Elector of Saxony, in a portrait painted by Lucas Cranach the Elder. Frederick sheltered Martin Luther at Wartburg after he was placed under an imperial ban in 1521.

The Peasants' War

Besides pillorying the clergy, Luther now also attacked the greed of the secular authorities, pointing out shortcomings in both society and education. In his *Address to the Christian Nobility of Germany*, for example, he specifically criticised Germany's wealthiest banking family, insisting that 'the excesses of the Fuggers and people like them must be curtailed'.

As Luther's ideas became more overtly political, they were taken up by people with social grievances who looked to him as a leader or an ally. Many of the farm labourers who rose up in the Peasants' War of 1524–5 took heart from Luther's attacks on the authorities.

The peasant uprising first flared in the southwest of Germany, then spread to the Tyrol, Franconia, Thuringia and Saxony. Its outbreak had a decisive effect on Luther. Forced to choose between the peasants and the princes, he came down on the side of order, unequivocally condemning the violence and calling the rebels 'fanatics with a mob mentality'. The uprising was finally put down, with much bloodshed, at the Battle of Frankenhausen on May 15, 1525.

The forces of the established Church now began to mobilise in the first stirrings of the movement that would become known as the Counter-Reformation. A series of imperial diets was convened, although these only served to underline the religious gulf in Germany. In 1526, at

Wittenberg was damaged during an outbreak of iconoclastic violence, Luther came out of seclusion and returned there in March 1522. In his Lenten sermons that year, he tried to steer the reform movement back to a more moderate path.

Two years later, another imperial diet, this one at Nuremberg, again condemned Luther. By that time, however, his ideas had so much support that no-one dared to arrest him. He travelled freely throughout central Germany, delivering his message in an earthy, everyday language that people understood.

Dissident's retreat
Built from 1067, Wartburg Castle in Saxony became a place of refuge for Martin Luther. He stayed there at the invitation of Frederick the Wise while working on his groundbreaking German translation of the Bible.

Speyer, the Lutherans offered to stay within the Church if they were given the freedom to accept only those doctrines that they considered the work of God rather than man. Charles V refused the compromise and the meeting broke up without a satisfactory conclusion.

The first Protestants

Another diet, held in the same city three years later, proved equally indecisive. When the Emperor again denounced Luther, the princes of Hesse and Anhalt, Brunswick-Lüneburg, Brandenburg and Saxony, along with the representatives of 14 imperial cities, all protested and hence were labelled 'Protestants'. A gathering called in Augsburg in 1530 also proved unable to come up with a mutually acceptable solution. The participants were confronted with a number of statements of faith, but again there was no agreement. Charles V specifically rejected Melanchthon's *Augsburg Confession*, a systematic exposition of Lutheran belief.

The Schmalkaldic War

In response, in 1531 the Protestant princes and cities formed the Schmalkaldic League to defend the faith politically and militarily. Faced with a united opposition, the Emperor wavered. He did not dare risk a military confrontation as his lands were under threat from the Ottomans at the time, so he concluded a settlement at Nuremberg in 1532, giving the Protestants free exercise of their religion.

The period of relative calm that followed was shattered in 1546 when Charles, with the support of Pope Paul II, took on the anti-Catholic forces militarily in the Schmalkaldic War. At the Battle of Mühlberg, fought on the banks of the River Elbe on April 24, 1547, the forces of the Counter-Reformation were victorious and the Protestant alliance was smashed.

Luther himself did not live to witness this defeat. He had written his last tract – provocatively entitled *Against the Papacy at*

▨	Catholic
▨	Protestant
▨	Predominantly Catholic
▥	Predominantly Protestant
●	Important towns and cities

Rome, Founded by the Devil – in 1545. The great reformer died on February 18, 1546, in Eisleben. His longtime friend and colleague Melanchthon was now the surviving champion of the new doctrine.

Although Charles's victory in the Schmalkaldic War was a serious setback for the Protestant cause, it failed to resolve the religious divide in the way the Emperor had hoped. When a settlement of sorts was

VIEWPOINT

Nailing of the Theses to the church door – myth or reality?

To publicise his criticisms of the Catholic Church, Martin Luther is said to have nailed his *95 Theses* to the door of the Castle Church at Wittenberg in Germany on October 31, 1517. But did this revolutionary event actually happen?

The principal source for the story was a text by Johann Schneider, a friend of Luther's, who was thought to have witnessed the act. However, in 1961, while examining Schneider's original Latin manuscript, a scholar found that there had been a misreading of the text and that the Latin word *modeste* ('modestly') had been wrongly transliterated as *me teste*, or 'as I can testify'. Schneider, it seemed, made no mention of Luther nailing up the theses on the church door, or of the traditional date of October 31.

The traditional view
Illustrators down the ages have popularised the image of Martin Luther nailing his *95 Theses* to the church door in Wittenberg. This one is from the late 19th century,

finally reached, in 1555, it came about mostly through mutual exhaustion. At the Diet of Augsburg that year, the two opposing sides agreed to differ, giving individual princes the right to determine the religion of the lands they ruled. Protestant and Catholic states were to coexist.

The Peace of Augsburg

The poet and historian Friedrich Schiller later described the Peace of Augsburg as 'essentially only a temporary relief, a measure born of desperate and turbulent times. It was not informed by the laws of justice, nor was it the fruit of considered deliberation on matters of religion and religious freedom'. In fact the settlement did not guarantee freedom of worship. Rather, it meant that rulers were free to determine the faith of their subjects, as in the maxim *Cuius regio, eius religio*: 'The ruler's religion is the state's religion.' The only option for citizens out of sympathy with their prince's decision was to leave.

Yet for all its limitations, the Peace of Augsburg brought 50 years of relative calm to Germany by accepting the religious divisions that existed in the country at the time. Thereafter the struggle returned to the field of religion rather than politics. The Roman Catholic Church redefined its beliefs at the Council of Trent, which met from 1545 to 1563. The council's decisions formed the core of the Counter-Reformation, condemning Protestant doctrines on original sin, confession, the role of priests and the sacraments. At the same time Pope Pius V ruthlessly enforced orthodoxy in the Catholic lands by reintroducing the Inquisition to persecute dissenters.

With the backing of powerful Catholic dynasties such as the Habsburgs and the Wittelsbachs, the Jesuits came to be the force behind the Counter-Reformation. Founded by the Spaniard St Ignatius Loyola in Paris in 1534, the Society of Jesus practiced asceticism and absolute obedience to the pope. Its members were soon playing a prominent role across Europe, especially in education.

The first German to join the order was St Peter Canisius, in 1543. He was active in fostering the order's growth, going with the Bishop of Augsburg to the Council of Trent and subsequently formulating the German Catechism as a counterpart to Luther's statement of belief. In just 10 years, this work was published in 55 editions and nine languages.

A nation divided

While much of the north joined the Protestant cause, southern Germany stayed loyal to Catholicism. No region promoted the Counter-Reformation more zealously than Bavaria, and its ruler, the Wittelsbach Duke Albert V, was the Jesuits' principal supporter in the imperial lands. With the Duke's encouragement, they founded a seminary at Ingolstadt, 70km (45 miles) north of Munich, in 1556.

Further north, the city of Cologne, a Catholic bastion, became a flashpoint in the conflict between the two faiths when its archbishop converted to Calvinism and took a wife. In 1583 Pope Gregory XIII declared him excommunicated and deposed, and war broke out between his followers and those of the loyal Catholic chosen to replace him. Ultimately, the Protestants were defeated with the aid of Bavarian and Spanish troops.

In 1597, the 24-year-old Maximilian I came to power in Bavaria. The new duke was a passionate supporter of the Catholic cause, and when Protestant states formed a new alliance under the leadership of the Elector Palatine, he responded by bringing Germany's Catholic rulers together in the Catholic League. Thus the battle lines were drawn, and the two sides would presently confront one another anew in the Thirty Years' War.

Courtly splendour
For all the turmoil that engulfed the German lands in the wake of the Reformation, the art of the gold and silversmiths blossomed in the 16th century. This decorative chalice is made of gold plated with silver.

The Ottomans at Europe's door

On the Mediterranean and in the Balkans, the rulers of the Ottoman Empire pursued expansionist policies that often brought them up against their arch-rivals, the Habsburgs.

Sultan and poet
Suleiman the Magnificent, the greatest of the Ottoman rulers, in a portrait painted around 1530. Renowned as a successful war leader, he also wrote poetry under the pseudonym Muhibi.

The 26-year-old who assumed the leadership of the Ottoman Empire in 1520 put the fear of God into the West. Sultan Suleiman I was tall and gaunt, with an aquiline nose, distinguished pallor and stately appearance. Tenacious and decisive, he was also a subtle and measured statesman. Turkish historians have dubbed him Suleiman the Just, or Suleiman the Lawgiver, but the West came to know him as 'the Magnificent'.

Suleiman the Magnificent

Suleiman's rule was blessed with good fortune from the outset. His accession passed off smoothly in rare peace and harmony. The young ruler was the sole surviving son of Sultan Selim I, and so ascended the throne unchallenged. His name recalled the Biblical King Solomon, respected as a great ruler in the Muslim tradition, as in the Judeo-Christian one. As the tenth Ottoman sultan he was inspired by the great achievements of his predecessors, who had started out as rulers of a tiny corner of Asiatic Turkey and built an empire stretching from the Crimea to southern Egypt, from Syria to the Adriatic Sea. Suleiman believed that it was his destiny to extend Ottoman power even further across Europe.

Western Christendom was soon to discover the scope of the Sultan's ambitions. He unleashed his armies in two main directions. One targeted Hungary by way of the Balkans, while the other had the Aegean as its objective. Having taken power in the autumn of 1520, he wasted no time in launching his first campaign in the spring of the following year.

His timing was perfect: France and the Habsburg-ruled Holy Roman Empire were at loggerheads with one another. King Francis I of France and the Emperor Charles V, heir to the Spanish throne as well as ruler of Germany, were engaged in a bitter struggle for power in Italy. Engrossed in their rivalry, each side effectively neutralised the other. Charles's brother

Ferdinand, installed in Vienna as ruler of the ancestral Habsburg lands in Austria, was not yet in control of his new domain. In Hungary itself the Ottoman forces would be confronted by King Louis II, a mere boy of 14.

So Suleiman felt confident of victory when, in 1521, he dispatched a force that included 300 artillery pieces and 3000 camels. This exotic army took the fortress of Subotica on what is now Serbia's northern border with Hungary, and the important stronghold of Belgrade. The way to Hungary itself was open, but Suleiman cautiously decided not to press his advantage further for the time being. After establishing a garrison of 3000 troops in Belgrade, he withdrew the rest of his forces to Turkey, where he made a triumphal entrance into his own capital, Istanbul.

Cut and thrust
The swords used by Ottoman warriors had an international reputation. As a general rule, Turkish weapons were lighter than those used by their European counterparts and had curved blades. This one is shown with its scabbard.

Ottoman forts (background)
A miniature painting depicts two Turkish strongholds on the Black Sea coast.

The Battle of Mohacs
Although the fall of Belgrade set alarm bells ringing across Europe, little was done to prevent a fresh Ottoman incursion. As King of Spain and Holy Roman Emperor, Charles V was the man best placed to organise a concerted response to the threat, but he was distracted by a host of other problems. Besides the ongoing war in Italy, the Habsburgs' German lands were suffering the impact of the Reformation and the Peasants' War, so no united effort was made to raise forces against the Turks. As a result, King Louis of Hungary was left to bear the Ottoman onslaught alone.

Suleiman finally renewed the assault in 1526. An Ottoman army almost 70,000 strong advanced across the Danube plains, undeterred by bad roads and heavy rainfall. At Mohacs, it was met by a smaller Hungarian force, reinforced by a few papal and Slavonian mercenaries. Outnumbered by at least three to one, Louis and his vassals suffered the worst defeat in all Hungarian history. Louis himself died in the battle, along with some 20,000 of his countrymen. Hungary was left defenceless, at the mercy of the Ottomans. Suleiman advanced with his army through the lowland plains until he reached the capital of Buda, where he set up his headquarters. For the first time since Charles Martel's 8th-century victory at Tours, Islamic armies were poised to strike at the heart of Europe.

The siege of Vienna
In spite of his overwhelming military success, Suleiman had no intention of directly annexing Hungary, since doing so would have stretched his supply lines to breaking point. Instead, he controlled the country through surrogate Christian kings. In the power vacuum that followed Louis's death, two principal candidates put themselves forward for the Hungarian crown. The victor was Janos Zapolya, a Hungarian nobleman already serving as *voivode* (lord) of Transylvania, who was chosen over Ferdinand I of Austria. Suleiman lent his backing to Zapolya, hoping to turn Hungary into a client state under his rule.

Ferdinand remained such a threat to the new king that, two years later, Turkish troops returned to Hungary at Zapolya's request to put his rival to flight. Suleiman's forces secured Buda for his ally before advancing to the very gates of Vienna. To the alarm of all Christendom, a huge

Ottoman army encamped outside the city walls in the autumn of 1529, in some 25,000 tents spread across the Danube plain. From vantage-points high on the spire of St Stephen's Cathedral, sentinels reported the enemy's manoeuvres to the fear-stricken citizens below.

Yet the siege failed and Suleiman never took the 'Golden Apple', as he called Vienna. Winter set in early that year, and heavy rain broke the Sultan's supply chain, leaving him short of heavy artillery and munitions. For the first time in his career, he had to accept defeat, lifting the siege after barely four weeks. To the relief of all Europe, the Habsburg capital was saved.

The fate of Hungary

Hungary's fate was decided after Janos Zapolya's death in 1540. Ferdinand was able then to claim a narrow strip in the west and north of the country, while the principality of Transylvania retained a degree of independence as an Ottoman protectorate under the rule of Zapolya's underage son. The rest of the country, including the capital of Buda, fell to Suleiman, who made it an Ottoman province. The annexation removed the last buffer between the Ottoman and Habsburg empires, which thereafter confronted one another as rivals across a frontier extending south via Lake Balaton to the Adriatic Sea.

Ottoman rule brought great change to the occupied territories. The long military campaigns in the Balkans had been accompanied by pillaging, burning, murder and mass deportation of the native inhabitants. Now a period of peace and good order ensued. The Ottoman rulers displayed a remarkably liberal attitude to their Christian subjects. Although they had to pay extra taxes, they were otherwise allowed to practice their religion unmolested under the Sultan's

The siege of Vienna
Following his victory over the Hungarians at Mohacs three years earlier, Suleiman led an Ottoman army right to the walls of Vienna in 1529. He gave up his attempt to capture the city, however, mainly because bad weather had prevented him from getting enough heavy siege engines into place before the onset of winter. In addition, he heard that a Christian relief force was on its way.

protection. Since Turks did not migrate in large numbers into the region, life for the peasants in the newly conquered lands was little better or worse than before.

Ownership of large tracts of land was given to Muslim landowners as a reward for their military service during the

Death on campaign
In 1566 an Ottoman force of 100,000 men under Suleiman's command laid siege to the Hungarian stronghold of Szigetvar, not far from the modern city of Pecs. Laid up with gout, the Sultan died during the course of the siege, but to avoid damaging morale his death was not announced until his troops had captured the town and Selim II had ascended the throne. This illustration is taken from a16th century manuscript devoted to the campaigns of Suleiman.

campaign. In general, the new owners turned out to be better managers of their estates than their Christian neighbours. Some Christian proprietors who did not want to be dispossessed by the new rulers chose to convert to Islam. In Bosnia and Herzegovina an indigenous Muslim popu-lation arose which soon took over the administration of the region.

Even at its most coercive, the Ottoman social system offered opportunities for able individuals to rise in the sultan's service.

Each year, in the so-called 'gathering of boys' (*devshirme*), a specified number of male children born into Christian families were recruited from the Balkans and sent to Istanbul, where they were raised as Muslims and given a thorough education. Many holders of high office in the empire began their careers in this way, among them Suleiman's own right-hand man, the Albanian Ibrahim. Rustem Pasha, a Bosnian who later succeeded to the post, was even permitted to marry a daughter of the sultan.

Renewal in the Balkans

As a result, Ottoman sovereignty over the occupied territories was not regarded as especially oppressive. Provincial governors such as Mehmed Pasha Sokoli, from the Bosnian mountain village of Sokolovici, built and decorated their palaces in a picturesque, Muslim-influenced style. The famous bridges at Mostar and Visegrad owed their construction to the Ottoman overlords of Bosnia, as did the mosques in Sarajevo and Banja Luka. Under the sultans, the most inaccessible Balkan valleys were brought firmly into the imperial sphere, to the benefit of the local economies. Sarajevo became an important commercial city with good transport links to Dubrovnik, Skopje and Istanbul.

The Mediterranean theatre

The Ottomans' other major theatre of war in Europe was the Mediterranean region. There, the sultans confronted not just the Spanish branch of the Habsburg dynasty but also the trading powers of Venice and Genoa, with their numerous military and commercial bases on the Aegean islands.

The Knights of St John (also known as the Knights Hospitallers) was a crusading order that had occupied the heavily fortified island of Rhodes off the coast of Anatolia since 1310. They had long been a thorn in the Ottomans' side, so to remove the threat, Suleiman sent an armada of 300 ships and 10,000 troops in 1522, just two years after he came to the throne. The

Hospitallers received no help from other Christian powers – the 700 knights had to defend the island's 5000 inhabitants alone. The knights could do nothing against Suleiman's heavy artillery; within 145 days, the island's defences had been breached and Ottoman forces stormed the walls. Suleiman accepted the knights' surrender on Christmas Day 1522 with magnanimity, ordering his troops to march silently into the fortress while allowing the knights to withdraw unharmed. The Hospitallers subsequently settled on Malta and in the Libyan port of Tripoli.

Barbarossa versus the Holy League

The conquest of Rhodes gave the Ottomans control over the entire Eastern Mediterranean. Yet the West did not abandon the region without a fight. A Genoese admiral called Andrea Doria took up arms in the service of the Holy Roman Emperor, and succeeded in retaking a number of bases in the Aegean. So Suleiman appointed a feared corsair based in North Africa, Khayr ad-Din Barbarossa, as supreme commander of his naval forces. Barbarossa had a powerful fleet and set sail for southern Italy. This Ottoman navy pillaged and burned many coastal settlements and launched raids on several western Mediterranean islands.

In response, Spain, Venice, the Papacy and the Knights of St John formed an alliance, the Holy League, that sent a combined fleet to confront the Ottomans in the Gulf of Prevesa in the Ionian Sea. The ageing Andrea Doria, now 72, was outmanouevred by Barbarossa and withdrew, giving the Ottomans a major victory. Venice subsequently had to accept extremely unfavourable peace terms, losing several bases to the Ottomans and being forced to pay large sums in tribute to the victors.

The alliance with France

The Ottomans increasingly challenged Spanish dominance in North Africa and were able to expand their power steadily.

Then, in 1542, by forging ties with the King of France, Suleiman achieved a diplomatic coup. Motivated by his bitter rivalry with the Emperor Charles V, Francis I agreed to launch a joint naval offensive with the Ottomans against the Habsburg ruler. So the forces of the Muslim corsair Barbarossa and the Christian King of France fought side by side in an assault on the port of Nice, which belonged to Savoy, a Habsburg ally. After putting up a brave defence, the duchy's ruler was forced to surrender the city. Francis then made his own harbour of Toulon available as a winter anchorage for Barbarossa's vessels.

The West was outraged that 'God's Scourge' – Barbarossa's nickname, won for sufferings inflicted on the Christian communities of the Mediterranean coastal lands – should find safe haven with a Christian ruler. Francis, however, was so immersed in his feud with the Habsburgs that he ignored the reproaches.

Seeking to gain naval supremacy across the Mediterranean, Suleiman next laid siege to Malta in 1565. The Knights of St John, who had moved there after leaving Rhodes, were charged with the task of defending

Decorative tiles (background)
A pattern of plum blossom decorates these ceramic wall tiles from the Turkish city of Iznik, which was renowned for its pottery.

Selim the drunkard
Suleiman's son and successor Selim II was widely known as 'the Drunkard' because of his fondness for alcohol. His reign marked the beginning of the Ottoman Empire's long decline.

TIME WITNESS

Battle of Lepanto

A member of the Knights of St John military order left an account of the part played by Don John of Austria, commander of the Christian forces in the great naval confrontation:

'As soon as the two admirals' flagships came within sight of one another, they engaged in a furious dogfight… A terrible pitched battle ensued, lasting for three hours; then, quite suddenly, it became clear that the Christian fleet was beginning to prevail on the left flank of the line. Accordingly, Don John turned his attentions to the right flank, where the Christian forces were most in need of support…'

War galleys

Lepanto was the last major naval engagement using galleys. A battle between these mighty warships inevitably involved hand-to-hand combat between crews.

Tripoli and other Spanish possessions in North Africa from Ottoman attack, as well as protecting the southern Italian coast.

The ageing Sultan laid his plans with care, ferrying heavy artillery and an invasion force of 40,000 men to attack the island in a fleet of 160 ships. But the order's grand master, Jean Parisot de la Valette, put up unexpectedly stiff resistance. The attackers managed, at the cost of heavy losses, to capture the Fort of St Elmo, recently built at the entrance to the Grand Harbour of Valetta, but they were unable to advance further. The threat of autumn storms, combined with delays in getting supplies across the Mediterranean and news of the imminent arrival of a Christian relief force, caused the Sultan to call off the siege after 105 days. In the following year Suleiman died, at the age of 72, while supervising the siege of the Hungarian town of Szigetvar.

The onset of decline

The death of Suleiman the Magnificent marked the turning point of the Ottoman Empire's power. His immediate successors were Selim II – appositely nicknamed 'the Drunkard' – and Murad III, both weak rulers who devoted themselves more to the pleasures of the harem than to affairs of state. Moreover, the size of the empire made it increasingly difficult to administer: the time that it took to deploy troops from Turkey to Hungary and the western Balkans increasingly restricted the scope for military action, while in the western Mediterranean the Ottomans lacked bases where a fleet could ride out the winter. Selim managed to chalk up at least one success with the conquest of Cyprus in 1570, but his victory only succeeded in uniting his enemies against him. After the island had fallen, a revived Holy League involving Spain, Venice, the papacy and the Knights of St John – this time joined by the Genoese and other Italian city-states – raised a 200-strong fleet against him. Command was given to the 25-year-old Don John of Austria, an illegitimate son of the Emperor Charles V.

The Christian and Ottoman fleets met on October 7, 1571, in the Strait of Lepanto, off the present-day port of

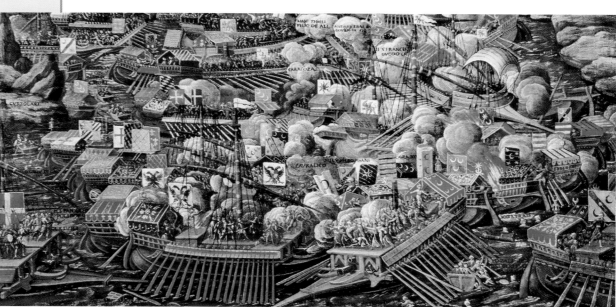

Navpaktos in the Gulf of Corinth. The battle raged for the entire afternoon, ship pitted against ship, gunpowder smoke shrouding the scene and reducing visibility, while the waters turned red with the blood of the dead. The Ottoman flagship became locked in desperate combat with the Spanish vessel commanded by Don John, and the Sultan's crack troops launched themselves into a hail of fire from Spanish marksmen. Finally, the Ottoman Grand Admiral Ali Pasha was brought down, and his ship fell to the Spanish. By nightfall, it was clear that the Holy League had won a resounding victory.

The defeat was a bitter blow for the Ottomans: 244 of their ships were sunk or captured and some 30,000 Turks had been killed, including almost all of the Ottoman admirals. In the aftermath of the battle, around 12,000 Christian captives and prisoners–of–war were freed from forced labour as slaves on the Turkish vessels.

Famous victory – or stalemate?

Christian Europe saw the Battle of Lepanto as a decisive victory that smashed the Ottomans once and for all, and they celebrated accordingly. Pope Pius V launched the Rosary Feast on October 7 and commissioned a magnificent vaulted ceiling for the Church of Santa Maria Aracoeli in Rome. In Barcelona Cathedral, the figurehead of Don John's flagship, a carved figure of Christ, was venerated, while in Ingolstadt in Bavaria a model of a galley made of chased silver was installed in the Church of Our Lady, built specially to house it. Famous painters, including Titian, Veronese and Tintoretto, were commissioned to portray the battle for posterity.

Yet the West failed to convert its military triumph into long-term political gain. Even though Ottoman naval domination of the Mediterranean had been well and truly broken, Cyprus remained in Ottoman hands and Venice was still obliged to pay large sums in tribute to Istanbul in order to retain its commercial rights in the eastern Mediterranean.

In the Balkans a similar stalemate situation set in along the Hungarian border. The advances that Suleiman's forces had made bogged down into a grinding guerrilla war in which control of every castle and town was bitterly contested. This war of attrition eventually ended with a ceasefire in 1606.

Breathing space for the Balkans

The ensuing Peace of Zsitvatorok regulated the relationship between emperor and sultan on the basis of new terms of equality, while the territorial status quo was to a large extent preserved. The principality of Transylvania was permitted to retain its independence under Ottoman patronage, as were large parts of northeastern Hungary, while the Habsburg Emperor, Rudolf II, retained control over imperial Hungary. However, the largest part of that country remained in the Ottoman sphere.

By mutually agreeing to recognise the situation that had long pertained on the ground the two rival powers were able to enjoy a period of peace that lasted for almost half a century. Yet the cessation of hostilities amounted to no more than a pause in a continuing struggle. The Ottoman threat to Europe continued and when, from the middle of the 17th century, control of the empire fell into the hands of a series of dynamic, reforming grand viziers, the conflict with the Habsburgs flared up once more.

Coffee and culinary delights
Modern gastronomes have the Ottomans to thank for introducing aubergines, globe artichokes, apricots, cherries, figs and coffee to the European table. This 16th-century miniature depicts a mobile Turkish coffee kiosk. In noble households, coffee was served from elegant vessels like this silver-plated coffee pot (background), which has a handle in the form of a dragon and a decorative pattern of intertwined flowers.

Swiss reformers – Zwingli and Calvin

The work of two religious reformers led the Swiss Confederation to split along denominational lines.

Puritan pioneer
Ulrich Zwingli, shown here in a portrait by the Dutch painter Pieter Pourbus that now hangs in Florence's Uffizi Gallery. Zwingli was a people's priest at the Great Minster in Zurich. The post carried little income or official influence, but provided the reformer with a pulpit for preaching his message.

A remarkable scene was played out in Zurich's City Hall on January 29, 1523. The city's Grand Council had convened a forum to discuss contentious religious issues that were dividing the population. The entire intellectual elite of the city and surrounding district – about 600 councillors and priests – had gathered to hear a battle of words between Johannes Faber, an expert on dogma representing the Bishop of Constance and the established Church, and Ulrich Zwingli, religious reformer. Zwingli was there to argue that, 'All those who claim that the gospels are invalid without confirmation by the Church are wrong, and defame God. The whole point of the gospels is that our Lord Jesus Christ made known to us the will of his heavenly father and delivered us from death through his innocence.'

The power of the Lord's word

Zwingli had studied the Scriptures in Latin, Hebrew and Greek, and had a major advantage over Faber, since the council had laid down that the Church's official champion should use biblical evidence alone to refute the doctrine that Zwingli was expounding. Before long it was not the reformer but rather the Catholic Church that stood in the dock. Where in the Bible, Zwingli demanded, was the Church so much as mentioned?

In his response, Faber began to cite the Acts of the Apostles and the epistles of St Paul, but Zwingli interrupted him: 'No, no, the true Church is the community of all believers. The Church of true Christians is invisible to mankind, since only God has the power to look into our hearts!'

It was soon clear to the council who had won the debate. Their judgment concluded that 'Although Master Ulrich

Zwingli has had many accusations flung at him, no-one has been able to disprove him through the holy scriptures. Thus, because nobody has been able to demonstrate that he is guilty of any form of heresy, the mayor and council henceforth announce, by way of preventing great unrest, that he is free to go his way and promulgate the holy gospels and the true word of the Lord until such time as he may be gainsaid.'

In a revolutionary move, municipal authorities had judged theological matters and weighed up which of two opposing factions – a representative of the legally established bishop of the area or an alleged heretic – was in the right. Nowhere else in Europe would such a scene have been possible. Since the swearing of the Rütli Oath in 1307, however, the Swiss had shown a determined political and intellectual independence, fighting off all attempts to deprive them of their rights with a combination of robust diplomacy and military action.

Fertile ground for reform

The Church abuses that had aroused Martin Luther's wrath in Germany had also displeased the Swiss, whose loyalty to Rome had never been particularly strong. In addition, the humanist movement, with its tradition of rational thought, had gained a strong following.

Towards the end of the 15th century, Basel emerged as the intellectual centre of the country – the first Swiss university

opened there in 1460. In 1521 the great humanist thinker Erasmus of Rotterdam arrived to teach in its schools, and spent the next eight years in the city. Although careful not to step outside the bounds of orthodoxy, his eloquent criticisms of the

existing state of the Church helped to prepare the ground for reform. Yet it was in Zurich that the Swiss Reformation got under way. Zwingli, who had been born in Zurich's Toggenburg district on January 1, 1484, had been preaching at the city's Great Minster since 1518.

Even more than Luther, Zwingli combined a gift for theological analysis with a commitment to social activism, and these qualities made him an energetic politician. He skilfully combined demands for an end to Church abuses with a call for economic and political reform. He criticised the moral failings of the clergy, particularly in regard to the peddling of indulgences, while also opposing the practice by which a single priest could hold multiple benefices. His principal

The Battle of Kappel
A copperplate engraving, by the Swiss artist Matthäus Merian the Elder, shows the battle between Catholic and Protestant forces in which Zwingli was killed in 1531.

Centre of dissent
In the 16th century Geneva, situated on the lake of the same name (below), was a free episcopal city contested by France and Savoy. The French-born theologian and statesman John Calvin (bottom) made it his base and turned it into a bastion of the reformed faith.

demand, however, was for the Church to give up its secular landholdings.

After the City Hall debate, the city of Zurich supported Zwingli's programme. Mass was replaced by a simple communion service, priests were no longer disbarred from marrying and Church lands were sold to commercial interests. Other cities, such as Berne, quickly followed Zurich's example in adopting the reforms.

Zwingli's attempts to create a Protestant ideology that was acceptable across Europe were less successful. He fell out with Luther over the issue of Christ's physical presence in the bread and wine of the sacrament, which Luther supported. The Protestant ruler Philip of Hesse brought the two together at the Marburg Debates in 1529 in the hope of affecting a reconciliation, but on this critical issue the two had to agree to differ.

Meanwhile, in the Swiss Confederation itself, opposition to the Reformation began to harden. The five forest cantons of Lucerne, Uri, Schwyz, Unterwalden and Zug joined to uphold traditional Catholic beliefs against Zwingli's doctrines. Part of their opposition was political, for the reformer condemned the practice of mercenary soldiering and its associated pension payments, a major source of income for the forest cantons' citizens.

War between the cantons

The first physical skirmishes between Catholic and Protestant factions broke out in 1529, and two years later the bloody War of Kappel began. Zwingli, serving as a military chaplain with the Protestant army, fell in battle on October 11, 1531.

One month later a peace treaty was signed confirming the division of the German-speaking cantons along denominational lines and setting the tone of the Confederation for the next 200 years. The Catholic Five Regions plus the cantons of Freiburg and Solothurn, which adhered to the old faith, were together able to outvote the Reformist cities of Basel, Berne, Schaffhausen and Zurich.

Calvin and predestination

The citizens of Berne, who had played no part in the war, subsequently extended their territory westward, helping to spread the Reformation message to the cities of Lausanne and Geneva. It was from Geneva that John Calvin carried on Zwingli's work in French-speaking Switzerland.

Born Jean Cauvin in Noyon, France, on July 10, 1509, he studied philosophy and jurisprudence. Influenced by Luther's teachings, he adopted the Reformist faith in about 1530 and had to leave France because of his beliefs. He arrived in Basel in 1535, changing his name to Calvin. At the heart of his theology stood the doctrine of the predestination of the elect, chosen for salvation by an all-knowing God. In the religious communities of this chosen minority, he believed, God's Kingdom would be realised on Earth.

Like Zwingli, Calvin regarded the eucharist as a liturgical act at which Christ was present in spirit, in contrast to the Catholic doctrine by which the communion bread and wine are believed to be transformed literally into the body and blood of Christ. This fundamental division between Catholic and Protestant doctrine survives to this day.

When Calvin moved to Geneva in 1536 he found the Reformation in full cry. Guillaume Farel, a reformist preacher, told him that God would not forgive him if he failed to lend his intellectual weight to the Protestant cause. Calvin drafted a confession of faith that stirred up much resistance because of the strictness of its provisions, and when, in 1538, Calvin and Farel refused to administer communion to their recalcitrant congregation they were driven out of the city. For the next three years Calvin ministered to a community of religious refugees in Strasbourg, before the Geneva city council invited him back.

A strict theocratic regime

Calvin devoted the remaining 23 years of his life to establishing a strict theocratic regime in both the city and its churches. A synod of church elders guarded public morals, monitoring whether the citizens were living in accordance with the Word of God. The synod enforced compulsory church attendance and banned all frivolities such as sports and dancing. Churches were stripped of all decoration so the faithful could concentrate on God's word without distraction.

Draconian punishments were imposed by the regime on apostates, heretics and dissenters. By 1564, 58 death sentences had been passed, including 34 against people convicted as witches. The most famous victim of the persecutions was the Spanish scientist and theologian Michael Servetus, who die at the stake in 1533.

The spread of Calvinism

In 1549, the followers of Ulrich Zwingli and of John Calvin reached agreement which was marked by signing the Zurich Accord. Ten years later Calvin founded a university of Calvinist Protestantism, the Geneva Academy, which helped to spread the teachings of the Reformation throughout the world. By adopting the Heidelberg Catechism of 1563 and the Second Helvetic Confession a year later, strengthened by the decrees of the Synod of Dordrecht in 1618-19, the reformed church firmly committed itself to the Calvinist strain of Protestantism. While Lutheranism initially remained confined to Germany and Scandinavia, Calvinism spread rapidly through much of western Europe. Independent and Presbyterian sects subsequently broke away from the Calvinist Church in Great Britain, from where their teachings reached North America in the 17th century.

Avoiding adornment

Calvinist meeting-places, such as this church in Lyon, had no ornament to distract worshippers from the word of God.

Calvin himself died on May 27, 1564. Two years later his followers joined with Zwingli's to agree a common faith, set down in the Second Helvetic Confession. This creed was subsequently also adopted in Scotland, Poland, Bohemia and Hungary.

Serious consequences

The Swiss Confederation was split by the Reformation: a league of mainly rural Catholic cantons was set against an alliance of Protestant cities. The reformist camp included Switzerland's most important economic centres along with two-thirds of the population.

Over time, religious differences between the Protestant cantons and the neighbouring Catholic regions of southern Germany caused a gradual loosening of Switzerland's remaining ties with the Holy Roman Empire. The break was finally confirmed in the treaty ending the Thirty Years' War in 1648, when the European powers formally recognised Switzerland's full independence.

Spain's Golden Age

Spain commanded a global empire in the 16th century, and in cultural terms the nation was at its peak. Politically and economically, however, the kings of Spain were powerless to prevent the start of the country's slow decline.

Royal retreat
El Escorial, Philip II's palace in the hills behind Madrid. The ground plan drawn up by court architect Juan Bautista de Toledo took a lattice pattern across a not-quite-square 200m wide by 160m deep (650ft by 530ft). The outer walls, protected by towers at the four corners, surrounded a series of internal courtyards. In the centre of the complex stands the basilica, its dome rising 95m (310ft) high, with cloisters adjoining. El Escorial served as a monastery as well as a palace.

For much of the first half of the 16th century, the Holy Roman Emperor, Charles V, was the most powerful man in Europe. Various well-chosen marriages arranged by his Habsburg forebears had made him ruler not just of imperial lands in Germany, but also of the Netherlands, large swathes of Italy, Spain and the newly conquered Spanish overseas colonies in Central and South America.

By the 1550s, however, the Emperor was growing tired. He had a son, Philip, born in 1527, who was ready to take his place, so the ageing ruler gradually handed over power, making Philip king of Naples and Sicily in 1554 and of the Netherlands in 1555. In 1556, at the age of 56, Charles handed over the greatest prize of all: Spain and its overseas colonies. Freed at last from the burden of duty, he then retired to the

monastery of Yuste in Spain to make his peace with God. He died two years later, on September 21, 1558.

The empire that Charles himself had inherited was too much for any one man, so he passed the German lands to his brother Ferdinand. Even so, Philip's inheritance was daunting, especially as the territory was accompanied by a long-running conflict with France, an ongoing struggle against the Turks in the Mediterranean, and an uneasy relationship with the papacy in Italy.

A conscientious monarch

Charles had every reason to feel confident in his heir – Philip was honest, upright and profoundly pious. He had been brought up with a keen sense of duty and he cared deeply for the well-being of his empire, seeing it as his lifelong duty to

preserve the legacy he had inherited. Yet he was also a limited man. Stiff and formal in his public manner, he lacked decisiveness and took refuge from the challenges of change in a backward-looking conservatism. Throughout his 42-year reign he set himself doggedly against the driving forces that were shaping a new era of European history: the Reformation, Dutch independence and the rising confidence of the French and English nations. His greatest concern was the preservation of the Catholic Church, and he made himself the chief secular champion of the Counter-Reformation.

Some of the King's difficulties sprang from his shyness, which stopped him meeting his subjects face to face. Instead he ran the empire from behind his desk in the monastery-cum-palace of El Escorial that he built for himself on the hills outside Madrid. He conducted affairs of

Ruler of worlds
Philip II (above) inherited the Spanish throne at the age of 29, having already assumed control of Milan, the Kingdom of Naples and Sicily, and the Netherlands. As king of Spain he also ruled over Spain's colonies in the Americas.

Pledging peace
Philip II of Spain and Henry II of France put an end to a long sequence of wars between France and Habsburg Spain with the signing of the Treaty of Cateau-Cambrésis in 1559. Philip married Henry's 15-year-old daughter Elisabeth of Valois to set the seal on the peace.

state there in an atmosphere of austere magnificence, surrounded by monks and holy relics and the tombs of his ancestors.

The politics of marriage

In the Habsburg tradition of dynastic marriages, Philip wed four times. At 16 he married his cousin Maria of Portugal; the couple had a disabled son, Don Carlos, who was kept away from positions of responsibility. Politically, the match led to the union of Portugal and Spain. When Maria's nephew Sebastian, Potugal's ruler since 1557, died heirless on crusade in Morocco in 1578, Philip put forward his own claim, and with the backing of a Spanish army was crowned king in 1580.

Maria died in childbirth in 1545 and Philip next married Mary, eldest daughter of England's Henry VIII. The marriage began as a diplomatic success: in 1553

Mary inherited the English throne and for five years, until her death in 1558, Philip ruled England with her as joint sovereign. He had hoped to bring England back into the Catholic fold, but this ambition failed when Mary died childless and her Protestant half-sister Elizabeth became queen.

Philip's third match, to Elisabeth of Valois, daughter of France's Henry II, was intended to put an end to the long rivalry that had divided the Habsburgs and the French monarchy. The marriage lasted for nine years, until Elisabeth died after giving birth to a second daughter. His last bride was Anna of Austria, fellow-Habsburg and daughter of the Emperor Maximilian II. She bore him the son who inherited the throne as Philip III. Anna was a strict Catholic and the marriage strengthened the Counter-Reformation alliance between Spain and the imperial house.

War on heresy

Philip dealt harshly with anyone who deviated from Catholic orthodoxy. Censorship was rigidly enforced, and Protestants were targeted by the Inquisition; Lutheran congregations were unearthed in Valladolid and Seville in 1558 and were mercilessly persecuted and destroyed. The King even had the primate of Spain, the Archbishop of Toledo, Bartolomé de Carranza, investigated for supposed Protestant leanings in his writings; Carranza ended up spending 17 years in prison.

Philip also vented his suspicions on the Moriscos, the descendants of Muslims forcibly converted to Christianity at the time of the reconquest of Spain from the Moors. The Moriscos numbered some 275,000 people out of a total population of about 8 million. Many who refused to give up their traditional customs and Arabic language suffered persecution, and tens of thousands emigrated as a result.

A classbound society

The Spain Philip ruled was rigidly classbound, in love with an aristocratic ideal. Up to 10 per cent of the population laid claim to some form of noble title. Grandees from the upper echelons of the aristocracy provided the country's political leadership and its highest-ranking state officials. Below them, the *caballeros*, or knights, also enjoyed extensive privileges. A third class of *hidalgos*, or gentlemen, made up the lower reaches of the nobility; often impoverished, they provided the Spanish crown with some of its proudest and most intrepid conquistadors. In addition, a growing class of scholars, the *letrados*, occupied many official positions. The Church and the

Act of faith
Individuals found guilty of heresy by the Spanish Inquisition were denounced and executed in a ceremony called *auto-da-fé* ('act of faith'). Thousands of Jews, Muslims and Protestant Christians were burned at the stake. The emerald pendant (inset) belonged to an inquisitor.

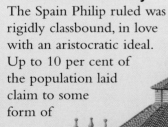

Bastion of Christianity
Built from 1523 onwards, the cathedral of Granada was a symbol of Christianity's triumph in the city that had until then been the last stronghold of Muslim Spain.

priesthood had about half of the country's total income at their disposal, even though they made up barely 5 per cent of the population. Standards of education among the clergy were low, and bishoprics were generally given to aristocrats for their family connections rather than any religious qualification.

Together, the Church and nobles owned most of the land, which was worked by farm labourers who were often mired in debt. Livestock farming was more profitable than arable, with the result that soil quality deteriorated and Spain had to import grain from England and the Netherlands. Powerful craft guilds hindered technological progress in once-significant industries such as textiles, leather and metalworking. Spanish shipbuilders were still building the old, top-heavy galleons and caravels when their English and French counterparts had long started building lighter, faster vessels.

From 1550 on, the Spanish economy was in decline. The constant wars that Spain fought throughout Europe and the high cost of government proved a ruinous drain on the state's finances. Even the immense haul of bullion that arrived from Spain's American colonies in annual treasure fleets could not fill the gap. In fact, the influx of precious metals had a negative effect, forcing up inflation and causing prices to spiral. On three separate occasions Philip was forced to declare the state bankrupt, and the nation's poor credit record caused interest payments on debts incurred on foreign loans to soar. Neither Philip nor his son ever found an effective policy to overcome these deep-seated fiscal problems.

Virgin's crown
Thought to be the work of a metalsmith from Madrid, this head-dress of gilded silver was made c.1620 to adorn a statue of the Virgin Mary.

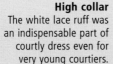

High collar
The white lace ruff was an indispensable part of courtly dress even for very young courtiers.

TIME WITNESS

Court protocol in Spain

Protocol in the Spanish court was much more than a simple matter of manners – it defined the way in which the Spanish court was organised. It dictated the entire hierarchy observed by all courtiers and state officials, as well as affecting such details of daily life as styles of dress and table manners. A grand master of ceremonies checked that correct procedures were always observed. The king himself was as much a prisoner of this etiquette as any of his subjects. He was expected to maintain a dignified, impassive demeanour at all times and was discouraged from displaying any human emotions whatsoever.

A failed foreign policy

Philip's foreign policy fared little better than his financial management. He could not suppress the Dutch struggle for independence, at least in the northern Netherlands, and he had to bear the loss of the Armada that he sent to conquer England in 1588. He fared better with the old enemy France. After the two nations had made peace at Cateau-Cambrésis in 1559, French rulers were distracted by the religious wars between Catholics and Huguenots. For 30 years the old sparring partners lived in peace, although at the end of his reign Philip could not resist being drawn into the struggle on the Catholic side, and hostilities resumed.

Outside Europe, Philip also suffered defeats in the colonies. Protecting not just Spanish possessions but also those of Portugal, after the union of the two crowns in 1580, was beyond his resources. After the outbreak of hostilities with the Netherlands, Dutch rebels targeted Portuguese possessions overseas, challenging the nation's trading dominance in Southeast Asia.

The reign of Philip III

Philip II died on September 13, 1598, and Spain's decline accelerated in the reign of his son and successor, Philip III, who was equally devout but lacked grand political ambition. Philip III continued the policy of creating an exclusively Catholic Spain, but went beyond anything his father had attempted by expelling the entire Morisco community in 1609.

Philip III was happy to delegate much of the business of government to chosen advisors, foremost among whom was the Duke of Lerma. Abroad, Lerma had some success. In 1604 he negotiated a long-delayed peace with England, and three years later brokered a ceasefire in the Netherlands that later became a 12-year truce. He was unable to reach a settlement with France, however, and during his ministry mutual animosities and rival claims flared up once more to embitter relations between the two old enemies.

At home, Lerma's regime was marked by corruption and favouritism. The duke himself took advantage of his position to amass a huge fortune. His wealth stirred intrigue at court and this eventually helped to bring about his downfall in 1618.

The Thirty Years' War broke out in the same year, and Philip responded by sending troops to support the Holy Roman Emperor, Ferdinand II, the champion of the Catholic cause. Spanish forces invaded the Rhineland Palatinate and secured the neutrality of the Protestant Union. However, Philip himself did not survive to see the effect of these interventions. He died in 1621 at the age of 43, having reigned for 23 years.

A great age in the arts

It is generally held that the period covering the reigns of the two Philips was the time when Spain's decline, which became more obvious over the course of the 17th century, first took root. Yet in one field at least the nation's glory shines as brightly now as it did at the time, and that is in the arts.

Literature reached a zenith in the plays of Lope de Vega and Pedro Calderón de la Barcain, and above all in the work of Miguel de Cervantes, whose *Don Quixote* remains the most widely read Spanish classic. Painters such as Velázquez, Murillo and El Greco easily rivalled the calibre of Spain's writers, creating masterpieces that have clearly stood the test of time. More than all the wealth in gold and silver garnered from the American colonies, this cultural flowering of the late 16th and early 17th centuries truly merited the appellation of Spain's Golden Age.

Mounted monarch
The pious but indolent Philip III was immortalised in the portraits of Diego Velázquez. This one of him on horseback can be seen in the Prado Museum in Madrid.

Tilting at windmills
The eponymous anti-hero of Miguel de Cervantes's *Don Quixote* attacks a windmill under the delusion that it is an evil giant. This illustration, by Antonio Carnicero, was produced for an 18th-century edition of the classic work.

The religious wars in France

Nowhere was the struggle between Catholics and Protestants more bitter and divisive than in France, where it led to decades of open warfare.

Queen of contradictions
As regent for Charles IX, Catherine de' Medici tried to mediate between Catholic and Protestant.

Merciless massacre
St Bartholomew's day, 1572, dawned in Paris to the ongoing slaughter by Catholic mobs of Protestants who had gathered to celebrate their leader's marriage.

In 1562 Catherine de' Medici, then regent for her young son Charles IX, signed an edict decreeing tolerance for France's Protestants. But the time had already passed for any real agreement between the nation's two mutually hostile religious camps. The new faith had become deeply entrenched since its arrival in the 1520s, and its adherents were now locked in a bitter ideological battle with the country's Catholic majority.

Non-reformers described the Protestants in their midst as 'Huguenots' a term that had previously been applied only to citizens of the Swiss Confederation. It was a corruption of the German *eidgenoss* or 'confederate', and was linked to the exiled French reformer John Calvin, who had established a model theocracy in his adopted home of Geneva. By the mid-16th century Calvinists made up around 10 per cent of the French population.

Catherine, daughter of Lorenzo de' Medici, had come to France as the wife of Henry, Duke of Orleans, who succeeded to the throne as Henry II in 1547. At a jousting tournament in 1559 to celebrate the marriage of his son Francis to Mary Stuart, the future Mary, Queen of Scots, Henry was wounded by splinters from a broken lance and later died of septicaemia.

The gathering storm

After her husband's death, Catherine became the true ruler of France. Francis was a sickly 15-year-old who survived his father by little more than a year. His successor was Charles IX, another of her sons by Henry, who was just 10 years old.

As regent for the young king, Catherine did her best to reconcile the opposing Catholic and Protestant factions, but this was no easy task. The Huguenots, under the leadership of Henry of Navarre, Louis Prince of Condé and Admiral Gaspard de Coligny, had established a strong presence at court, where they were bitterly opposed by a Catholic party led by the Guise family, who thwarted Catherine's attempts at conciliation. By making concessions to the Protestants, she sparked a campaign of revenge by the Catholics. Followers of the Duke of Guise attacked a Huguenot church service at Vassy, near Langres in the province of Champagne, in 1562 and massacred the congregation. This event lit the fuse that started the religious wars.

St Bartholomew's Day Massacre

The next eight years saw a series of three short wars, each ended by a truce. When a more lasting peace was finally arranged at St Germain in 1570, the supporters of reform won limited freedom of worship, guaranteed by the temporary cession of four strongholds, among them the bastions of La Rochelle and Montauban, where they could find refuge from persecution.

In a spirit of conciliation intended to cement the peace, Charles now arranged a marriage between his sister, the Catholic Margaret of Valois, and the Protestant leader Henry of Navarre. The ceremony took place on August 18, 1572, and thousands of Huguenots made their way to Paris to celebrate the wedding.

The influx of so many Protestants into the capital alarmed Catherine de' Medici, who feared a conspiracy. A rumour reached her that the prominent Huguenot Admiral de Coligny planned to intervene on the side of the Dutch rebels in the Netherlands, so fomenting war between France and Spain. She responded by persuading Charles to sanction Coligny's assassination. The initial attempt, on August 22, failed but the following night Coligny was murdered and the massacre ensued. Armed bands of Catholics stormed through the streets of Paris, killing any Huguenots they found – many were still in Paris following the wedding celebrations. The slaughter spread to the provinces and continued for over a month, despite a royal order against it. The final death toll may have been as high as 70,000; some 3000 died in Paris alone.

The bitter aftermath

No one knows whether Catherine intended this escalation of the conflict. Her policy had been one of conciliation, so perhaps she simply panicked. The Guise faction was always ready to take advantage of any sign of weakness on her part.

A fresh war – the fourth – broke out soon after. Fighting concentrated on the Huguenot stronghold of La Rochelle, which refused to admit a royal governor in the wake of the massacre. Charles's brother Henry, Duke of Anjou, then laid siege to the port, which held out for six

Display armour
A magnificent Renaissance helmet that once belonged to France's Charles IX. Coming to the throne at the age of 10 in 1560, Charles was a weak and sickly king. He had a passion for hunting, but the helmet was never put to use.

An extravagant monarch
Henry III, shown below on a bronze medallion, was an intelligent but extravagant monarch who surrounded himself at court with a coterie of male favourites. He won the bitter hostility of the zealots of the Catholic League, one of whose supporters assassinated him in 1590.

Impregnable fortress
In 1573 a royal army laid siege to the Huguenot stronghold of La Rochelle, firing some 34,000 cannonballs at its walls. Eight successive attempts to storm the bastion failed at a cost of almost 20,000 lives. The besiegers eventually withdrew in defeat.

months against attempts to take it. Henry eventually lost interest in the enterprise when he was elected King of Poland, and a fresh truce confirming the terms of the 1570 treaty was arranged. For the most part the Protestant ranks held firm, although some Huguenots emigrated to England, Germany and the Netherlands.

An eccentric ruler

Charles died in May 1574 at the age of 24, and his brother Henry hurried back from Poland, abandoning his title there in order to claim the French throne as Henry III. He turned out to be a somewhat eccentric king, not well suited to ruling in crisis. In his brief sojourn in Poland he had experienced an atmosphere of religious freedom that inclined him towards toleration. Like his mother, he was repelled by the zeal of the Catholic faction gathered around the Duke of Guise. In April 1576 he brought to an end the fifth war against the Huguenots by signing the Peace of Monsieur (so titled from his own nickname) in which he granted the most substantial concessions that the Protestants had ever won.

Yet despite the quick intelligence that had always made him Catherine's favourite son, Henry was ultimately too frivolous to impose his will on a divided nation. To celebrate the peace, he organised a transvestite ball at the Château of Chenonceaux in the Loire Valley in which he greeted his guests dressed as a woman, resplendent in jewellery and a dress with a plunging neckline. By that time Henry was making no secret of his homosexual tendencies, surrounding himself with a group of handsome young

favourites known as his *mignons* ('darlings'). His marriage to a princess from the ruling family of Lorraine was childless, and he was to be the last king of the Valois line.

The rise of the Catholic League

Henry's morals did nothing to placate the Catholic zealots, already outraged by the tolerance he had displayed towards their Huguenot opponents. In 1578 they banded together under the leadership of Henry, Duke of Guise, in the Catholic League to oppose Henry III's measures, forcing the king to revoke the concessions he had made in the Peace of Monsieur.

The conflict intensified in 1584 when the Duke of Alençon, Henry's brother and the heir to the throne, died of tuberculosis. Next in the line of succession was the Huguenot Henry of Navarre, the very same bridegroom whose wedding celebrations had sparked the massacre on St Batholomew's day.

The War of the Three Henrys

The Catholic League responded by demanding that the King exclude his brother-in-law from the succession. However, the French ruler refused to let himself be browbeaten. The result was the last of the Huguenot wars, known as the War of the Three Henrys, for it set King Henry and Henry of Navarre against the Catholic League's Henry, Duke of Guise.

The Paris mob rose up in support of the League, forcing the King to flee his own capital and take refuge in the Loire Valley. He responded with treachery. On the pretext of conducting negotiations he lured Henry of Guise and his brother, Cardinal Louis, to the Chateau of Blois. There, on December 23, 1588, he had them murdered by his guards in the corridors of the royal apartment.

On her deathbed the following year, Catherine de' Medici told her son that he would come to regret the murders, and she was soon proved right. A few months later a Dominican monk named Jacques Clément, a fanatical supporter of the League, stabbed the King to death at Saint-Cloud on the outskirts of Paris.

Peace at last

Following the assassination, Henry of Navarre duly ascended the French throne as King Henry IV. At first he continued the struggle against the Catholic League but came to realise that the policy had little support in the country at large. To restore peace, he then performed an extraordinary political U-turn: he announced that he was rejecting his long-held Protestant beliefs to convert to Catholicism.

Despite widespread public cynicism about the sincerity of his conversion, the move worked. Catholic towns that had held out against the royal army now opened their gates, and on March 22, 1594, the King finally entered Paris itself. He celebrated his return in Nôtre Dame Cathedral, memorably remarking of the ceremony that 'Paris is worth a Mass'.

By that time Henry had already been formally crowned in Chartres Cathedral as the first monarch of the new Bourbon dynasty. Much work remained to be done, however, before he could reunite the

whole kingdom. Spanish forces had intervened on the Catholic side, and it took Henry another four years of fighting before the invaders finally withdrew.

The last step needed to bring the strife to a close was a religious settlement acceptable to all. In 1598 Henry issued the Edict of Nantes, guaranteeing Huguenots the freedom of conscience they had long sought and the right to hold public worship across much of France, although not in ultra-Catholic Paris. They were also granted full civic rights and were permitted to hold on to all their remaining strongholds. Although the edict was controversial with the Catholic majority, a war-weary nation agreed to the proposals in the edict, and so the long wars of religion were finally over.

Bringing peace at last
Seen here in a painting of the Flemish School, Henry IV eventually brought the religious wars to an end by denying his own Protestant beliefs and joining the Catholic Church. One unforeseen benefit of his action was that it paved the way for France to emerge in the following century as the dominant European power.

The Dutch struggle for independence

Opposition to Spanish rule spawned a revolt that saw the northern Netherlands finally emerge as the Dutch Republic.

Man of war
The Duke of Alba – seen here in a portrait by Titian – was a highly successful military commander. His intervention in the Battle of Mühlberg in 1547 won the day for Emperor Charles V against the German Protestant forces of the Schmalkaldic League, and in 1580 he conquered Portugal for Philip II. But his brutal rule as Spanish governor of the Netherlands provoked determined revolt.

In the summer of 1567, the army of King Philip II of Spain marched into the southern Netherlands. Earlier in the century a series of dynastic marriages had brought the Low Countries into the hands of the Habsburgs. Philip had inherited the crowns of both the Netherlands (in 1555) and Spain (in 1556), and now ruled from Madrid. Trouble had broken out in the previous year, when Dutch Calvinists had destroyed images in some churches, and the fiercely Catholic Philip had sent troops to restore order. The mercenary forces he dispatched made an undeniably impressive sight as they marched through the villages of Flanders on their way from Lorraine to Brussels. French chronicler Pierre de Brantome described them as 'strapping fellows one and all, battle-hardened and so well equipped with splendid kit and weapons that you would have taken them to be officers rather than just common soldiers… Moreover, you might even have thought them to be great noblemen, so haughty was their behaviour and such detachment and dignity did they display on their arrival.'

This proud army entered Brussels under the command

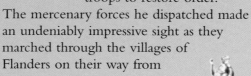

of Fernando Álvarez de Toledo, the Duke of Alba, and over the next six years it spread terror in its wake. As the new governor of the Netherlands, the duke rode roughshod over the traditional rights of provinces and cities and introduced new taxes that were so resented they were never actually imposed. By the time Alba was recalled to Madrid, in 1573, a region that had been merely unruly was in open revolt, launching a lengthy struggle for independence that was not finally resolved until 1648, when Spain at last formally recognised the Dutch Republic, formed from the Low Countries' northern provinces, as a separate state.

First signs of trouble

When he took over from his father Charles V in 1555, the province had some 3 million inhabitants, among whom Protestantism had already made substantial inroads. Charles had been born in Flanders, but Philip II had no local roots and spoke neither Dutch, Flemish nor French, the main languages of the region. He visited the Netherlands in 1559 to install his half-sister Margaret of Parma as governess, but never returned in the remaining 39 years of his reign. Margaret had the difficult task of enforcing often unpopular orders from Spain, which both the wealthy municipalities and the aristocracy deeply resented. They stood firmly by their ancient rights; the nobility in particular took an attitude of defiance, refusing to serve at Margaret's court.

Real trouble began with an argument over money – specifically, who should pay for the Spanish troops garrisoned in the Netherlands. Religion was another bone of contention, for Philip was as keen to impose his authority by appointing local bishops as he was

Imposing façades
Ornate housefronts like these in Antwerp were a sign of the wealth and self-confidence of the trading cities of the Netherlands in the 16th and early 17th centuries. Antwerp lost its commercial ascendancy to Amsterdam during the Dutch Revolt, when territorial gains by rebels cut the city off from the sea.

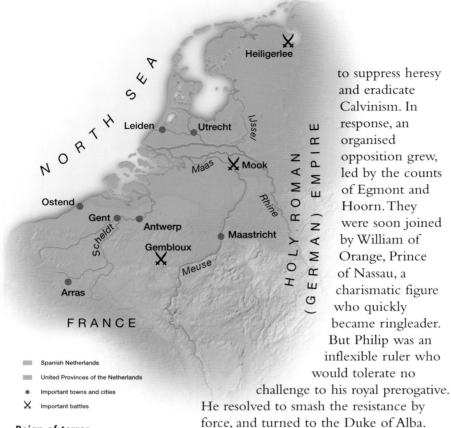

North Sea

Heiligerlee

Leiden · Utrecht

IJssel

Maas · Mook

Ostend

Gent · Antwerp

Scheldt

Gembloux · Maastricht

Rhine

Meuse

Arras

HOLY ROMAN (GERMAN) EMPIRE

FRANCE

- ▇ Spanish Netherlands
- ▇ United Provinces of the Netherlands
- ● Important towns and cities
- ✕ Important battles

Reign of terror
The campaign launched by the Duke of Alba in 1573 to win back towns conquered by the rebel Sea Beggars was marked by atrocities. This coloured engraving records a massacre of civilians in Haarlem.

to suppress heresy and eradicate Calvinism. In response, an organised opposition grew, led by the counts of Egmont and Hoorn. They were soon joined by William of Orange, Prince of Nassau, a charismatic figure who quickly became ringleader. But Philip was an inflexible ruler who would tolerate no challenge to his royal prerogative. He resolved to smash the resistance by force, and turned to the Duke of Alba.

Alba's rule of terror

Within a year of his arrival in the Netherlands, Alba had the rebellious counts of Egmont and Hoorn publicly executed. He also revoked the ancient constitutional privileges accorded to the *Staten-Generaal*, or States-General – the parliamentary body that brought together representatives of the 17 provinces of the Netherlands. Instead he ruled despotically through a newly established Council of Troubles, soon to become known as the Council of Blood. And in order to pay for the military occupation he imposed new taxes on property and land, plus a 10 per cent levy on the sale of goods.

Resistance in the early days of the revolt focused on the Sea Beggars – members of the minor nobility who staged piratical raids on the coast. Their counterparts on land raised the flag of rebellion from 1568 onwards, but the small forces at their disposal were at first no match for the Spanish troops. In 1572 the Sea Beggars captured the port of Brill, after which the insurrection spread rapidly in the north. Alba responded with a brutal campaign of reconquest that bogged down outside Haarlem. The town surrendered after a seven-month siege and its citizens paid a heavy price for their resistance.

Other cities took heart from Haarlem's brave example. Leiden saved itself by breaching the dykes that held back the sea, flooding the surrounding land. The rebel leaders rewarded the city by choosing it as the site of the Netherlands' first university. Subsequently, so many refugees from Antwerp, Brussels and other cities in the Spanish-held south sought safety there that the city had to extend its walls.

The religious divide

In the early years the rebels fought mainly to regain ancient rights rather than to reject the authority of the Spanish king. As the war dragged on, however, the conflict broadened. The insurgents began to seek allies abroad, forging ties with the French Huguenots and with Protestant England. Gradually the rebellion took an increasingly militant direction, stimulated by Calvinists in the north who totally rejected a Catholic monarch.

The recall of Alba to Spain in 1573 came too late to halt the tide. The secessionist movement had by that time gathered such momentum that the duke's successor, Luis de Requesens, had great difficulty asserting his authority. When Requesens died three years later, Philip tried to shore up his faltering authority by sending his half-brother, Don John of Austria, as the province's new governor.

Don John came fresh from his triumph over the Ottoman fleet at Lepanto. In this new situation he found himself faced with a newly united opposition. Thanks to tireless diplomacy by William the Silent, the Catholic southern Netherlands had come together with the mainly Protestant northern provinces to sign the Pacification of Ghent, a joint demand for religious toleration and the withdrawal of Spanish forces. Another condition insisted that the new governor should only rule in cooperation with local authorities. William's achievement was all the more remarkable in that the northern Calvinists were themselves showing increasing intolerance, having banned the holding of Catholic services in the provinces they controlled since 1574.

Don John's intention was to exploit the differences between the northern radicals and the southern conservatives. But before he could make much headway he succumbed to a typhoid epidemic that was raging through the occupation forces, and died at the age of 31, in October 1578.

Separating north from south

The task of separating the Catholic south from the Protestant north fell to Don John's successor, Alessandro Farnese, Duke of Parma, a skilful diplomat. He played on southern fears of northern radicalism to bring the mostly French-speaking southern lands back to the King.

Thanks to Parma, the Pacification of Ghent was the last document that all 17 provinces signed in unison. In 1579 the two halves of the Netherlands split into separate alliances. The seven northern provinces of Holland, Zeeland, Utrecht, Groningen, Friesland, Gelderland and Overijssel joined the Union of Utrecht. Their southern counterparts formed the Union of Arras which reaffirmed support for the Catholic religion and loyalty to the King, while reiterating the need for cooperation as spelled out at Ghent.

Independence for the north

The northern provinces proclaimed their independence from the Spanish crown in 1581. With wealthy Holland taking the lead, they appointed William of Orange as

William the Silent
Shown here in a portrait by Antonio Moro, William of Orange, prince of Nassau, won his sobriquet 'the Silent' for his habit of keeping his own counsel. A nobleman with extensive estates in Germany and France as well as the Netherlands, he made the Low Countries' struggle for independence his life's work.

TIME WITNESS

The siege of Leiden

The town of Leiden in the province of Holland achieved glory in rebel mythology by holding out against the Duke of Alba's troops for just a few days short of a year in 1573–4. In the last stages of the siege, the town's mayor stirred the courage of the defenders by offering his own arm, if necessary, for food. Thousands died of starvation.

The city was finally saved by the momentous decision to breach the dykes that held back the sea, flooding the surrounding countryside. When storm winds carried the waters up to the Spanish guns, the besiegers were forced to withdraw.

Legend has it that when a Dutch relief force finally entered the starving city, they brought with them herrings and white bread, along with a large pot of carrot and onion stew rescued from the abandoned Spanish camp. Ever since, the people of Leiden have celebrated their deliverance on October 3 each year by distributing bread and fish and holding a banquet with a carrot stew as the main course.

their *stadholder* or military leader, responsible to the States-General. By this act, they transformed what had previously been an insurrection against arbitrary rule into an out-and-out struggle for self-determination.

The north-south divide was not clear-cut, for the northern provinces were never entirely united, while there were southern provinces that favoured the cause of independence. Over the course of two more decades of war, the Spanish were able to secure their hold on the south, along with some eastern provinces that had not originally joined the Union of Arras. They owed their success, again, to the astute policies of the Duke of Parma, who took care to conciliate local opinion. Perhaps the most significant factor, however, was the assassination of

Money masters
This portrait of a money-changer and his wife by the 16th-century Flemish master Marinus van Reymerswaele now hangs in the Prado Museum in Madrid. Banking and other commercial activities provided the prosperity on which the great age of Dutch and Flemish painting would be built.

William of Orange at the hands of a Catholic fanatic in 1584. This deprived the nationalist camp of its wisest and most trusted leader. William's son and successor, Count Maurice of Nassau, could not prevent the Spanish from notching up

some quite notable military successes, in particular the capture of Antwerp in 1585.

Beset on all sides

Spain's last chance of regaining the northern provinces disappeared with the defeat of the Spanish Armada, sent to invade England in 1588. That disaster, combined with the nation's ongoing involvement in other theatres of war around Europe, stretched Spain's resources to breaking point. Parma even had to withdraw troops from Flanders to intervene in France's religious wars. At the same time the breakaway provinces were receiving increased support from abroad, particularly from England, which offered financial and military aid.

Yet the rebel forces did not have an easy ride. Before his death in 1598, Philip gave control of the Netherlands to his daughter Isabella and her husband, Archduke Albert of Austria. Under their stewardship the Catholic cause made some gains. One notable victory was the capture of Ostend after a lengthy siege in 1601, which deprived the Dutch States-General of its last foothold in Flanders.

Peace at last

The war dragged on for another 11 years under the new monarch, Philip III, until both sides recognised that they had no realistic chance of breaking the deadlock. With bankruptcy threatening, Philip made peace with England in 1604, and three years later suspended all military operations in the Netherlands.

Even so Spain still could not bring itself to recognise the sovereignty of the States-General, and when a ceasefire was finally signed, in 1609, it was only for 12 years. The truce ran out in 1621 and sporadic fighting resumed, but by that stage the Dutch Republic was strong and wealthy enough to hold its own. The final settlement came in 1648, when the Spanish recognised Dutch independence as part of the Treaty of Westphalia that ended the Thirty Years' War.

Europe in chaos – the Thirty Years' War

The religious war that was unleashed on the territories of the Holy Roman Empire in 1618 permanently changed the balance of power in Europe and left behind a devastated land.

The first act of the Thirty Years' War took place on May 23, 1618. In an event that has become known as the Defenestration of Prague, two imperial councillors appointed by the King of Bohemia, Count Martinic and Count Slavata, were thrown from a window at Hradcany Castle. The imperial secretary Fabricius soon followed. With the laughter of their tormentors ringing in their ears, the three victims landed in a pile of dung, which broke their fall from a height of 17m (55ft), preventing serious injury.

This act showed the contempt that the representatives of the Protestant estates of Bohemia felt for the policies of the Habsburgs who had ruled them for almost a century. Time and again, the Habsburg kings had tried to restore Catholicism in the country. The last straw had come when two Protestant churches were closed on orders of the Habsburg regents and the Habsburg Emperor in Vienna refused even to accept a written protest sent by the Protestant representatives. Having made their feelings clear in the Hradcany Castle

The Winter King
The Calvinist Elector Palatine, Frederick V was persuaded by the Protestant estates of Bohemia to accept the crown of Bohemia and Moravia. He paid for this unwise move when he was deposed, just 15 months later, losing both the Palatinate and Bohemia.

Trigger for war
Imperial officials being flung out of a high window in Hradcany Castle in Prague. Such acts of protest already had a history in Bohemia: almost 200 years earlier the Hussite Wars had also begun with a similar act of defenestration. This time, the defenestration sparked the Thirty Years' War.

A soldier's tools
The mercenaries who fought in the Thirty Years' War went into battle wearing protective helmets and armed with pikes, swords and muskets. Their armour was generally lighter than that used in the Middle Ages, giving them far greater mobility.

incident, they elected Frederick V, the Calvinist Elector Palatine, as their new king, so ending the power of the Habsburg, Ferdinand.

The Europe-wide conflict sparked by these developments was not just a religious war, even though this was the immediate cause. The predominantly Protestant estates in Bohemia were in political conflict with their Catholic emperor, whose ambitions clashed with their own desire for autonomy.

International power politics also had a role, for many European states feared any further extension of Habsburg power. Denmark and Sweden both saw the Holy Roman Emperors as their rivals for control over the Baltic region, and France had long feared encirclement by the Habsburgs, who controlled Spain, Milan and the Spanish Netherlands as well as the imperial lands in Germany.

Ousting the Winter King

The Prague revolt was doubly explosive because Ferdinand was elected Holy Roman Emperor directly after his ejection from Bohemia. Such humiliation in his

ancestral homeland undermined his authority throughout the empire. He also realised that with the crowning of Frederick as King of Bohemia, the balance of power among the electors responsible for choosing future emperors was now in favour of the Protestants. So he had good reason, over and above his Catholicism, to stake everything on a military trial of strength with his rival.

Short of money and allies, Ferdinand turned to Duke Maximilian of Bavaria, a leading champion of the Catholic cause. Maximilian's reward for helping Ferdinand to defeat Frederick was to be the Palatinate region, plus the imperial

electoral vote that went with it. Ferdinand also won the support of Albrecht von Wallenstein, who would be a defining character of the Thirty Years' War.

Wallenstein had been born into a poor but aristocratic Protestant family and had converted to Catholicism in Vienna to advance his career. Fiercely ambitious, he improved his prospects yet further by marrying a rich widow whose estates made him Moravia's largest landowner. By putting his resources at the Emperor's disposal, he duly gained imperial favour.

On November 8, 1620, an imperial army under the command of Johann Tserclaes, Count of Tilly, won a

BACKGROUND

Provisioning the mercenary armies

The task of supplying a mercenary army presented military commanders with horrendous logistical problems. To feed an army of 40,000 men, for example, 40 tonnes of bread had to be baked each day, 20 tonnes of meat butchered and 120,000 litres (25,000 gallons) of beer brewed. To provide for the soldiers' needs, an extensive baggage train of butchers, cooks, traders and field surgeons followed the army as it marched to war, along with herdsmen marshalling large flocks of sheep and oxen. This severely restricted the force's mobility.

Soldiers' wives made up an important part of the train. They served as nurses caring for the wounded, but also played a significant part in the pillaging and looting that accompanied the army's progress, cashing in their booty with sutlers (camp followers who sold provisions). Because soldiers' pay and catering arrangements were often neglected, troops often had to rely on pillaging expeditions for their survival.

Catholic commanders
In Tilly (right) and Wallenstein (far right), the imperial camp had two military leaders of genius. The 72-year-old Tilly, shown here in a portrait by Van Dyck, was mortally wounded at the Battle of the Lech River fought against the Swedes in 1632. Wallenstein fell victim to a murder plot hatched within the imperial court itself in 1634, after the Emperor became concerned that he had grown too powerful.

resounding victory over the Bohemian army at the Battle of the White Mountain, west of Prague. Frederick abandoned his new capital, in disarray. He would go down in history as the Winter King, since his reign had lasted barely a year.

In the wake of the defeat, Bohemia's resistance quickly collapsed. Imperial troops occupied Prague and set about dispensing rough justice; 27 ringleaders of the rebellion were executed, some 700 noblemen were dispossessed, and 150,000 people chose to emigrate. Wallenstein was one of those who profited, buying up a number of adjoining Bohemian estates and merging them into a domain the size

of a principality, which was duly granted to him by a grateful Emperor. Ferdinand crowned his victory by issuing a new edict that made him absolute ruler of Bohemia, depriving the estates of their claims to autonomy.

The conflict spreads

Ferdinand's triumph was so complete that the conflict might have ended there, had he not promised the Palatinate to Maximilian, so spreading the war into the heart of the empire. Tilly's army ravaged the disputed territory, capturing the Calvinist centres of Mannheim and Heidelberg. By 1623 the conquest was complete, and Ferdinand conferred the electorship on the ambitious duke.

By now Habsburg success was ringing alarm bells, not just in Protestant German lands but right across Europe. Protestant princes, backed by the deposed Frederick, turned for help to neighbouring powers who had reasons of their own to view the weakening of Protestantism in the empire with concern. One of their principal hopes was James I of England and VI of Scotland, the father-in-law of the Winter King, who provided some financial help, as did the French and the Dutch.

Big guns
Heavy artillery came to play an increasingly important role in the Thirty Years' War. Armies brought heavy cannons onto the battlefield to punch holes in the enemy's ranks.

The Protestant counter-offensive only really got under way in 1624, when King Christian IV of Denmark sent an army to join the frey on the side of the Protestants. As Duke of Holstein, Christian had extensive interests in northern Germany, and he was also eager to extend his influence eastward along the southern Baltic coast. His intervention escalated the war into an international conflict.

Christian's venture turned out to be ill-judged. His armies came up against imperial forces under Wallenstein, who put 24,000 troops in the field at his own expense – a gesture he could well afford, having developed his new fief in eastern Bohemia into a model state, the Principality of Friedland, whose entire economy was geared to the production of armour, weapons, munitions and cavalry mounts.

Wallenstein the warlord

Wallenstein represented a new kind of military figure north of the Alps. Making his career out of the business of war, he attracted like-minded followers from across the German lands. Disinherited younger sons, unemployed craftsmen's apprentices and day-labourers all flocked in droves to be recruited. Delighted, the Emperor made Wallenstein commander of the imperial forces in 1625, with the title of Duke of Friedland. At the head of an army that eventually swelled to 100,000 men, Wallenstein joined forces with Tilly and advanced to engage with the Danish army. The imperial armies pushed steadily across northern Germany, dispossessing the Duke of Mecklenburg, who had allied himself with the Danes, and eventually forcing Christian himself to sue for peace. In recognition of his services, the Emperor granted Wallenstein fresh titles: Duke of Mecklenburg and General of the Baltic and Oceanic Seas.

The Edict of Restitution

By 1629, with the Danish king defeated, Ferdinand seemed to have swept his enemies before him, but then he made a cardinal error. Instead of concluding an advantageous peace, he embarked on a grand plan to transform the empire's religious make-up. That March he issued the Edict of Restitution, requiring that all

Lion of the North
Gustavus II Adolphus of Sweden was vaunted in Protestant propaganda as the man who would free Germany from the yoke of popery. His intervention in the war came to be associated with an old prophecy, according to which a 'lion from the north' would come to vanquish the eagle – the heraldic symbol of the Habsburg dynasty.

The siege of Magdeburg
The sack of the prosperous city of Magdeburg in May 1631 was one of the worst of many atrocities that took place in the Thirty Years' War. The naturalist Otto Guericke, who survived the massacre, recalled that 'Murder, arson, pillage, torture and beatings were the order of the day'. Some 20,000 people perished in a devastating fire that finally destroyed the city.

New weapons
Wheel-lock pistols, like this 17th-century example, were awkward to operate but often gave their users an advantage in battle. The musket was the principal firearm of the war, but it was still cumbersome, usually fired from a forked rest with the aid of a match that had to be kept permanently burning.

EVERYDAY LIFE

Atrocities of war

The bands of mercenaries who fought in the Thirty Years' War introduced a new dimension of brutality to the business of warfare. Sparing no thought for civilians, they indiscriminately burned fields, villages and crops. The result was widespread famine in Europe and waves of refugees attempting to flee the conflict. Mass rape, torture and murder were common occurrences. Arguably, no other civilian population in history has ever suffered so much for so long as the people of central Europe during the Thirty Years' War.

Hangman's tree

As they passed through villages, bands of mercenaries often meted out summary justice on suspected enemies as well as on their own.

ecclesiastical lands that had been disappropriated since 1552 should be restored to the Catholic Church, depriving Protestants of all the gains they had made since the Peace of Augsburg. It meant the restitution of a dozen or more archbishoprics and bishoprics and over 100 monasteries. The edict also deprived Calvinists of all political rights, recognising the legitimacy only of Lutheranism among the Protestant denominations.

The edict went too far, even for the Catholic princes, who saw it as a Habsburg bid for autocratic power, so at the Diet of Regensburg in 1630, the electors showed their disapproval by refusing to name the Emperor's son Ferdinand as his successor. At the same time they demanded the dismissal of Wallenstein and, under pressure, the Emperor agreed.

Sweden enters the fray

On a stormy day in the early summer of 1630 the Swedish king, Gustavus II Adolphus, landed on the island of Usedom off Germany's Baltic coast at the head of a well-trained army of 10,000 foot soldiers and 3000 cavalry. Gustavus's supporters claimed that he had been forced to act by the desperate plight of his Protestant co-religionists in Germany. In fact, he was intent on securing sovereignty over the Baltic, and felt his position was threatened by the extension of Habsburg imperial power in northern Germany. He was supported in his actions by France, the Habsburgs' old enemy, which had watched the growth of Ferdinand's power with growing anxiety.

The recall of Wallenstein

The Protestant princes were unsure about the Swedish king's motives. But the devastating news of the sacking of Magdeburg by Tilly's troops, and the brutality that the imperial army displayed in pillaging and razing this prosperous city on the Elbe, sent shock waves through the empire and drove the Protestant princes into Gustavus Adolphus's arms. In a lightning campaign the Swedes chalked up victory after victory, advancing to the banks of the Rhine and the River Main, and even capturing Munich in 1632. Horrified, the Emperor recalled Wallenstein to stem the tide of conquest.

The encounter between the new champion of the Protestant cause and Wallenstein's forces took place at Lützen on November 17, 1632. Gustavus Adolphus was killed during the fighting, but the imperial army was forced to withdraw. When Wallenstein subsequently tried to break the stalemate between the warring parties, negotiating on his own initiative, the Emperor suspected him of treason and determined to eliminate him. On February 25, 1634, Wallenstein was murdered in the Hungarian city of Eger.

War without bounds

Sweden's military success and the possible entry of France into the war stimulated a national reaction in Germany that crossed the religious divide. Calls for a peaceful settlement to the conflict grew louder, but with the internationalisation of the war, the ability to make peace was no longer in the Emperor's hands. Intent on taming Habsburg power, France and Sweden played out the final act of the drama on German soil. The French took on Spanish and Bavarian troops in southwestern Germany while, in the north, Swedish forces continued to confront the imperial armies.

When peace negotiations finally got underway, from 1644 onwards, it was only because the opposing forces had fought themselves to a standstill. Mutual animosity between the different religious groups was still so great that representatives of France and Spain, the Catholic adversaries, met in Münster, while the German Protestant princes and their protector Sweden gathered separately in Osnabrück.

The Peace of Westphalia

A total of 148 delegates, including 37 foreign envoys, took part in the discussions to end the war. When the Peace of Westphalia was finally signed, in Münster on October 24, 1648, it established a division of power in Germany that held until Napoleon's day.

The Holy Roman Empire continued to be an elective monarchy whose ruler was chosen by electors from the ruling estates. Having fought off Ferdinand's bid for autocratic power, the princes who governed the empire's constituent parts retained a free hand to govern their own realms as they saw fit, while agreeing to remain under the imperial aegis. The only parts of the old imperial lands to quit the imperial union were the Netherlands and the Swiss Confederation, both of which had long regarded themselves as independent states. In religious matters, Calvinism was granted equal status with

Protestantism and Catholicism within the empire, and all imperial posts were to be assigned on a basis of equal representation. Religious lands were assigned to the denominations that held them in 1624.

The Habsburgs were the big losers in the war. The Emperor's attempts to impose absolutism in Germany had failed, and Spain's dominant position in Europe was gone for good. In contrast, France and Sweden won reparations payments and territorial concessions that lifted them to the status of major European powers.

The most immediate beneficiaries of the peace were the long-suffering people of the war-ravaged lands. All the church bells in Prague rang out to celebrate the signing of the accord, bonfires were lit on the banks of the River Main and in Münster people sang the *Te Deum*. A long task of reconstruction still lay ahead, for when the troops finally went home they left behind them scenes of devastation that took decades to put right.

Peace charter
In Münster in October 1648, Philip IV of Spain concluded a peace agreement with the States-General of the Netherlands (above). Set down in an extensive treaty (background), the Peace of Westphalia thus brought to an end not only the Thirty Years' War but also 80 years of hostility between Spain and the Netherlands. Every European power except Russia, England and the Ottoman Empire took part in the negotiations that lead to the peace.

AMERICA

The westward voyages of Columbus

While searching for an alternative route to access the treasures of the Orient, an inspired Italian seafarer discovered a new world in the west.

A man of conviction
From his studies of classical and contemporary geographers, Christopher Columbus was convinced that a steady westerly course across the Atlantic Ocean would lead to Asia. He had no conception of the undiscovered continent of America that barred the way. This portrait is by the Spanish artist, José Roldan.

At daybreak on October 12, 1492, Christopher Columbus set foot on a small island in the western Atlantic Ocean off the southeast coast of Florida, vindicating a dream of decades. Even on his deathbed 14 years later, Columbus still believed that on that auspicious morning he had reached the Indies and discovered a western sea route to Asia. In fact, he and his companions had landed in the Bahamas, opening the path to the European exploration of the Americas. In doing so, they revolutionised previously held views of the world and set the stage for the fresh colonisation of the New World.

An idea takes shape

Columbus – a Latinisation of his real name, Cristoforo Colombo – was born in Genoa, Italy, the son of a weaver. He first went to sea as a young man and at 25 was shipwrecked off the Portuguese coast. Portugal was then the leader of maritime exploration, and he was happy to stay. Three years later, in 1479, he married into a Portuguese aristocratic family; his bride's recently deceased father had been the original coloniser of the island of Porto Santo in the Madeiras. Columbus duly inherited his father-in-law's collection of nautical charts and logbooks, which he studied avidly.

Columbus pored over the works of ancient geographers and contemporary explorers – in particular, the travel journals of an earlier Italian, the Venetian Marco Polo, and his accounts of the fabulous wealth of China and the Indies. He became fascinated by the views of the Greco-Egyptian astronomer Ptolemy, who claimed that the Eurasian landmass took up half the northern hemisphere, implying that the remaining half was filled by the western ocean. He also read the theories of Florentine geographer Paolo Toscanelli, who in 1474 had written a letter to the king of Portugal proposing a western sea route to the Indies. Columbus took a copy of this letter on his first voyage.

A man with a mission

Columbus's plan was to put Toscanelli's theories into practice and sail west to Asia. At first he had no luck in finding backing for his project. In 1484 he obtained an audience with the king of Portugal, but was turned down: Portugal's resources were committed to finding an eastern seaway to the Indies around Africa.

Two years later Columbus made an appearance at the Spanish court in Córdoba, seeking to persuade the nation's joint rulers – Ferdinand II of Aragon and Isabella I of Castille – to supply him with money and a small fleet of ships. At first he fared little better than he had in Portugal. The Spanish royal couple were preoccupied with the reconquest of southern Spain from the Moors. Even so, Queen Isabella was impressed by the eloquent young explorer and told him to put his proposal to a panel of experts. Initially these royal advisors were sceptical. For six years Columbus tried to persuade them of the feasibility of his plan. His last visit to the Queen, in January 1492, came fortuitously only days after the fall of the last Moorish enclave of Granada. The mood at court was so buoyant that Isabella disregarded her advisors and finally gave her consent to the scheme.

Columbus could now get on with fitting out and manning the ships he needed. Six months later, he was ready to go. On August 2, 1492, he put to sea from

the small port of Palos, north of Cadiz. He had a crew of about 90 men in a fleet of three vessels – the *Santa María*, Columbus's flagship, and two smaller caravels, the *Niña* and *Pinta*. He had two court officials aboard and large stores of provisions. Just as importantly, he carried a royal document according him the rank of admiral and appointing him viceroy over all the lands that he discovered, which he was to govern in the name of the rulers of Spain. He was also officially granted the right to one-tenth of all the goods that he succeeded in bartering on the voyage, including precious metals.

Columbus' estimate of the distance between Europe and Asia proved over-optimistic. After almost five weeks had passed without sight of land, the crew grew mutinous; some even talked of turning for home. Then, at dawn, on October 12, 1492, land was sighted. The explorer's effort and faith had not been in vain.

Exploring a new world

Although history records that Columbus discovered America in 1492, he had actually reached a small island in the Bahamas group. Claiming the newly found territory for Christianity, Columbus christened it San Salvador, 'Holy Saviour'. Going ashore in company with royal officials and armed sailors, he hoisted the Spanish flag, claiming the territory in the name of the crown. Inquisitive islanders hastened to the spot to see the marvellous scenes unfolding there. Convinced he had reached Asia, Columbus dubbed them 'Indians', a name that has stuck to the indigenous inhabitants of the Americas.

In the ship's journal that he kept aboard the *Santa María*, Columbus described the native people as well-built and handsome, observing that they willingly bartered

Coconut cup
The bowl of this elaborately decorated cup is in the shape of a coconut shell clasped in silver-gilt mountings. Made in England around the time of Columbus's voyages, the goblet reflects the taste for the exotic that the age of exploration opened up.

New map, new name
(background) Drawn up in 1507, this map of the world is by the German cartographer Martin Waldseemüller. It features the first known use of the word 'America', named for the navigator Amerigo Vespucci, a contemporary of Columbus who was among the first to suspect that the new-found lands were not Asia at all.

spears, cotton and parrots for the glass beads and colourful fabrics that the Spaniards had brought as trade goods. He was shocked by their lack of clothes, but was more disappointed to discover that they had no precious metals, for he had set his heart on finding gold.

From San Salvador the little fleet travelled on, first to Cuba and then to Hispaniola, driven by the urge to find the wealth of the Indies. Then, on Christmas Eve, with an inexperienced boy at the helm, the *Santa María* ran aground on a coral reef and was damaged beyond repair. Columbus was forced to abandon ship. Reaching shore safely with his crew, he used the wreckage to build the first European settlement in the New World. Located on the north coast of Hispaniola,

it was named La Navidad (The Nativity) in memory of the day. Leaving 39 men behind with a promise to return as soon as he was able, Columbus transferred the rest of the crew to the *Niña* and set off homeward to Spain, arriving back in Palos after a gruelling 10-week voyage.

Planting settlements

On his return Columbus hurried to the royal court, then in Barcelona, to report on his adventures. He received a hero's welcome. The King and Queen greeted him in person, rising from their thrones to salute him and offering him a seat at Isabella's right hand. Columbus presented them with six native Hispaniolans that he had taken captive, along with 40 parrots and other brightly coloured birds. Despite the lack of more marketable treasures, the royal couple promised to equip a second, larger expedition for him to follow up his discoveries.

Columbus lost no time in planning the new voyage. He remained convinced that there were untold riches to be found in the new territories, and still hoped to make direct contact with the lands that Marco Polo had called Cathay (China) and Cipanagu (Japan). After the initial triumph of discovery, he wanted to extend the policy of settlement begun at La Navidad, and turn the region into a thriving centre of trade.

This time he had little trouble finding men to crew his fleet. The royal treasury provided the money to equip 17 ships loaded with livestock, seeds and tools, and more than a thousand potential settlers. Besides sailors, there were peasants,

Welcome to the New World
A late 16th-century copperplate engraving shows native inhabitants of the Bahamas greeting Columbus with gifts when the Europeans made their first landfall on October 12, 1492. Columbus named the island San Salvador – its native name was Guanahani – and claimed it in the name of Christianity: his men raise a cross, symbolising the conquest.

miners and soldiers, including horsemen with their mounts. Priests, a doctor and a surgeon completed the manpower needed for a successful colonisation.

Columbus put to sea once more in September 1493. This time he landed in the Lesser Antilles, claiming the islands of Dominica, Guadeloupe, Antigua and Puerto Rico for Spain. Anxious to keep his promise to the 39 men at La Navidad, he pressed on to Hispaniola, only to learn that the Spaniards had all been killed in a dispute with local tribes. Undaunted, Columbus founded a new town, named Isabella after his royal patron, further along the coast. He then dispatched 12 of the 17 ships back to Spain. He remained with the other five and their crews to continue exploring.

Unfortunately, the natural aggression of his companions led bands of armed horsemen on forays inland accompanied by baying bloodhounds, removing any hope of peaceful coexistence with the native inhabitants. The Spaniards justified their own cruelty with tales of the bloodthirsty customs of the native peoples. Columbus had already heard on his first visit of the feared *caniba*, the word from which 'cannibal' derives. These were the warlike Caribs, recent arrivals from the South American mainland who raided native villages, taking the women as slaves and killing and eating male prisoners.

EVERYDAY LIFE

A hard life on board

While out at sea, whether in the teeth of a storm or in searing heat, sailors had to trust in the navigational skills of the captain. Only officers or noblemen enjoyed the luxury of a private cubicle. The rest of the crew lived on deck, preferring the open air to the foul-smelling holds, crawling with rats, lice and maggots.

Poor hygiene and diet led to epidemics and illness. Fresh food was quickly consumed or went rotten, leaving crews short of vitamin C and liable to scurvy. All that was then left to eat was salted meat or fish and ship's biscuits, usually infested with weevils. Drinking water was stored in wooden barrels, and soon became unpalatable.

In such conditions it was not uncommon for an on-board crisis to escalate into full-blown mutiny.

Growing unrest

Discontent quickly spread among the colonists when the promised gold failed to materialise. Rather than cultivating the land as intended, the hungry settlers, eager for instant wealth, fell to fighting among themselves.

Columbus still clung to the conviction that he was on the edge of Asia. Leaving the malcontents behind, he set off again westward, discovering the island of Jamaica before scouting the Cuban coast, which he mistook for the long-sought Asian mainland.

Steering by the stars
Columbus relied on wind directions, cloud formations and the flight of birds to find land, but for general navigational purposes he had some rudimentary instruments. One was the magnetic compass, which indicated due north. Another was the astrolabe (above), which could be used to find the latitude of the sun and stars.

Columbus's flagship
The *Santa María* was a high-sided carrack. Equipped with three masts and heavy cannon, she carried 52 men.

When he finally returned to Spain, in June 1496, it was with only a fraction of the gold he had promised. Along with some spices and a few hundred native prisoners, it was a poor return for all the money and effort expended on the trip.

The third crossing

Although Columbus received another royal welcome on his return, and his titles and privileges were reconfirmed, the initial enthusiasm for his ventures had waned, and he had greater difficulty attracting volunteers for a third voyage. When he finally set sail with six ships, in May 1498, many of his crew were ex-convicts, although there were also 30 women, the first to make the crossing.

This time Columbus took a more southerly course. He landed on the island of Trinidad before probing the coast of a country he named 'Little Venice' on account of houses built on piles he could see on its shoreline – the future Venezuela. Mistaking what was the South American

Changing worldview
A map made in 1508 by the Italian cartographer Francesco Rosselli, showing the islands of Hispaniola and Cuba lying off the coast of China, as Columbus imagined them. The vast landmass to the south represents *terra incognita australis*, the unknown southern continent fabled since antiquity. Curiously, Rosselli labelled it 'Antarcticus', even though the continent of Antarctica would not be identified and named for another three centuries.

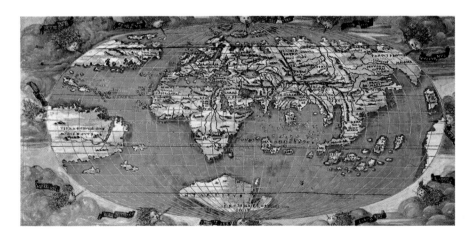

mainland for another island, Columbus turned northwards for Hispaniola and the colony of Isabella, where he had left his brother Bartolomé in charge. When he got there he found a rebellion in progress, with the small Spanish community split into two warring groups.

When news of the strife reached Spain, Ferdinand and Isabella decided that their viceroy, however able he might be as an explorer, was not the man they needed to administer their new possessions. So they dispatched a new governor, Francisco de Bobadilla, to the island. When Columbus and his brother refused to recognise the authority of the royal envoy, Bobadilla had them put in chains and sent back to Spain. Meanwhile Bobadilla imposed law and order in the new colony, treating the native Hispaniolans particularly brutally.

The Spanish monarchs were shocked by the humiliating treatment meted out to their former favourite and received him warmly, without in any way changing their views as to his limitations as a colonial administrator. Yet Columbus himself had lost none of his ambition. Less than two years later he personally raised the funds needed for a fourth voyage. The King and Queen agreed to let him go, but specifically prohibited him from landing on Hispaniola lest his presence there stir up further trouble.

The last voyage

Despite failing health, Columbus set sail once more, and this time made landfall on the island of Martinique in the Lesser Antilles. Next he headed for Jamaica before once more probing westward.

So began a wild odyssey that took the ailing admiral to the coast of Central America. With his ships barely seaworthy and his crew mutinous, he wandered down the coasts of Honduras, Nicaragua, Costa Rica and Panama, still convinced that he was on the threshold of China. Eventually he found his way back to Jamaica, where the boats had to be scrapped. He spent a year there, hungry and ill, before fresh vessels arrived from Hispaniola to carry him and his remaining men back to Spain. He arrived in November 1504, racked by arthritis and just in time to hear of the death of his patron, Queen Isabella. He lived for a further 18 months, lonely and embittered, convinced that he had been cheated of his rightful dues and still believing that he had discovered a westerly route to Asia.

The conquistadors in Mexico and Peru

Driven by greed and a sense of missionary zeal, Spanish warriors used guns and horses to overrun and obliterate the thriving civilisations of the Aztecs and the Inca.

In the summer of 1496 Bartolomé Colombo, a brother of Christopher Columbus, led a force of 10 mounted men into the interior of the Caribbean island of Hispaniola, the first island that Europeans had attempted to settle in the New World. A chief of the indigenous Taino people, Caonabo, awaited their arrival in his village. He had set his heart on acquiring a horse, a gift that the two men had promised to bring him.

The Spaniards had only just introduced horses to the Caribbean, and the chief had no previous experience of riding. So the conquistadors easily persuaded him to let himself be handcuffed to the saddle, supposedly for his own safety. When he was firmly secured, his captors dug their spurs into their horses' flanks and galloped off at speed. Caonabo had fallen into the Spaniards' trap and was now their prisoner. He was transported to Spain, and his tribe, along with all the other indigenous communities on the island, were enslaved. Most fell victim to a combination of brutal treatment and imported diseases; by 1531, their numbers had plummeted from hundreds of thousands to just 600.

The ruse employed by the Spanish officers established a pattern that later adventurers would successfully copy.

Golden sun
Some of the finest Inca artefacts were platters, dishes and plaques made of gold, intricately decorated and often depicting the Sun god Viracocha, legendary ancestor of the Inca royal line. The Spanish conquerors showed little appreciation of the artistry, generally choosing to melt gold artefacts down to simplify the task of dividing the spoils.

Unequal struggle
A manuscript illustration from a codex now in the National Library in Madrid shows Cortés and his men charging Aztec warriors. Despite the vast numerical superiority of the Mesoamerican armies, the Spanish conquistadors usually emerged triumphant thanks to their guns and metal armour.

Pathfinders and conquerors
While Hernán Cortés (right) returned
to Spain in 1540 with great riches and
fame, Francisco de Córdoba (far right),
who led the first Spanish expedition to
the American mainland in 1517, paid
for his audacity with his life.

Weapon of choice
In hand-to-hand fighting the
conquistadors relied on their swords,
which were usually about 1.1m (3½ft)
long and weighed up to 2.5kg (6lb).

In the ensuing decades, the two richest
cultures of the Americas, the Aztec realm
in Mexico and the Inca Empire in Peru,
would both be brought down by
conquistadors who boldly forced their
way into their heartlands and then seized
their emperors. Each time, resistance
crumbled once the ruler had been taken.

The Spanish conquest of the New
World followed soon after Christopher
Columbus's voyages of discovery. In the
decade following the explorer's death in
1506, the Spanish roamed far and wide
through the Caribbean, driven by the
hunt for gold. A force led by Juan Ponce
de Léon overran Puerto Rico between
1508 and 1511, Jamaica fell to Juan de
Esquivel the same year, and Cuba was
conquered from 1512 onwards by Diego
de Velázquez, one of the wealthiest
conquistadors in Hispaniola.

From Cuba to the mainland
Cuba itself was sparsely populated and had
no gold, but it became an embarkation
point for further expeditions westwards
and the first contacts with the great
civilisations of the American mainland. In
1517 Francesco Hernández de Córdoba
sailed a fleet to the Yucatán Peninsula of

southern Mexico and brought back news
of cities with huge buildings as well as of
warriors armed with spears, slings and
bows and arrows who repelled his men in
a bloody skirmish; he himself died of his
wounds soon after his return to Cuba. He
had unknowingly made the first European
contact with the Maya.

A second expedition set out at
Velázquez's behest the following spring,
this time commanded by Juan de Grijalva.
His fleet sailed northward from Yucatán
up the shores of the Bay of Campeche,
where they met some natives and
exchanged gifts, receiving some gold
artefacts. The local people had no way of
knowing that their golden trinkets were
an irresistible lure to the white men.

Cortés takes ship
Without more ado, Velázquez assembled a
fresh expeditionary force, appointing one
of his chief aides, Hernán Cortés, as its
leader. Cortés was 34 years old at the
time, a minor nobleman who had made
his fortune on Cuba but whose ambitions
were still not filled. He started his
campaign by establishing a base at
Veracruz on the Mexican coast, the first
permanent European settlement on the

American mainland. Far exceeding the authority that Velázquez had given him, he proclaimed himself governor of the lands he was setting out to conquer – a clear act of insubordination that underlined the independent nature of his enterprise.

To help in his dealings with local chiefs, Cortés was lucky to have a young Amerindian woman, Malinche, who had been presented to him as a gift by a coastal chief. A woman of noble birth who had been sold into slavery in childhood, Malinche converted to Christianity and became Cortés' mistress. She turned out to be an invaluable adviser, providing information on the inner workings of the Aztec realm.

Armed with the intelligence Malinche supplied, Cortés secured the cooperation of a number of neighbouring peoples. The most formidable were the Tlaxcalans, tough mountain-dwellers and longtime foes of the Aztecs. Cortés won their respect by taking on their army of several thousand warriors with his small force. The bloody engagement lasted several days and Cortés eventually emerged victorious.

The battle for Mexico

From Malinche, Cortés learned of an Aztec legend about the god Quetzalcoatl, who had been driven out

TIME WITNESS

History in pictures

An illustrated manuscript known as the Florentine Codex was compiled in the16th century in both Spanish and Aztec under the direction of a Franciscan friar, Bernardino de Sahagún.

Sahagún devoted his life to promoting the Christian faith among the native Amerindian peoples, and he was a keen student of their languages and local customs.

To this end, he asked former Aztec rulers and noblemen to recount their oral histories to him in the form of pictures and to annotate them in the Aztec language, Nahuatl. To accomplish the task, he taught them the Latin alphabet. The Codex is an invaluable guide to a vanished way of life.

of Mexico but was expected one day to return from across the sea as a white-complexioned man with a beard. Cortés encouraged the belief that he himself was that returning deity.

Meanwhile, in his capital of Tenochtitlán located on islands in Lake Texcoco in the Valley of Mexico, the Aztec Emperor Montezuma II was kept informed of every move that the Spaniards made. Yet from a combination of fear, arrogance, resignation and plain carelessness, Montezuma allowed Cortés and his army to advance deeper into Aztec territory. On November 8, 1519, Cortés marched over the causeway across the lake into Tenochtitlán itself. Montezuma received him at the head of his royal household and formally bade him welcome.

Within a week of their arrival the Spanish had found a pretext for taking Moctezuma hostage. The royal prince was

Promising gifts
A manuscript illustration shows Tlaxcalans greeting Hernán Cortés with gifts. The lavish presents that the Aztec Emperor Montezuma sent to the conquistadors on their first arrival in Mexico only served to fire the Spaniards' lust for conquest and more gold.

Tragic ruler

The ill-fated Aztec ruler Montezuma II never found a consistent strategy with which to confront the Spaniards. Swayed by prophecies of impending doom, he eventually adopted a fatalistic attitude to the newcomers that weakened the resistance of his people to the benefit of the invaders.

Temples of blood

The Spanish were horrified by the Aztec practice of large-scale human sacrifice. Prisoners of war and other victims had their hearts cut out in shrines set on top of temple-pyramids, and their bodies were then thrown down the steps.

forced to call in special tribute payments from all the provinces of the empire, and Cortés and his men amassed great hoards of treasure. They would doubtless have continued their extortion if disturbing news had not reached them. Diego de Velázquez had sent a fresh expedition under Panfilo de Narváez to bring the insubordinate Cortés to heel. Cortés now had to divide his force, leaving half of his army in Tenochtitlán under the command of Pedro de Alvarado while he marched off with the rest to meet Narváez.

Narváez's expedition was responsible for introducing smallpox to the Central American mainland. In no time the disease wrought havoc among the native population: never having encountered the disease before, they had no immunity to it. The Aztecs called the epidemic *huizáhuatl*, 'the great leprosy', and it spread through them like wildfire. In the space of a few months, the populations of entire regions were wiped out.

Meanwhile, Cortés staged a night attack on Narváez, taking him completely by

surprise. Narváez's men surrendered, agreeing to join forces with Cortés. No sooner had they done so than alarming news arrived of a general uprising in Tenochtitlán. Hotheaded Alvarado had used a religious festival as an excuse to launch an attack during which many people, including leading noblemen, were killed. The residents of Tenochtitlán reacted to the provocation by taking up arms and besieging Alvarado's men.

Cortés returned to Tenochtitlán where he was besieged by thousands of angry citizens. He tried to calm the crowds by putting the captive Montezuma on the roof of the building, but when the ruler tried to address his subjects they stoned him, incensed by his submission to the foreigners. Refusing treatment for the wounds he had received, he died three days later.

Realising that his small force could not defeat the enraged Aztecs, Cortés decided to fight his way out. On the evening of June 30, 1520, he and his men broke out and fled to safety across the partly destroyed causeway, all the while under attack from both the town and the lake.

The Aztec downfall

The price of retreat was heavy. Cortés lost more than 600 Spanish soldiers and more than 2000 of his Tlaxcalan allies. Much of the Spanish loot was left behind in the city or lost in the lakeshore mud. The event went down in Spanish history as 'The Sad Night'.

Over the following months, reinforcements came from both Cuba and Jamaica, but Cortés's greatest ally was the raging smallpox epidemic, which depleted the Aztec ranks. In 1521 he returned to the shores of Lake Texcoco to besiege Tenochtitlán. For nearly three months the citizens put up a desperate resistance, but eventually hunger and disease wore them down. In August the conquistadors launched a final assault, capturing the city and its new ruler Cuauhtémoc, who was tortured and eventually hanged. Barely a year after the Sad Night, the Aztec Empire was in Spanish hands.

Lost city
Cortés had Tenochtitlán completely razed to the ground. Mexico City was built on its ruins. The old Aztec ceremonial centre (below) is now an archaeological site.

Pizarro in Peru

While Cortés and his lieutenants were extending their power through the length and breadth of Mexico, conquistadors in South America were opening the door to a fresh realm of gold. In Panama, at that time the southernmost Spanish bridgehead in Central America, an elderly lawyer named Luque joined with two middle-aged conquistadors, Diego de Almagro and Francisco Pizarro, to found a joint-stock company in 1524. Their aim was to conquer an as yet undiscovered land known as Birú, rumours of which had reached them from the first Spanish explorers to probe down the Pacific coast. Birú was reported to be rich in precious metals, its rulers were said to live a life of luxury and its cities were all but paved with gold.

Inca chalice
Probably used in rituals and religious ceremonies, this painted wooden chalice was found on an island in Lake Titicaca, now on the border of Peru and Bolivia.

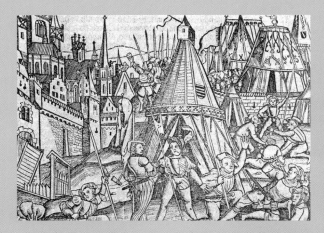

Fighting over the spoils
An illustration prepared for a 16th-century chronicle of the conquest of the New World shows the rebel conquistador Diego de Almagro taking control of the city of Cuzco in defiance of the Spanish governor Francisco Pizarro. Almagro subsequently paid for his insubordination with his life.

Mountain stronghold
The ruins of Machu Picchu give some impression of the Incas' formidable building skills. On an Andean peak, some 2430m (8000ft) above sea level, they carved out the living quarters and ceremonial buildings of this impressive royal stronghold. Built around 1460, Machu Picchu was not found by the conquistadors; it lay undisturbed until 1911 when it was discovered by the American archaeologist Hiram Bingham.

In 1532 Pizarro and Almagro set out from Tumbes, now on the Peru–Ecuador border, with a force of just 185 men and 37 horses. This small force was regarded with disdainful curiosity by the Inca ruler Atahualpa, so the Spanish were able to advance deep into his realm. There the pattern set by previous conquests was repeated. Atahualpa accepted an invitation to parley with the Spanish, walked into a trap, and was ambushed and taken captive along with his entire bodyguard.

An emperor's ransom
After taking Atahualpa hostage, the Spanish demanded the highest possible ransom for his release – enough precious metals to fill a hall 7m long, 5m wide (23ft by 16ft) and as tall as a man. The emperor's capture paralysed Inca society, which ran on strictly hierarchical lines, with a godlike ruler at the top.

With no-one to command or organise resistance, Spanish scouting and raiding parties encountered little opposition.

At the end of August 1533, Pizarro had Atahualpa executed anyway, and then divided up the treasure he had amassed among his lieutenants – it amounted to 4.8 tonnes of gold; even after a fifth had been deducted for the Spanish crown, an amazing 1.6 million gold pesos remained.

Subduing the Inca lands
Despite their huge rewards, the victorious conquistadors fell to squabbling over the sharing of the booty. Almagro and others felt cheated and contemplated revenge. Meanwhile Pizarro busied himself with mopping up native resistance, resurgent after Atahualpa's death. Having captured the Inca capital of Cuzco, he withdrew to the coast, where he founded the city of Lima in 1535.

Meanwhile, Almagro and another of Pizarro's lieutenants, Sebastián de Benalcázar, prepared expeditions of their own. The two marched north and overran what is now Ecuador,

previously an Inca province. Returning overland, they encountered Pedro de Alvarado – Cortés' former second-in-command, who had marched south after the conquest of Mexico, subjugating Guatemala along the way. He planned to take a share of the Inca wealth, but his men were exhausted by seven months of constant marching through difficult terrain. Deciding to cut his losses, Alvarado accepted 100,000 pesos and returned with his men to Guatemala.

Consolidating Spanish power

Benalcázar waged a series of bloody campaigns across the northern Inca lands, which had already been weakened by recent Inca wars of conquest and by an epidemic of smallpox, which had crossed the Isthmus of Panama. The present-day Ecuadorian capital of Quito was founded as San Francisco de Quito in 1533, and the port of Guayaquil on the Pacific coast was established the following year.

Meanwhile, Pizarro's conquest of Peru was going according to plan. With Benalcázar occupied in the north, in 1535 Pizarro dispatched the still-unreconciled Almagro on a fruitless southern expedition that took him as far as the modern states of Argentina and Chile.

Inca rule had been well and truly smashed by that time – to the extent that Pizarro felt sure enough of his own position to install a native ruler, Manco Cápac, to govern as his puppet. Although Cápac would eventually rebel, Spanish authority in the region was by then so firmly secured, it would not be seriously threatened for centuries to come.

A perfidious spectacle
In a staged show trial, the captured Inca ruler Atahualpa was at first condemned to be burned alive. After he agreed to be baptised, the sentence was commuted to garrotting, which preserved his body – a precondition for entry to the afterlife in Inca belief.

Conqueror by royal appointment
A bronze statue commemorating Francisco Pizarro's role as a soldier and conqueror. One copy is in Lima, another in Trujillo, Spain.

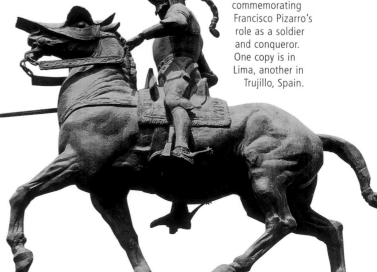

The struggle for Brazil

Having discovered Brazil by accident, the Portuguese had trouble finding settlers for their new colony and also struggled to defend it against rival European powers.

The first Portuguese fleet to reach Brazil arrived in April 1500. Led by Captain Pedro Álvares Cabral, it was headed for India in the wake of Vasco da Gama's trail-blazing voyage of 1499. Da Gama had advised his successors that the key to avoiding the becalmed waters of the Gulf of Guinea was to sail far out into the Atlantic, but Cabral's course took him so far west that he reached uncharted waters. It was there, on the evening of April 21, that his lookouts sighted land.

First they saw a high, round-topped mountain, then lower mountain ridges, and finally flat, densely wooded countryside. Cabral made the sign of the cross and gave thanks to God before christening the peak Monte Pascoal – Easter Mountain – and the newly found land Isla de la Vera Cruz, the Island of the True Cross. In fact, he had reached the South American mainland, near the present-day city of Porto Seguro in what is now the Brazilian state of Bahía.

First ashore was Nicolau Coelho, one of Cabral's captains, who took some boats from the ship to reconnoitre a nearby river mouth. Naked indigenous peoples lined the banks, and Coelho and his crew offered them three of their hats as a gesture of goodwill. In response one of the Indians threw back his headdress of long birds' feathers.

A slow start to settlement

In fact, Cabral was probably not the first European to make landfall on the coast of Brazil. Christopher Columbus had reached Venezuela in 1498 during his third voyage, and in his wake two separate Spanish fleets – one commanded by Columbus's old sailing companion, Vicente Yáñez Pinzón, the other by Diego de Lepe – are thought to have both reached Brazil a few weeks before Cabral. The newly discovered land, however, lay to the east of a line established by the 1494 Treaty of Tordesillas, which demarcated the Spanish and Portuguese spheres of influence in the New World: Brazil was out of bounds for Spain.

A Portuguese map of Rio de Janeiro Bay made in 1579 shows the recently founded city of São Sebastião do Rio de Janeiro, abbreviated here as 'Cidade des Sebastiam'.

The brazilwood trade
One of the most valuable trade goods that the new land had to offer was brazilwood, which Vespucci first brought back to the Portuguese court. The red pigment that it contained was used for dyeing wool and cotton. Europe's commercial world was soon abuzz with talk of the newly discovered 'land of brazilwood', a term that eventually became shortened to Brazil. This woodcarving shows logs being loaded onto a ship for transport back to Europe.

Pioneer navigator
In 1500 the Portuguese navigator Pedro Álvares Cabral, shown in this engraving, claimed the coast of Brazil for Portugal. A few weeks before, the Spanish captain Vicente Yáñez Pinzón had visited the same stretch of coast.

Cabral formally took possession of the territory for the Portuguese crown on May 1, 1500. Thereafter there would be both Spanish and Portuguese power blocs in South America, but for more than 30 years after Cabral's arrival Brazil was very much the poor relation of Portuguese colonial politics. King Manuel I was far more interested in exploiting the richer pickings of India and Southeast Asia, and he did little to assert Portugal's rights. Spanish, Dutch and French ships all freely plied the waters off Brazil's shores. Only the presence of brazilwood, used in the dyeing industry, attracted a few entrepreneurs to trade with the local Amerindians. The first serious attempt at colonisation came in 1532

when Martin Alonso de Sousa founded São Vicente near the present-day city of Santos. Even so, the increased Portuguese presence did little to deter traders of other nations, particularly the French and Dutch, who continued to make contacts with the coastal natives.

To counter the threat of foreign incursions, the Portuguese crown decided to develop the country through private endeavour. The entire Brazilian seaboard was divided up into parallel strips running inland as far as the notional demarcation line with Spanish lands. Each of the 12 'captaincies' so created included about 280km (175 miles) of coastline, as well as all the undeveloped hinterland beyond, and each was then offered to individuals with the means to exploit them. In return for promising to settle the land, they were granted complete military and political autonomy, including the right to enslave the native people and to establish their own jurisdiction within their territories.

In practice, because of a general shortage of settlers and the growing hostility of the local people, there were few individuals with the means to take on the captaincies. By the 1540s it was

obvious that Brazil needed a more centralised administration with a crown-appointed leader. In 1549, Thomas de Sousa sailed for Brazil to take up his new post as the nation's first governor-general, administering executive and judicial power that were vested in the crown. He arrived with six Jesuit priests, 300 soldiers, 300 volunteer settlers and 400 freed convicts who had been offered the chance to build a new life in the New World. Reaching All Saints' Bay, he founded Brazil's first city, Salvador de Bahía.

A boom based on sugar

By that stage an economic boom was driving the country's growth. Sugar had replaced dyewoods as Brazil's chief export. The first sugar mills were set up in São Vicente in 1533 and in Pernambuco in 1542. These enterprises, which were funded with Dutch capital, were in the hands of powerful sugar barons.

The development was fraught with implications for the colony's future, for sugar cane was grown on plantations worked by slaves. At first bands of slave-hunters staged raids into the interior in search of indigenous people to do the

work. But as in the Caribbean, the native population proved unsuitable, with many of the conscripts choosing flight or even suicide in preference to forced labour for European masters. As a result, the plantation owners ultimately came to rely on slaves imported from Africa. In time, São Salvador de Bahía became the world's largest slave market as well as the chief export outlet for sugar, with an annual turnover of up to 20,000 tonnes.

Portugal's heyday as a colonial power came to an end in the summer of 1578, when young King Sebastian was killed fighting the Moors on a North African battlefield, prompting Philip II of Spain to put forward a claim to the vacant Portuguese throne. For 60 years, from 1580 to 1640, Portugal fell under Spanish rule, a situation that had profound implications for Brazil. Following the defeat of the Spanish Armada in 1588, Philip closed Portuguese ports to English and Dutch shipping. The two nations responded by seizing

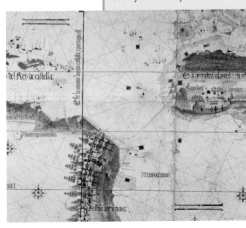

Portuguese bases in the Far East. By the beginning of the 17th century, much of Portugal's overseas empire was gone, leaving Brazil as the nation's only substantial surviving colony.

The Dutch arrive

Brazilian ports, too, came under assault. In 1593 Dutch and English corsairs raided Pernambuco, and in 1604 the Dutch

Dancing warriors
A painting by the Dutch artist Albert van der Eeckhout shows people of the Tarairiu tribe of northern Brazil performing a traditional dance. Eeckhout accompanied Maurice von Nassau to Brazil in 1637 and kept a visual record of everything he saw.

attacked Portuguese ships in the Bay of Bahía and sailed up the lower Amazon. These early raids were the work of bold privateers, but with the foundation of the Dutch West Indies Company in 1621, a major new player entered the scene. Equipped with its own troops and granted both a trading monopoly by the Dutch government and a charter authorising it to found colonies in Africa and the Americas, the company's establishment was almost a declaration of war – a threat that was realised in 1624 when Dutch forces conquered Bahía and occupied six of the former Portuguese captaincies.

Three years later, a combined Spanish and Portuguese fleet succeeded in retaking Bahía, repelling a subsequent Dutch attempt to win it back. Nonetheless, the interlopers retained a firm foothold in Pernambuco, the northern region where

the lucrative wood and sugar industries were concentrated; in 1630 they even captured the regional capital, Olinda. Driven from their homes, the displaced Portuguese settlers conducted a prolonged guerrilla war against the Dutch.

The burden of running the newly conquered lands proved too much for the Dutch West Indies Company. By 1636 it had run up debts of 18 million guilders, and it was becoming obvious that the conquered territories in Brazil could not be maintained without state intervention.

A far-sighted governor

The Dutch government responded by dispatching Maurice von Nassau to the colony as *stadholder* or governor, with extensive powers. Under his prudent leadership, Dutch power in Brazil reached its zenith. Maurice secured control of the whole of the northeast of the country, transforming Recife into an imposing city that attracted scientists and artists from Europe. He sought to diversify the colony's economy by encouraging coffee-growing and the cultivation of tropical and European cash crops as an alternative to the monoculture of cane sugar, which was destroying the soil. The governor also promoted religious tolerance, encouraging Catholics, Jews and Calvinists to live side by side in peace.

In 1640, von Nassau called the first parliament in the Americas, with 43 seats set aside for Portuguese representatives to speak for their fellow-countrymen. Yet the colony was still a drain on resources, and in 1654 the Dutch withdrew. They took the knowledge they had gained of sugar and tobacco production to their existing West Indian colonies, which subsequently became dangerous competitors of the restored Portuguese planters.

The expansion of the Spanish colonial empire

In a second wave of conquest, the Spanish crown established control over vast territories in Central and Southern America.

The Spanish conquest of the New World did not begin as a state enterprise. Most of the original ventures were private initiatives, although the government sometimes lent its support or actively promoted the expeditions – after all, a fifth of all gains were set aside for the king. In return, the Spanish monarch gave splendid titles to the entrepreneurs and conquistadors – Columbus was named Admiral of the Ocean Sea – and granted them great estates in the lands they claimed for the crown.

The early conquistadors had a great deal of freedom. The huge distances that separated the colonies from the mother country, together with the length of time needed to cross them, allowed them to do whatever it took to seize and secure the new lands. They had the right to found cities, as Pizarro and others did, once they had brought extensive territories under their control.

The labour was provided by the defeated Amerindians, without whom the colonists would never have been able to build or maintain the settlements.

The most spectacular gains were made in the first wave of exploration and conquest, from Columbus's pioneering voyage in 1492 through to Pizarro's conquest of Peru, culminating in the foundation of Lima in 1535.

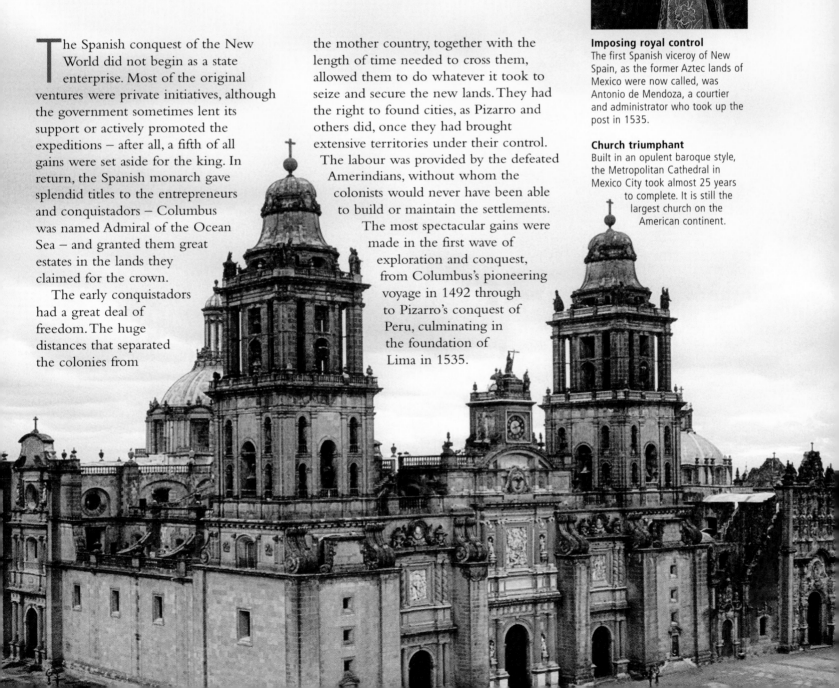

Imposing royal control
The first Spanish viceroy of New Spain, as the former Aztec lands of Mexico were now called, was Antonio de Mendoza, a courtier and administrator who took up the post in 1535.

Church triumphant
Built in an opulent baroque style, the Metropolitan Cathedral in Mexico City took almost 25 years to complete. It is still the largest church on the American continent.

Further expansion

The extension of Spanish penetration to north and south continued long after that date. These ventures proved less lucrative than the conquest of Mexico or Peru, but they vastly extended the territory under Spanish rule, from southern Chile and Argentina stretching northward into what is now Texas, California and New Mexico in the United States.

The task of pushing north from the Aztec heartland began even before Peru had fallen to Pizarro. In 1530 Nuño de Guzmán marched to Mexico's northern Pacific coast with 500 men, wiping out 800 native settlements on the way. Nine years later Francisco de Ulloa became the first Spaniard to reach the northern end of the Gulf of California. In 1540 Francisco Coronado was dispatched with 300 Spaniards and hundreds of Amerindians into the desert lands to the north of Mexico, drawn by legends of the Seven Golden Cities of Cibola. Although the cities turned out to be imaginary, Coronado discovered and pillaged the Pueblo civilisations of New Mexico on his travels. One of his lieutenants became the first European to see the Grand Canyon of the Colorado River.

Further east, Hernando de Soto, one of Pizarro's comrades-in-arms in Peru, sailed from Spain to Florida in search of a legendary spring of eternal youth. In 1541 he travelled through the region that would later be known as Georgia, the Carolinas, Tennessee and Alabama, discovering the Mississippi River and venturing as far as the present-day state of Oklahoma. In 1598 Juan de Oñate established a colony of several hundred people in New Mexico. A brutal commander, he was subsequently put on trial and exiled from the colony for his crimes as governor. In 1610 his successor, Pedro de Peralta, founded Santa Fé.

Opening up the south

In South America, too, the second phase of the conquest brought vast new areas under Spanish control. In 1535 Pedro de Mendoza embarked from Spain with a fleet of 16 ships and some 2000 men heading for the Rio de la Plata region of South America. Eager to expand his dominions, Emperor Charles V (who then ruled Spain) had granted Mendoza the right to claim all territories lying between the 25th and 30th degrees of latitude – now northern Argentina – for the Spanish crown. Sailing up the river, Mendoza founded what was to become Buenos Aires: the original settlement consisted of a modest church set in the midst of a few reed-thatched adobe houses.

Across the Andes Mountains, on the western side of South America, Pedro de Valdivia ventured south from Peru in 1540 with 11 Spanish companions and several hundred Amerindians. He founded the city of Santiago on Valparaiso Bay, and then used it as a base to penetrate further south in what is now Chile.

In the north, Gonzalo Jiménez de Quesada conquered the Chibcha Indian civilisation of present-day Colombia and explored the area around the upper reaches of the Orinoco River. In his capacity as governor of

Recording the Aztec past
Now the state symbol of Mexico, the image of an eagle holding a snake and perched on a cactus makes an early appearance in this illustration for the *Codex Mendoza*, a chronicle of Aztec history drawn up for New Spain's first viceroy, Antonio de Mendoza. He commissioned the work from native scribes in 1541 as a way of informing Emperor Charles V about his new colony.

Efficient statesman
A contemporary woodcut by an Inca artist, Felipe Guaman Poma de Ayala, shows Francesco de Toledo, who was appointed viceroy of Peru in 1569. A harsh disciplinarian who enforced compulsory labour on the native population, Toledo was also an efficient and impartial administrator. Under his guidance the Viceroyalty of Peru became the most important colony in the Spanish overseas empire.

Quito, Gonzalo Pizarro – a half-brother of Francisco, the conqueror of Peru – embarked upon an expedition that crossed the Andes eastwards and ventured into the inhospitable jungle of the Amazon Basin. Pizarro himself turned back, losing most of his men on the return journey, but his lieutenant Francisco de Orellana pressed on. He and his companions eventually completed their journey across the entire continent, floating down the Amazon on a raft built from rainforest timber to reach the Atlantic in August 1541. Finding his way to Trinidad and so back to Spain, Orellana took with him stories of encounters with tribes of women warriors like the Amazons of ancient Greek legend, giving the mighty river its present name.

Exploiting the native population

The conquistadors who carved out the Spanish empire in America were driven by many motives, but lust for wealth and glory dominated. Military success brought with it social advancement in the form of titles, land and privileges. No reward was more lucrative or more sought-after than the granting of an *encomienda* – the right to claim tribute and forced labour from a specified Amerindian group, usually the

The fate of native peoples
As this 17th-century engraving suggests, the conquistadors often displayed appalling cruelty towards the peoples they conquered. On one occasion Pedro de Valdivia, conqueror of Chile, had the hands and noses cut off 400 prisoners. Ten years later he himself died in Indian captivity – according to legend, his Araucanian captors forced him to drink molten gold.

Local coinage
From 1566 silver coins such as this one from the West Indies, worth eight Spanish *reales*, were minted in the colonies themselves rather than in Spain.

inhabitants of a village but sometimes of an entire region. In theory, the holders of an encomienda took on responsibility for the welfare of the natives, providing them with security and with the services of a parish priest to instruct them in the Christian religion. In practice, the system was a brutal form of slavery.

Complaints about the system led to its replacement by the *repartimiento*, under which Amerindian labour could be called on only temporarily for the duration of specific works, yet this, too, proved open to exploitation. As the native population plummeted in the course of the 16th century, killed by disease and demoralisation, the survivors found themselves subjected to ever-increasing demands that only hastened the downward spiral of death and despair.

In time a rigid class system developed. African slaves were at the bottom, with the Amerindians barely better placed just above them. *Mestizos* – citizens of mixed European and native ancestry – provided a middle layer. Then came two grades of white colonists: those born in the colonies had inferior status to immigrants from Spain – the so-called *peninsulares*.

Establishing royal control

Despite ongoing exploration, the heyday of the conquistadors was over by 1535. A new age was dawning in which power would pass to office-holders: governors, lawyers, administrators, bishops. The extent of the territories under Spanish control by that time required a carefully designed hierarchy of authority, so the Spanish crown tightened its grip by appointing viceroys. These royal deputies represented the monarchy in the colonies, exercising almost regal powers.

In 1535 Antonio de Mendoza became the first viceroy of New Spain, as the former Aztec lands in Central America were now called. In contrast to the early adventurers, the 45-year-old governor was a man of education and culture. His office combined the powers of a supreme military commander, the chief justice, treasurer and head of the Church. In practice, however, a welter of petty regulations restricted his ability to take decisions, and he was also aware that, on

Working the mines
An engraving by a Flemish artist, Theodor de Bry, shows native workers labouring in the famous silver mines at Potosí in Bolivia. At first 7000 Amerindians were employed in the mines; by the end of the century this had risen to 160,000. Forced to work in appalling conditions at high altitude, most died of malnutrition and disease.

the expiry of his designated term, crown representatives would subject his performance to thorough scrutiny.

Mendoza's arrival marked the end of the days when the conquistadors set their own rules. Even Hernán Cortés, the conqueror of Mexico, had to fall into line. By the time of Mendoza's arrival Cortés had retired to his estates at Cuernavaca, south of Mexico City. Five years later he returned to Spain, where he died, worn out by endless litigation.

The New Laws
Spanish churchmen began to campaign for improvements in the lot of the native population, and in 1537 Pope Paul III announced in the bull *Sublimus Deus* that the indigenous peoples should be treated humanely and received into the Christian faith. In response Emperor Charles V drew up fresh legislation, the so-called New Laws, which came into effect in 1542 and 1543. Henceforth 18 separate decrees regulated the treatment of indigenous peoples, bringing the granting and operation of encomiendas under the control of the colonial authorities.

The new measures unleashed a storm of protest in the colonies that in some cases broke out into open revolt. In Peru in 1544 Gonzalo Pizarro refused to recognise the authority of the newly appointed viceroy, Blasco Núñez Vela, or to acknowledge the jurisdiction of the high court in Lima. Vela was executed in 1546, and Pizarro moved to have himself proclaimed king of an independent Peru.

Even though Pizarro had the support of almost all the holders of encomiendas, who considered their livelihoods to be at stake, the revolt was nipped in the bud by Vela's replacement, Pedro de la Gasca. The new viceroy won over many of the rebels by offers of conciliation, then took on and defeated the rest in battle. Pizarro was captured and executed. La Gasca then reformed the existing encomiendas, but stopped short of abolishing the system altogether.

By that time the viceroyalty was enjoying an economic boom triggered by the discovery, in 1545, of rich silver deposits at Potosí Mountain in what is now Bolivia. As a result, the southern lands experienced an influx of immigrants both from Spain itself and from the other colonies. In the 1550s at least 8000 Europeans arrived, but they could no longer expect encomiendas to assist them as these were no longer being granted.

The work of the missions
By 1580 Spain's colonial empire had reached its furthest limits. Spanish control was firmly established across the South American continent and effective systems of administration were in place. The next phase of colonisation was marked by missionary activities by the Christian religious orders, such as the Franciscans, Dominicans and Jesuits. Thanks to their efforts in setting up schools and printing presses, the colonies enjoyed a cultural flowering in the following century. The missionary effort reached a peak in the settlements founded by the Jesuits in Paraguay. Within these so-called *reducciones* (reductions), native peoples farmed the land in peace, producing cotton, tobacco, hides and other products, and white settlers were barred from entry.

Christian cause
Bartolomé de las Casas (below right) campaigned to improve the treatment and conditions of the indigenous people. Many converted to Christianity. A page from the Lienzo de Tlaxcala, a mid 16th-century manuscript from Mexico, shows indigenous people being baptised by Christian missionaries.

Privateers in the Caribbean

The riches of Spain's New World colonies drew smugglers and privateers from other European nations keen to plunder some of the wealth for themselves.

Seafaring hero
Francis Drake was the most famous privateer of the 16th century. Originally from a Devon farming background, he worked his way up through the ranks to serve as ship's captain under John Hawkins. He was eventually knighted for his exploits by Queen Elizabeth I.

When the French corsair Martin Cote and his 1000 heavily armed men came ashore, they were met with a hail of bullets, but their Spanish adversaries soon ran out of ammunition and withdrew to the mountains, leaving Cartagena, Spain's chief port on South America's Caribbean coast, at the mercy of the raiders. Cote's men spent several days pillaging the city then set sail, allowing the citizens to return to their devastated homes.

Cote's raid on Cartagena in 1559 alerted the Spanish government to the fact that many people coveted the riches of their American colonies. Portuguese, Dutch and English privateers as well as French conducted raids against Spanish ports and shipping. Every year, the Spanish took thousands of tonnes of silver from the mines at Zacatecas and Guanajuanato in Mexico and from Potosí in Bolivia to the ports of Peru and Mexico, where they were weighed and stamped; sometimes coins were minted in situ. Then the Spanish silver fleets carried the treasure to Europe, departing from Nombre de Dios in Panama or Veracruz in Mexico.

Breaking Spain's monopoly

Initially, it was not the promise of gold or silver that lured ships to the Caribbean. At first they came simply to trade. Then, in 1556, Spain placed a general embargo on all non-Spanish merchants in order to protect the monopoly of the state-run *Casa de Contratación* (House of Trade) in Seville. At a stroke, the English, French and Dutch who had been doing business in the region found themselves cut out of the action completely. The only course left to them if they wished to go on trading was to disregard the ban and deal illegally, a practice that sometimes escalated into violent acts of piracy. Many a law-abiding sea captain simply wishing to trade ended up becoming a raider and privateer.

Spain's decision fell particularly hard on English merchant captains, who were accustomed to conducting trade freely on the high seas around the globe. Their indignation at the measure grew as a political divide opened up between Protestant England and Catholic Spain following Elizabeth I's accession in 1558. The Queen was sympathetic to their cause, and soon lent support, tacitly at first but then in public. The freelance traders and raiders styled themselves privateers; their Spanish victims called them pirates.

Colluding with the colonists

In the early years of the Spanish ban, foreign captains overcame the embargo with the aid of complaisant local officials. One Spaniard ruefully commented of his countrymen at the time, 'No punishment on Earth can restrain them from buying everything they need'. Dutch merchants even devised a special form of commerce known as 'sloop trade'; at a pre-arranged signal, their Spanish counterparts would row out to the Dutch ships under cover of darkness to load up with goods.

Once the authorities were alerted to the situation, however, fresh stratagems to get around the ban were required. Sometimes captains would pretend they needed urgent repairs, providing local officials with the excuse to allow their vessels into port. Mayors sometimes encouraged foreign traders to feign attacks on their cities, then claimed that they had only agreed to exchange goods under threat of force.

In time the lucrative pickings on the Spanish Main drew in corsairs who had previously operated in European waters, intercepting Spanish ships on their way to Flanders. Some of them moved their operations to the Caribbean. At the same time, England's policy of expanding maritime trade made many English seafarers set course for Central America.

The first privateer

The pioneer in the field, whose methods would be emulated by all who came after him, was John Hawkins. Hawkins came from a long-established Devon seafaring family – his father had successfully (and legally) imported dyewood to Europe from the Portuguese colony of Brazil as early as 1530. The son made his first trading voyage to the Caribbean in 1562. With the help of a Spanish helmsman from the Canary Islands, he found his way to the Caribbean island of Hispaniola, where he openly but illegally conducted a lucrative trade in slaves, picked up en route from Africa's Guinea Coast. Hawkins found a ready market on the island, for the local landowners wanted cheap labour to man their plantations but were unwilling to pay the head tax of 30 ducats charged on all slaves by the Spanish crown.

Drake's drum and flagship
Francis Drake captured this drum, dated 1596, on one of his expeditions as a privateer. It is now on display at his former home, Buckland Abbey in Devon. Drake's flagship vessel, the *Pelican* (below), had 18 guns and a dead-weight of 100 tonnes. It was the only one of a fleet of five ships to complete the circumnavigation of the globe in 1577. In the course of the voyage Drake renamed it the *Golden Hind*.

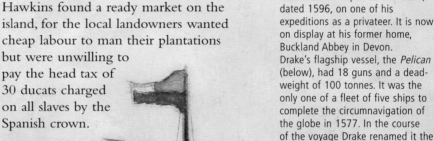

Merchant adventurer

John Hawkins was the pathfinder for all English privateers in the Caribbean. In the course of four major trading voyages he amassed huge riches, advertising the wealth to be had for the taking in the ports of the Spanish Main.

Besides turning a handsome profit, Hawkins returned with valuable knowledge of the sea lanes leading to the heart of the Spanish empire.

Hawkins' second voyage was backed by some of England's wealthiest people. Queen Elizabeth herself took the largest share by putting one of her own ships at Hawkins' disposal, the massive and cumbersome *Jesus of Lübeck*, bought by her father Henry VIII from the Hanseatic League 20 years before. With three smaller ships making up his fleet, Hawkins once again sailed to the Guinea Coast of West Africa, where he and his men captured or bartered a fresh

textiles, wine and other goods, before setting sail with a handsome profit of 12,000 gold pesos. Moving on to the offshore island of Curaçao, Hawkins had to use force to ply his trade. The governor sought to bar entry to the English ships, so Hawkins and his men took him hostage then proceeded to conduct their business undisturbed.

Continuing along the coast they came next to Rio de la Hacha, now in Colombia, where Hawkins landed 100 men and some artillery. After a brief confrontation with a local militia, in which no-one was injured, the port authorities agreed to let the English sell their goods. The captain happily disposed of the rest of his cargo for a handsome profit, then set sail for home.

The Spanish reaction

Hawkins' success, trumpeted in England and abroad, provoked a reaction from the Spanish ambassador in London, who warned mariners not to attempt to repeat the venture. But Hawkins was not to be discouraged. Two years later he assembled another fleet in Plymouth. When a Spanish squadron appeared in Plymouth Sound in an attempt to deter him, it was seen off with a furious cannonade of fire.

Hawkins set sail in October 1567, but from the beginning things went badly. The Portuguese were by now enforcing a monopoly on the West African slave trade, and he had difficulty in finding slaves to fill his ships. When he finally arrived on the Spanish Main, he found ports that had once been keen to trade now closed against him, and he had to use force to persuade the reluctant authorities to allow him to do business. Even that did not work at Cartagena, the most important port on the coast, where he and his fleet were forced to withdraw empty-handed after a siege lasting seven days.

Native hunters

An illustration from a 16th-century French travel journal shows Carib Indians returning from a successful wild boar hunt. Hispaniola and Cuba were rich in game, including domesticated pigs and cattle that ran wild when island landowners abandoned their estates for a more lucrative life on the mainland.

cargo of slaves. He was in for an unpleasant surprise when he arrived in the Caribbean, however, for the authorities on Hispaniola denied him landing rights and forbade him to trade in any way. Diverting his fleet to the mainland coast of what is now Venezuela, he finally managed to make a landfall at the port of Borburata, where he sold 151 slaves, along with

Disaster at San Juan de Ulúa

Even though Hawkins had not sold all his cargo, he decided to cut his losses and head for home. But his bad luck continued. Caught in a storm, his fleet was driven toward the Mexican coast. Several ships were badly damaged and needed repairs. The captain of a Spanish merchantman commandeered in the Gulf of Mexico told Hawkins that San Juan de Ulua, near Veracruz, was the nearest port, but also warned him that a Spanish silver fleet was due there shortly on its way to Spain.

Hawkins reached the port safely and took local leaders hostage as a guarantee that his men would not be attacked while the repairs were being carried out. A day later, however, the Spanish fleet arrived. Its commander heard of the presence of English ships and dropped anchor outside the harbour, while military reinforcements were rushed overland from nearby Veracruz.

Hawkins met his nemesis on the morning of September 23, 1568. Almost all of his ships were either captured or sunk, and he was lucky to escape with his life on the last seaworthy vessel. Short of supplies for the return journey, he was forced to leave half of his men behind on the Mexican coast. Many of the rest died of starvation or disease on the journey back to England. When the ship finally limped back into Plymouth Sound, 15 months after its departure, only 15 of its crew were left alive.

While the battle had been raging at San Juan de Ulúa, however, one other ship from Hawkins' fleet had escaped: the *Judith*, under the command of Francis Drake. As well as rescuing all of his crew,

EVERYDAY LIFE

The wild world of the buccaneers

In the 17th century several Caribbean islands became homes to a multinational population of buccaneers. The word came from the Arawak term *buccan*, meaning a grill on which meat was smoked over a slow fire, for at first the buccaneers supported themselves by hunting, living off the wild cattle and pigs that roamed the islands. An all-male community, they made their living by selling the dried meat and skins, often to the crews of privateering ships. In time some took to sea-raiding themselves, and their base on the island of Tortuga off Hispaniola's north coast eventually became a famous pirate haunt.

the 28-year-old captain managed to bring his cargo safely home, making him the only commander to realise a profit from the expedition.

Around the world

In the years that followed, Drake was to become the most renowned of all the privateers. Hawkins had been a trader willing to adapt his methods to the lawless conditions of the Spanish Main, but Drake made stealing from Spain into a respectable and even patriotic way of life. His outstanding gifts as a sailor and his unquestioned loyalty to Queen Elizabeth helped him to become a legend in his own lifetime, and his fame only increased after his death.

Drake first emerged from Hawkins' shadow in 1572. On the first major expedition under his own command, he ambushed a mule train carrying bullion across the Isthmus of Panama to the port

A seagoing fortress
Spanish warships of the 16th century, like the *Sancta Trinitas* (below), were floating fortresses. The galleons served as escorts for the annual treasure fleets carrying bullion from the New World colonies.

Raid on Santo Domingo
A map painted in 1588 shows Francis Drake's expeditionary force off the port of Santo Domingo, in January 1586. The explorer and sea-farer Martin Frobisher (below) sailed with Francis Drake on the expedition to Santo Domingo and Cartagena.

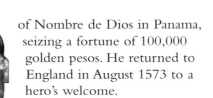

of Nombre de Dios in Panama, seizing a fortune of 100,000 golden pesos. He returned to England in August 1573 to a hero's welcome.

Four years later Drake had an even more ambitious plan: to sail far to the south around Cape Horn in order to attack the relatively undefended Spanish ports on South America's Pacific coast. He lost four vessels navigating the stormy Straits of Magellan, but sailed on with his one remaining ship, the *Golden Hind*. In Valparaiso harbour in Chile he looted a merchantman before going ashore with his men to sack the city. Off Panama, he captured a galleon, the *Nuestra Señora de la Concepción*, heavily laden with treasure from Peru.

Soon after, two experienced helmsmen fell into Drake's hands from another commandeered Spanish vessel, along with ship's charts showing routes across the Pacific to the fabled Spice Islands. These precious documents enabled him to undertake a daring return voyage via the Pacific and Indian oceans and around the Cape of Good Hope in Africa. He thus became only the second captain, after Magellan, to circumnavigate the globe. Drake arrived back in Plymouth in September 1580 after a journey of 35 months. The Queen herself came on board the *Golden Hind* and, to the resounding cheers of the assembled crowd, knighted him on the spot.

Six years later another adventurous English mariner, Thomas Cavendish, reprised Drake's voyage. He too plundered Spanish shipping in the Pacific and came back unscathed to England around the Cape of Good Hope, having completed the third circumnavigation of the world.

A final voyage

Drake and Hawkins became the models for a whole generation of English corsairs, yet their careers ended unhappily with a disastrous joint venture. In 1595, Hawkins and Drake, now aged 63 and 55, set off once more for the Caribbean with a fleet of 28 ships. The expedition met with one disaster after another. Forewarned of its arrival, the Spanish secured the treasure that the privateers had hoped to capture. Hawkins died of a fever as the fleet came in sight of the Puerto Rican port of San Juan. A later attack on the Isthmus of Panama proved fruitless, and Drake and much of the rest of the crew contracted dysentery on an island off the Mosquito Coast. Drake himself died a few days later, and the fleet limped back to England having lost 10 ships and 1500 men.

The end of an era

By then the golden age of privateering was at an end. The Spanish had learned to group their treasure galleons in large convoys that made twice-yearly voyages across the Atlantic accompanied by warships. Daredevil English commanders and explorers like Sir Walter Raleigh and George Clifford, the 3rd Earl of Cumberland, sought to seize these fleets in vain.

There were still plenty of spoils to be had in the Caribbean – in 1598, for example, Clifford led a fleet of 27 ships with 2000 men to attack Puerto Rico, capturing and sacking several ports on the island. The vessels returned to England with a haul that included 1000 baskets of sugar, 2000 quintals of ginger, a cargo of slaves and crates full of pearls.

Raleigh undertook one final, unsuccessful, expedition to South America, in the course of which he captured the capital of Trinidad, then moved on to the coast of Guiana, where he hoped to establish a gold mine. Like Drake, he was struck down by illness and the expedition ended in personal tragedy when his son was killed on an expedition up the Orinoco River. Raleigh returned home with no booty

and just two of his original 14 ships. On arrival, he was arrested and executed on a trumped-up charge of conspiracy.

The last great coup

The last great plundering expedition in Caribbean waters was by the Dutch seafarer Piet Hein. As admiral of the fleet for the Dutch West Indies Company, he had been responsible for challenging Spanish ships in the western Atlantic for some years. Once, while privateering off Brazil, he captured 22 Portuguese vessels.

Hein's greatest feat came in 1628. At the head of a corsair squadron in Matanzas Bay off Cuba, he achieved every

privateer's dream by capturing the entire Spanish silver fleet of 27 ships. Hein transferred the bullion to his own vessels and set all but four of the galleons ablaze. The total haul was estimated to be worth more than 12 million florins – enough to pay his crews two years' wages in advance, distribute a 50 per cent dividend to the company's shareholders, and fit out an entire new fleet of 61 ships.

Doomed island idyll
A French privateer who served with Drake's expeditionary force is thought to have made this drawing of Arawak Indians. Peace-loving and hospitable, the Arawaks shared the fate of their long-time enemies, the warlike Caribs, at the hands of European settlers – both groups were all but wiped out within a generation.

Europeans start to settle North America

Eager for a share of the promised riches of the New World, England, France and the Netherlands set about colonising North America. England quickly gained the upper hand.

The first lasting settlement
Founded in 1607, Jamestown in Virginia was the first permanent English colony in North America. Named in honour of King James I, the settlement was plagued by disease and starvation in its early years, but later flourished as a centre of the tobacco trade.

The opening up of North America to European settlement began with a voyage of discovery. Five years after Columbus reached the Caribbean another Genoese-born mariner, Giovanni Caboto, better-known as John Cabot, probed the coast of Newfoundland for the English crown. After his voyage, calls for a colony to be established grew more insistent. The prospects of trade with Native Americans were irresistible: the continent had rich resources of fish, fur and timber, and there was also the possibility that gold and silver might be found in the interior. And in those early years, merchant adventurers still hoped that America might prove a convenient way-station on the long-sought western sea route to the Indies.

The first attempt at permanent settlement was made in 1584. Sir Walter Raleigh, courtier, poet and entrepreneur, persuaded Queen Elizabeth I to give her blessing to a New World colony, to be called Virginia in her honour as the Virgin Queen. Raleigh dispatched two ships at his own expense in search of a suitable site. The expedition picked Roanoke Island, off the coast of present-day North Carolina.

A year later, the first 108 volunteers made the Atlantic crossing and erected a fortified settlement on the site, but within a year the enterprise ended in failure. Worn down by hunger and illness, the settlers were only too happy to take advantage of the chance arrival of a fleet commanded by Francis Drake, who called

Native village
A Native American village, one of the first to be visited by Europeans. It was painted from life sometime in the 1580s by John White, a talented artist who was later to become the first leader of the lost colony of Roanoke Island. The villagers belonged to an Algonquian-speaking group in what is now southern Virginia.

in on his way back from privateering in the Spanish Main. All the colonists chose to return with him to England.

The lost colony

Undeterred, Raleigh recruited a second group of settlers who arrived in Roanoke in July 1587. Their fate remains one of the great mysteries of early American history. Finding themselves inadequately equipped, the colonists sent their leader, John White, back to England for supplies. White left behind his daughter and newborn granddaughter, Virginia Dare, the first English child to be born in the New World. He arrived in England to find the country gearing up to confront the Spanish Armada, however, and three years passed before he was able to return.

When White finally put into Roanoke in August 1590, he found the settlement abandoned. The colonists had disappeared without a trace but for one clue, the word 'Croatoan' carved on a wooden palisade. No sign of the settlers was ever found again. Croatan was the home village of a

neighbouring tribe, and historians have assumed that the settlers were either assimilated into the Native American community or were killed.

Despite this disaster, the dream of an American colony lived on. Travellers returning from the continent brought reports of good soil, extensive forests for timber, and plentiful stocks of fish and animal pelts. In response, a group of merchant adventurers set up the Virginia Company in London in 1606. Its founding charter, signed by Elizabeth's successor James I, entitled it to establish two colonies, one in the area of the present-day state of Virginia and the other in the northern region that would later be known as New England.

Prosperous merchants provided the venture capital for the enterprise, recruiting colonists and undertaking to support them in the difficult early years while they were finding their feet in the

Skilled bowman
The Dutch engraver Theodor de Bry drew on John White's work to produce this engraving of an Algonquian hunter. The indigenous Virginians lived by a combination of hunting, trapping, fishing and slash-and-burn agriculture: maize (known to British settlers as Indian corn) was their staple crop.

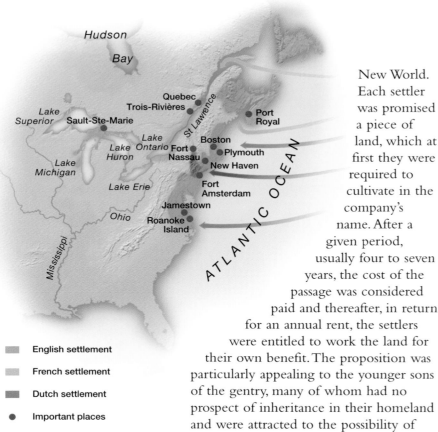

Hudson Bay

Quebec
Trois-Rivières
Lake Superior
Sault-Ste-Marie
Port Royal
Lake Ontario
Lake Huron
Boston
Fort Nassau
Lake Michigan
Plymouth
New Haven
Lake Erie
Fort Amsterdam
Jamestown
Ohio
Roanoke Island
Mississippi
St Lawrence
ATLANTIC OCEAN

- ▪ English settlement
- ▪ French settlement
- ▪ Dutch settlement
- ● Important places

Uneven conflict
A 1629 engraving shows French troops attacking a fortified Iroquois village. The Iroquois bows and arrows were no match for guns.

New World. Each settler was promised a piece of land, which at first they were required to cultivate in the company's name. After a given period, usually four to seven years, the cost of the passage was considered paid and thereafter, in return for an annual rent, the settlers were entitled to work the land for their own benefit. The proposition was particularly appealing to the younger sons of the gentry, many of whom had no prospect of inheritance in their homeland and were attracted to the possibility of making their fortune elsewhere. As a result, the settlements suffered in the early days from too many well-bred young men and not enough carpenters, blacksmiths and other skilled craftsmen and labourers.

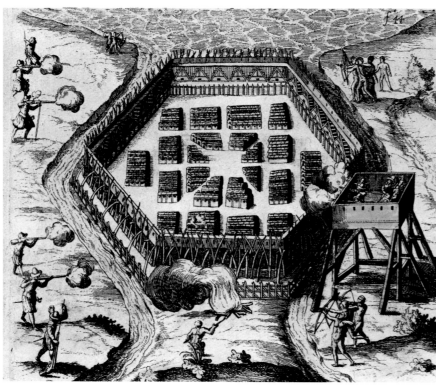

The first permanent settlement

On May 14, 1607, a party of 105 colonists arrived on the coast of present-day Virginia. The site chosen by their leader, John Smith, lay on the estuary of a wide river north of Roanoke that they named the James in honour of James I. The colony itself was called Jamestown.

Survival turned out to be just as tough a proposition for the Jamestown colonists as it had been for the earlier Roanoke settlers. Food and clean drinking water were in short supply, and illnesses soon decimated the small community. By the end of the first winter, despite the arrival of about 100 more settlers, their numbers were down to 38.

In these difficult times Smith held the group together. He learnt the Algonquian language to establish relations with the local tribe and its chief, Powhatan, and undertook lengthy exploratory journeys along the coast north of Jamestown. Reports of his findings were carried back to England by intermittent ships.

Saved by tobacco

The colony's fate hung by a thread, the more so after Smith left for England in October 1609. The arrival of more new settlers from England was taxing resources to the limit, but disease took the greatest toll. The winter of 1609–10 became known as the 'starving time': only 60 were still alive when the arrival of fresh supplies saved the settlement from extinction.

The situation finally began to improve from 1612, when an enterprising newcomer, John Rolfe, planted tobacco seeds, brought from the Caribbean, on Virginian soil. An indigenous strain of tobacco already grew there, but it was not to the taste of English consumers. By contrast, the aromatic Caribbean plant was an instant success. Within five years the colonists were shipping 8500kg (19,000lb) of tobacco to England annually, to the chagrin of King James and others who considered smoking a noxious habit. Thereafter the Virginia settlers geared their economy largely to cultivating tobacco, importing slaves from Africa to work the plantations.

France stakes its claim

Meanwhile, to the north, settlers from France and the Netherlands had secured a foothold on the continent. The French presence dated back to Jacques Cartier, who sailed up the St Lawrence River in the 1530s as far as the future site of Montreal, taking possession of the surrounding lands in the name of France.

In 1603, Samuel de Champlain followed Cartier's route up the St Lawrence, also reaching the Lachine Rapids at Montreal. Champlain was to devote his life to establishing an enduring French presence in Canada. In 1608, on his third expedition, he founded the fort of Quebec to serve as a stronghold dominating the St Lawrence Valley as well as a base for exploring the great lakes that he had heard lay around the river's headwaters. Over the next 27 years he worked tirelessly to develop the town, which grew from a small settlement surrounded by a protective ditch into a major centre of the fur trade.

Initially the pelts traded in Quebec were supplied by native hunters and trappers from the Huron tribe. Champlain was at pains to foster good relations with the indigenous population, using Native American guides to help him to explore the Canadian interior. In 1609 he reached the body of water that was to become known as Lake Champlain (now on the Canada–USA border). Six years later he

pushed on through the territory of the Ottawa people into the Great Lakes region, visiting Lake Huron and Lake Ontario.

Missionaries and hunters

By the time of Champlain's death in 1635, a new breed of French woodsman was working alongside the Native American hunters, travelling far and wide in the search for pelts. Living almost outside the law, these young trappers became known as *coureurs de bois* ('wood wanderers'), and their journeys into the wilderness to supply the European demand for beaver fur – used to make hats, muffs and capes – steadily widened the area of French penetration.

The fur hunters were joined by Jesuit priests, who ventured into the interior with native guides to bring the Christian message to the indigenous population. These intrepid missionaries ventured far

Father of French America
The explorer and statesman Samuel de Champlain (top) was also an excellent artist and cartographer who published several richly illustrated accounts of his expeditions. This woodcut, taken from one of his drawings, shows the engagement that took place between the Iroquois and the French at Ticonderoga on July 30, 1607. It ended in resounding defeat for the native tribes.

Colonial cradle
Cradles like this one, made from wicker, oak and maple, were in great demand in the colonies. Couples married earlier than in the mother country and the birth rate soared. This one was made in the Netherlands in the 17th century.

Symbol of a nation
After the rigours of a two-month Atlantic crossing, the first Puritan settlers arrived in New England on November 21, 1620, on board the two-masted *Mayflower*. The vessel carried a crew of 25 as well as the 102 settlers.

and wide, making important discoveries on the way; the first European to set eyes on Niagara Falls came from their ranks. However, the French colonies attracted fewer settlers than their English rivals, giving the British an overwhelming advantage when armed conflict eventually broke out between the two sides.

The Dutch on the Hudson

The Dutch presence in North America was almost accidental, for the merchants who initially sponsored it were more interested in finding a new route to Asia. In 1609 the directors of the Dutch East India Company commissioned the English explorer Henry Hudson to take on this task. Hudson's voyage took him to New York Bay and into the estuary of the river that now bears his name. Hopeful that the stream might provide a through route to the Pacific Ocean, he

sailed 250km (150 miles) upstream, almost to the site of the modern city of Albany. Although he didn't find the route he sought, his voyage gave the Dutch a claim to settle the region.

On his return to England, Hudson was forbidden to undertake any further voyages in the interests of foreign powers, but by that time the damage was done, and the Dutch had established a presence. Founding the West India Company as a New World counterpart of the existing East India Company, they set up a number of permanent trading posts on the Delaware and Hudson rivers.

One such site, located at the mouth of the Hudson River on an island known to the local Native American people as Manhattan. It not only offered a sheltered natural harbour but was also ideally placed to control traffic upriver. In 1626 the company's governor, Peter Minuit, purchased the island for a few woollen blankets and some cheap glass beads. On it he established the settlement of New Amsterdam, which became the centre of all Dutch colonial activity in North America. New Amsterdam itself rapidly became a prosperous community doing a brisk trade in furs. With its red-brick architecture, it was reminiscent of a small Dutch provincial town, even boasting a windmill. Yet New Holland, like New France, remained short of colonists, and this prevented it in the long term from effectively fending off English competition. In 1664 four English warships descended on New Amsterdam, giving the governor, Peter Stuyvesant, no choice but to surrender. The town was subsequently renamed New York, and with its fall the whole colony passed into British hands.

The Puritans in New England

The English owed their numeric advantage first and foremost to the successful colonisation of New England, and the force that drove the first settlers there was religion. They were Puritans, strict Calvinists whose views put them at odds with the established Church of England. The king and his ministers feared them as potential rebels. Unwilling to compromise over their convictions, they saw emigration as the only course open to them, even though they were never, in fact, actually persecuted in England.

Accordingly, in early 1620, a group of 102 men, women and children set sail from Plymouth, Devon, on board the *Mayflower* in the hope of establishing a promised land on the other side of the Atlantic. The Pilgrims, as they became known, landed on the Massachusetts coast, where they founded the settlement of Plymouth in the lee of Cape Cod. Ten years later a second wave of Puritans arrived under the aegis of the Massachusetts Bay Company, and established Boston about 50km (30 miles) to the north.

Sadly, the colonists' hopes of creating a realm of peace and harmony in the New World was not to be fulfilled. The new settlers soon fell to quarrelling among themselves. One troublesome spirit, Roger Williams, broke away in 1636 to establish the

colony of Rhode Island; and another, Thomas Hooker, founded the town of Hartford in Connecticut.

The British predominance

Despite the squabbles, New England prospered. The early settlers created a thriving cod fishery, and before long Boston developed as the main hub of North America's maritime trade. Economic prosperity, coupled with the chance of a new life, attracted a growing throng of settlers. Between 1620 and 1640 some 50,000 people left Britain for New England. By that time the population of Virginia had increased to over 10,000.

The undoubted losers in this territorial expansion were the Native American peoples. In 1622, local tribesmen fell on the inhabitants of Jamestown, killing almost a third of the colony's population before they were beaten back. Similar scenes were played out 15 years later in New England in the Pequot War, in which some 500 tribesmen were killed. The long-term advantage lay with the settlers, and as European colonisation went on, America's original inhabitants found themselves remorselessly pushed back from their traditional lands.

Princess Pocahontas

In 1614, Pocahontas, the beautiful daughter of the local Algonquian chief Powhatan, married the tobacco planter John Rolfe. The match marked the high point in relations between the two communities. In 1616 Pocahontas travelled with her husband to London, where she charmed the court of King James I with her regal bearing. A year later she died of smallpox and is buried at Gravesend.

Court dress
A portrait of Pocahontas wearing the European dress she wore for her presentation at the English royal court.

The Pequot War
In 1637 fighting broke out between settlers and the Pequot people. The Pequot stockade at Mystic was burnt down and more than 500 defenders were killed.

Discovering a wider world

The main motive that drove the European voyages of discovery in the 15th and early 16th centuries was the search for a direct sea-route to Asia. The traditional overland routes had been cut by the Ottoman Empire's expansion in the Middle East, and a new link was needed. Portuguese and Spanish ships pioneered the first wave of exploration, with English, French and Dutch following in their wake.

Prince Henry of Portugal, known to history as Henry the Navigator, sponsored the first exploratory voyages down the west coast of Africa. Following this route, Vasco da Gama reached India in 1498. Columbus blazed a trail west across the Atlantic: he never reached his goal of Asia, but his quest led to the discovery of the Americas.

The search continued

Columbus went to his grave believing that the lands he had found were outlying regions of the Asian mainland. It took the experiences of other explorers such as John Cabot and Amerigo Vespucci – two more Italians exploring for foreign masters – to convince people that the new discoveries were part of a vast unknown continent.

The next quest was to find a route round the Americas. The first to succeed was Portugal's Fernão de Magalhães (anglicised as Ferdinand Magellan) who in 1519 rounded South America's tip through the straits that now bear his name. The ship went on to make the first circumnavigation of the globe, though Magellan himself was killed on the voyage.

Other navigators probed for a northern route. The Dutchman Willem Barents made three voyages to the Arctic Ocean, reaching the island of Novaya Zemlya off the north Russian coast. On the other side of the globe another Dutch seafarer, Abel Tasman, discovered Tasmania and New Zealand while sailing from Indonesia in 1642, and later explored the north coast of Australia.

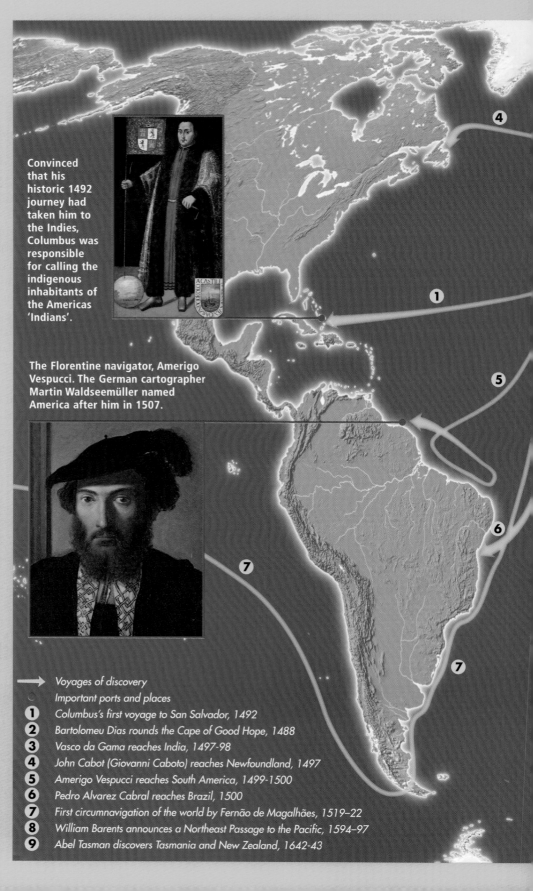

Convinced that his historic 1492 journey had taken him to the Indies, Columbus was responsible for calling the indigenous inhabitants of the Americas 'Indians'.

The Florentine navigator, Amerigo Vespucci. The German cartographer Martin Waldseemüller named America after him in 1507.

→ Voyages of discovery
○ Important ports and places
① Columbus's first voyage to San Salvador, 1492
② Bartolomeu Dias rounds the Cape of Good Hope, 1488
③ Vasco da Gama reaches India, 1497-98
④ John Cabot (Giovanni Caboto) reaches Newfoundland, 1497
⑤ Amerigo Vespucci reaches South America, 1499-1500
⑥ Pedro Alvarez Cabral reaches Brazil, 1500
⑦ First circumnavigation of the world by Fernão de Magalhães, 1519–22
⑧ William Barents announces a Northeast Passage to the Pacific, 1594–97
⑨ Abel Tasman discovers Tasmania and New Zealand, 1642-43

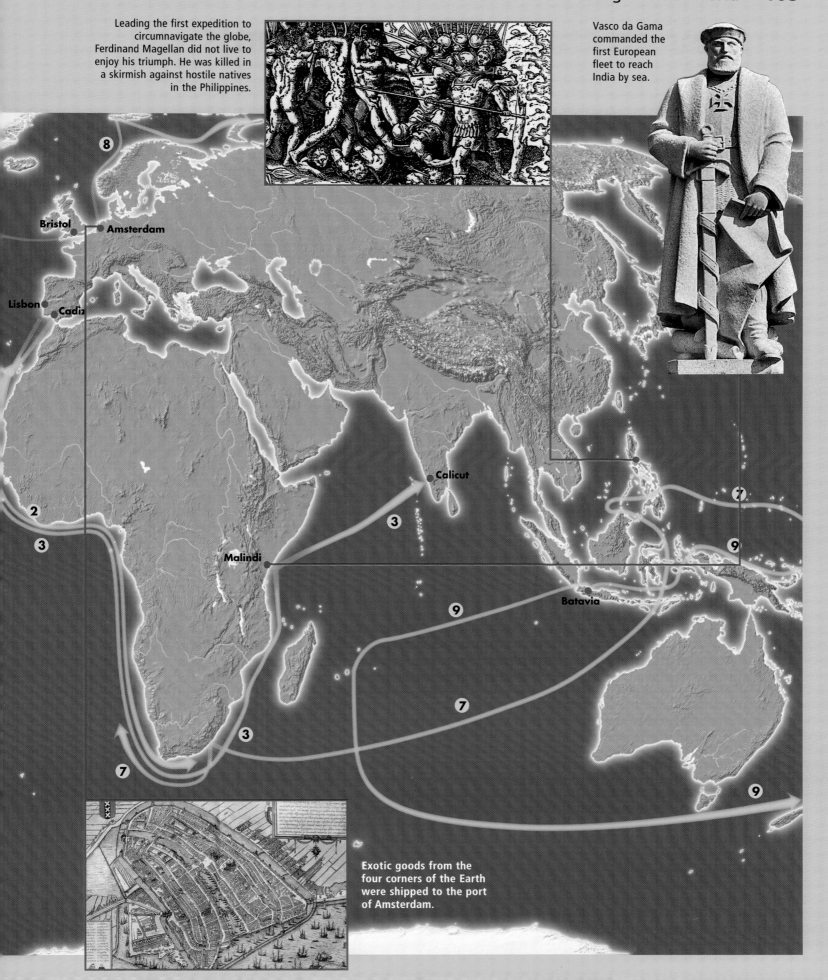

Leading the first expedition to circumnavigate the globe, Ferdinand Magellan did not live to enjoy his triumph. He was killed in a skirmish against hostile natives in the Philippines.

Vasco da Gama commanded the first European fleet to reach India by sea.

Bristol

Amsterdam

Lisbon

Cadiz

8

2

3

3

Calicut

3

Malindi

9

Batavia

7

3

7

9

7

9

Exotic goods from the four corners of the Earth were shipped to the port of Amsterdam.

Improving the navigator's tools

g'ensuict la demonstrance de lus

DELLE
NAVIGATIONI
ET VIAGGI
RACCOLTE DA M. GIO. BATTISTA RAMVSIO,
IN TRE VOLVMI DIVISE:

Nelle quali con relatione fedelissima si descriuono tutti quei paesi, che da
già 300. anni sin'hora sono stati scoperti, così di verso Leuante, &
Ponente, come di verso Mezzo di, & Tramontana;

Et si hà notitia del Regno del Prete Gianni, & dell'Africa fino à Calicut,
& all'Isole Molucche.

Et si tratta dell'Isola Giappan, delle due Sarmatie, della Tartaria, Scitia, Circasia, &
circonstanti Prouincie: della Tana, & dell'Indie tanto Occidentali, quanto
Orientali, & della Nauigatione d'intorno il Mondo.

Con Discorsi à suoi luoghi, & imprese diuerse d'Imperatori di Tartari, di Turchi, & di Persiani, de
Soldani di Babilonia, & d'altri Prencipi; & alcuni Capitoli, & Tauole di Geografia secondo le
carte da nauicare, co' nomi de' popoli, Porti, Città, Laghi, Fiumi, & altre cose notabili.

Et nel fine con aggiunta nella presente quinta impressione del viaggio di M. Cesare
de' Federici, nell'India Orientale, nel quale si descriue le Speierie, Droghe,
Gioie, & Perle, che in detti Paesi si trouano.

Et le tre Nauigationi vltimamente fatte da gli Olandesi, & Zelandesi verso il Regno de' Sini,
& la nuoua Zembla, & paese della Groenlandia:

VOLVME PRIMO.

Con due Indici, l'vno de' nomi di tutti gli Auttori, che hanno scritto le dette Nauigationi, & Viaggi;
L'altro delle cose più notabili, che in esso Volume si contiene.

CON PRIVILEGIO.

IN VENETIA, APPRESSO I GIVNTI.
M DC XIII.

A French book illustration of 1583 (above) shows a navigator using an astrolabe to take a bearing on a star. Such devices were cumbersome and not suitable for use on the swaying decks of ships, so portable astrolabes that could be suspended from string were developed.

Following the invention of the printing press, navigational knowledge was more easily disseminated. This Italian volume on the subject (left) was published in 1613.

Cosmographers and cartographers (above) incorporated the discoveries made by seafarers into new nautical charts and maps of the world.

From early times through the age of the Vikings, seafarers used simple observation – of landmarks on shore, of the sun's position and the constellations of the night sky – as their basic navigational tools, taking care also to note natural phenomena such as cloud formations and the flight of birds. From the 14th century on, seafarers began supplementing the evidence of the naked eye by the gradual introduction of specialised instruments. One of the first was the magnetic compass, invented in China and introduced to Europe by the Arabs. With its aid sailors could plot their course independently of weather conditions, even in thick fog.

To determine their position at sea, captains still relied first and foremost on dead reckoning – this was essentially educated guesswork based on the direction and speed of the ship and the likely effects of ocean currents. Such calculations were liable to cumulative error unless they could be checked against a fixed measure – in practice, some reckoning of latitude.

Calculating latitude

Several instruments were employed for this purpose, the simplest being the cross-staff, which took the form of a rod marked with a scale calibrated in degrees and equipped with sliding wooden cross-pieces known as transversals. Other tools used to do essentially the same job were the astrolabe, the quadrant and (later) the sextant. Navigators used the instruments to measure the angle of elevation of a given celestial body above the horizon – usually the Sun or (in the northern hemisphere) the North Star. With the aid of charts or fairly simple calculations, they could then work out the approximate position of the ship in degrees north or south of the Equator.

Toward the end of the Age of Discovery, advances in optical technology produced the first telescopes. These instruments increased the accuracy of observations and soon became essential equipment on all ocean voyages.

The compass came into use among European navigators from the 14th century on.

Both marine astrolabes (top) and quadrants (above) served similar purposes: they were used to measure the angle of the stars above the horizon. By taking bearings on the Pole Star, which lies almost due north, mariners could take a reasonably accurate measurement of their latitude.

Seafarers and their ships

Seaworthy ships were an essential prerequisite for undertaking long voyages into unknown oceans. The oared galleys that had long been used to ply the relatively calm waters of the Mediterranean were hardly suited to the purpose. From the early 15th century on, shipwrights sought to meet the challenge by developing new types of vessel to cope with the demands of long voyages in the open ocean.

Portuguese artisans brought together different traditions of Mediterranean and northern European shipbuilding, combining the triangular lateen rigs originally introduced from the Arab lands with the straight sternpost and stern rudder familiar in medieval English and Dutch cogs. The result was the caravel, which was the vessel of choice for the early voyages of discovery, employed by Bartolomeu Dias, Christopher Columbus and Vasco da Gama among others. Typically only 25m (80ft) long, these small, nimble craft were sturdy and easy to handle, but they offered little room for the crew and their provisions. Some combined lateen and square sails for extra versatility.

The discomforts of life aboard

Life on board ship was extremely cramped, and harsh discipline was usually imposed to forestall the risk of mutiny. In addition, a lack of fresh water and food often led to the outbreak of vitamin-deficiency diseases such as the dreaded scurvy.

Another factor that weighed almost as heavily as the seaworthiness of the ships was their armaments. Non-European adversaries had nothing to match the firepower of the many cannons carried on board Portuguese and Spanish ships of the period. These weapons gave the explorers a significant strategic advantage, especially in the Indian Ocean where Portuguese merchantmen used their weapons to counter the numerical superiority of their Arab competitors, quickly outstripping them.

In the 16th century large galleons supplanted the smaller, lighter caravels that had been the workhorses of the early Age of Discovery. Sir Francis Drake circumnavigated the globe in the *Golden Hind* (left).

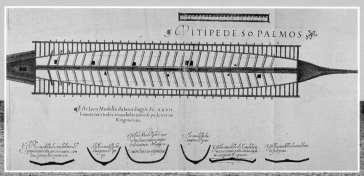

Sketches of a galley and of different hull designs (left) illustrate an early work on shipbuilding. Printed books helped to circulate technical knowledge.

A sign painted for the Marangoni family shipyard in Venice (below) shows some of the tools and techniques used to build vessels early in the 16th century.

A sketch by Hans Holbein the Younger depicts the cramped conditions on board the small warships and merchant vessels of the age.

Riches from far-flung lands

A painting by the 17th-century Dutch artist, Anthonie Palamedesz, shows a gentleman enjoying a pipe. Tobacco smoking spread across the world from the 16th century on.

Jean Nicot originally brought the tobacco plant (left) back to France as a medicinal herb. Nicotine was named after him.

The driving force behind the first voyages of discovery was Europe's demand for Oriental spices and for gold. For all the risks involved, the spice trade generated huge profits, the more so since many of the imported seeds and roots were used for medicinal purposes. In the early years the commodities most in demand in Europe – pepper, cinnamon, cloves and nutmeg – all came either from India or from the islands of Southeast Asia.

The spice trade already had a long history. Arab and Indian captains had long shipped condiments, aromatic woods and precious stones across the Indian Ocean, but now these local merchants found themselves outstripped by European competitors. After the Portuguese reached China from 1520 on, tea became a major feature of the export market: countless merchantmen shipped huge quantities of the dried leaves back to Europe.

Fruits of exchange

Along with trade goods, technological innovations also spread along the sea routes. New methods of steel production reached India from the Islamic world, and there was an upsurge of iron-working in sub-Saharan Africa. Previously unknown crops reached Europe – maize, potatoes, tobacco, cocoa beans and tomatoes all originated from America. Initially, tobacco and cocoa were luxury goods reserved for the wealthy classes; in contrast, the hardy potato rapidly became a staple food.

In the early days, Europeans were fascinated and astonished by reports of indigenous peoples and their lifestyles in the new lands. Explorers sometimes brought natives back with them, usually against their will, to be exhibited as curiosities at royal courts. Other wonders – stuffed animals, exotic artefacts, everyday objects – also aroused interest, attracting the attention of scholars and artists. Viewing Aztec artworks for the first time, the great German painter Albrecht Dürer noted: 'I have seen nothing that so rejoiced my heart as these things, for I saw in them strange and exquisitely worked objects and marvelled at the subtle genius of men in distant lands.'

A Flemish tapestry from Tournai (far left) celebrating the riches of the Orient.

A Japanese screen (left) dating from 1600 depicts the arrival of the first European traders.

Europeans quickly established trading settlements in the Spice Islands of Southeast Asia, such as this one at Bantam on Java (below).

A new vision of the world

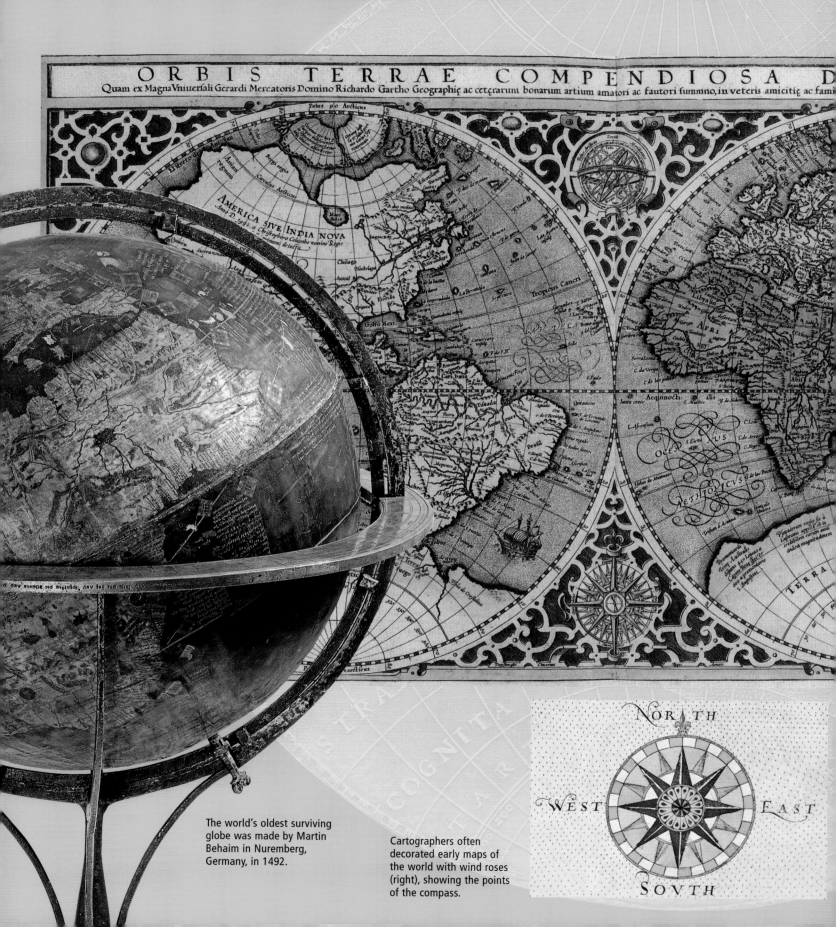

ORBIS TERRAE COMPENDIOSA D

Quam ex Magna Vniuerfali Gerardi Mercatoris Domino Richardo Gartho Geographiç ac cetçrarum bonarum artium amatori ac fautori summno, in veteris amicitiç ac fami

AMERICA SIVE INDIA NOVA

The world's oldest surviving globe was made by Martin Behaim in Nuremberg, Germany, in 1492.

Cartographers often decorated early maps of the world with wind roses (right), showing the points of the compass.

Improved printing techniques meant maps could be reproduced quickly and accurately. Copperplate engravers prepared the plates (background).

A map of the world (above) from a compendium of Mercator's works published the year after his death in 1594. The frontispiece of such books often featured an image of the giant Atlas bearing the globe on his shoulders, as described in Greek myth, and this is how they got the name of 'Atlas'

The voyages of discovery were a crucial watershed separating modern times from the Middle Ages. They did away with the medieval worldview that put Jerusalem at the centre of the universe, and proved conclusively that the Earth was round, as informed scientific opinion had long maintained.

Europe's horizons suddenly became much wider, and with the new geographical knowledge came an increased awareness of foreign cultures and peoples. Many of the native tribes that the early explorers encountered were living Stone Age lives, even if their lifestyles were often well adapted to their environments. Other races, though, particularly in eastern Asia, were at least as technologically advanced as the Europeans themselves. Contact with these unfamiliar civilisations stimulated a new interest among European scholars in the origin and growth of cultures, not least their own.

New maps for a new world

Maps and atlases were crucial tools helping to disseminate the new image of the world. At first, the picture of the globe that they presented was often wildly inaccurate, partly because they were based on incorrect measurements but also due to a general ignorance about large sections of the Earth, including substantial parts of the newly discovered lands.

The draughtsmen who produced the maps showed great ingenuity in filling in gaps in their knowledge. Often they made wild guesses as to the courses of rivers, the contours of coastlines or the location of settlements, filling in empty spaces with drawings of fantastic plants and animals. Their task was made harder because information concerning new discoveries was often treated as a closely-guarded state secret by governments eager to keep competitors out of promising new markets.

In 1569, the Flemish cartographer Gerardus Mercator achieved a significant breakthrough in the method of preparing nautical charts. For the first time, the Mercator projection that bears his name allowed the three-dimensional Earth to be accurately portrayed on a two-dimensional planar map.

The Flemish cartographer Gerardus Mercator (a Latinised version of his real name, Gerhard Kremer) was the best-known mapmaker of the 16th century. His most brilliant innovation was the Mercator projection, which compensated for the curvature of the globe and allowed direct sea-routes to be shown as straight lines.

ASIA

Japan – civil war and reunification

After almost 100 years of civil war, three men succeeded in reunifying Japan. The military regime they imposed finally brought peace to a divided nation.

Japan was an anomaly in the 16th century, and had been so for some time. Supreme power was vested in an emperor, enthroned in the imperial capital of Kyoto, who traced his ancestry back to the sun goddess Amaterasu herself. Yet real power, from the late 12th century on, had been wielded by an entirely different figure, the *shogun* or military leader.

In the early days the shoguns kept a close watch on the power of the nation's feudal nobility, headed by warlords known as *daimyo*. By the mid 15th century, however, the system was failing. The Ashikaga clan, who had controlled the shogunate since the 1330s, was fatally weakened by the outbreak of the Onin War in 1467, sparked by rivalry within the family over succession to the office of shogun. Rival daimyo aligned themselves with one or other of the contending parties, and in the ensuing 10-year civil war Kyoto itself became a battleground. Although Ashikaga shoguns continued to hold office for another century, they lost control of the provincial tax revenues that supported them and became mere figureheads. Deprived of central leadership, Japan was split between competing daimyo, who exercised absolute

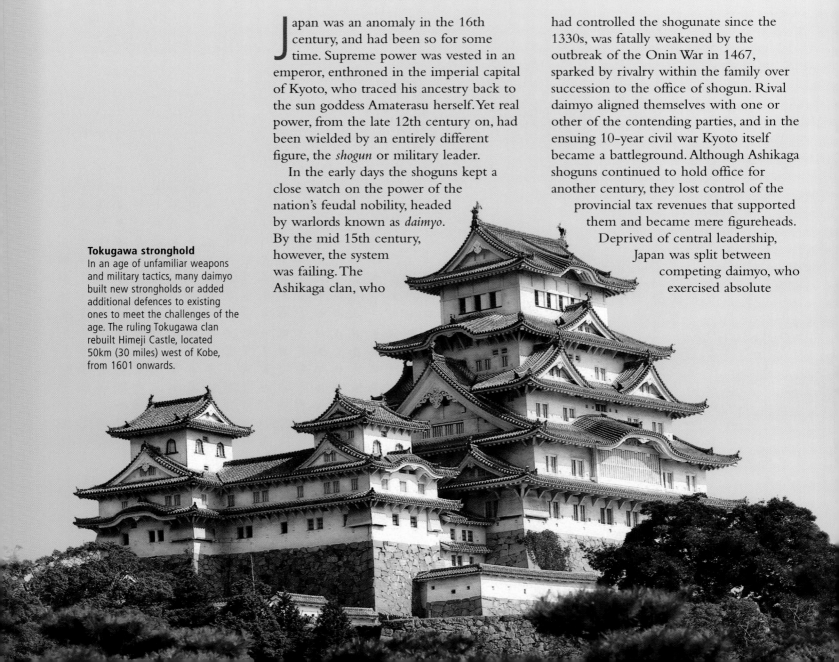

Tokugawa stronghold
In an age of unfamiliar weapons and military tactics, many daimyo built new strongholds or added additional defences to existing ones to meet the challenges of the age. The ruling Tokugawa clan rebuilt Himeji Castle, located 50km (30 miles) west of Kobe, from 1601 onwards.

power within their domains and gave out lands as fiefs to members of their retinue. To meet their costs they imposed taxes of their own on the villages under their control. In return they provided protection, defending their territories against hostile neighbours.

Despite the lack of political cohesion, Japan prospered. The daimyo generally encouraged the growth of fortified towns within their territories, since taxes paid by craftsmen and traders contributed to their own prosperity. Merchants – long a despised class in Japan – flourished in port cities, using the wealth made from trade with China to fit out armed merchant fleets and provide loans to noble families in financial difficulties.

Buddhist monasteries whose inmates had repeatedly intervened in the nation's politics. Although the warrior-monks put up stiff resistance, Nobunaga's troops captured one monastery after another, razing them to the ground. The battle for Nagashima, a stronghold of the powerful Ikko sect, turned out to be especially murderous.

Man of the people
Toyotomi Hideyoshi (below) was a fearsome military commander, but he also had a reputation as a companionable man who was fond of all forms of entertainment.

Warlord and nation-builder
In his efforts to unify Japan, Oda Nobunaga (left) made many enemies. He was killed by one of his former attendants.

A new age dawns

The man who first reunited Japan began his career as a daimyo. Oda Nobunaga came from a noble but insignificant family with estates in the central province of Owari. In 1560 a mighty neighbour, Imagawa Yoshimoto, attempted to cross Nobunaga's territory with an army on his way to Kyoto. Nobunaga's men took Yoshimoto's force by surprise in a defile, killing Yoshimoto himself and setting Nobunaga on an unstoppable rise to become the most powerful man in Japan.

By 1573 Nobunaga had taken control of the imperial capital and deposed the last Ashikaga shogun. Declining to take the title for himself, he nonetheless left no doubt that he was now the military controller of the nation. To strengthen his position, he ruthlessly eliminated all competition, notably from the powerful

Nobunaga's forces heaped up piles of dry wood against the enemy fortifications; when the wind was in a favourable direction, they set them alight. Some 20,000 people perished in the firestorm that ensued.

The Portuguese arrival

In 1542 a seemingly inconsequential event took place that was to have a profound influence on the future course of Japanese history. In that year the first Europeans set foot on Japanese soil, landing on the island of Tanegashima, off the southern coast of Kyushu. The daimyo who presided over the region extended a warm welcome to the Portuguese adventurers, who sought to impress their host with a demonstration of the deadly firepower of their matchlock muskets. Realising the huge significance

Sea
of
Japan

JAPAN

Edo (Tokyo)

Azuchi
Kyoto   Nagoya
Kobe
Osaka   Yoshida

KOREA

Pusan

PACIFIC OCEAN

Hirado

Nagasaki

▬ Heartland under Oda Nobunaga

▬ Conquests under Nobunaga and Hideyoshi

▬ Heartland under Tokugawa Ieyasu

● Important places

of the new weapon, the daimyo lost no time in having his craftsmen copy it.

Guns challenge the samurai

Muskets quickly found their way into battle, contributing to the rise of large forces of foot-soldiers, known as *ashigaru* ('nimble-footed'), who challenged the superiority of the mounted samurai. In the course of the civil wars, increasing numbers of peasant farmers had been driven from the fields to serve one or other of the many warring parties, some no doubt tempted by the prospect of a share in the spoils of war. These soldiers gradually augmented their original light weaponry with arms they captured from opponents, initially bows and spears.

When matchlock muskets were added to the ashigaru's arsenal, the balance of power on the battlefield tipped in their favour. A foot-soldier with a gun could bring down even the most skilled samurai

warrior. Infantry forces had been seen as little more than support for the mounted samurai; now they were transformed into disciplined troops whose intervention often decided the outcome of battles.

In 1575 at Nagashino, Oda Nobunaga stationed a force of ashigaru marksmen behind a palisade, protected by pikemen, to await an attack by the samurai cavalry of the Takeda clan. He let the enemy get within 50m (160ft), then gave the order to fire. The musketmen's intervention played a major part in winning the battle.

Merchants and missionaries

European influences were felt in other fields besides warfare. At first, the growing numbers of Portuguese merchants were welcome guests, since they imported precious commodities like silk from China in large quantities. The daimyo who controlled the ports profited hugely from the trade and became enthusiastic patrons of the foreign presence.

Missionaries soon followed in the merchants' footsteps. At first many were impressed by what they found. In 1549 St Francis Xavier, the Spanish co-founder of the Jesuit order, wrote enthusiastically, 'Of all the peoples we have hitherto come across, those whom we have encountered here are by far the best, and I am convinced that we shall never find a race among the heathen that is the equal of the Japanese'.

Before long the Christians were recording their first successes, winning converts not just among the common people but also in the ranks of the samurai and daimyo. One reason for the

Arrival of the foreigners
Portuguese ships armed with cannon caused a great stir in Japan on their arrival in 1542. The guns made it easy to repel attacks by pirates, who haunted the nation's coasts at the time. This detail from a Japanese wall screen shows a Portuguese ship arriving at Nagasaki harbour.

new faith's popularity may have been the depredations of the Buddhist warrior-monks, whose aggressive behaviour had alienated some supporters. Also, some nobles hoped to gain economic and military advantages by cementing relations with the prosperous, technologically advanced foreigners now in their midst.

For a time all things European became fashionable. Genteel society in Kyoto sported clothes in the Portuguese style and carried crucifixes and rosaries. Blacksmiths fashioned metal armour in place of the samurai warriors' traditional lacquered silk and bamboo, and loan-words from Portuguese – for example, *pan* for bread – even found their way into the Japanese language. Oda Nobunaga himself granted the Portuguese missionaries an audience, during which they noted that the building materials for his new castle came from demolished Buddhist shrines.

Hideyoshi at the helm

Oda Nobunaga's career ended abruptly in 1582, when he was killed trying to quell a rebellion led by one of his own former retainers. His work in unifying Japan was carried forward by Toyotomi Hideyoshi, a man who had risen through the ranks from a simple ashigaru to a leading general. He soon showed that no military commander knew better than he how to deploy ashigaru forces in battle.

Although Hideyoshi came from humble stock, one of his first acts was to exclude Japan's peasants from military service. He issued a decree specifying that all citizens other than samurai were to hand in their weapons under pain of severe punishment. The ensuing sword hunt was intended to make Japan a safer place. As a sweetener, Hideyoshi promised that an enormous statue of the Buddha would be cast from the metal of all the weapons collected.

Enforcing a rigid social hierarchy

Soon after taking power Hideyoshi authorised a comprehensive land survey, assessing the rice yields on which people were taxed. The peasant farmers who made up the bulk of the population were forced to hand over up to 50 per cent of their crop, but in return were relieved of all other obligations to the state. There was no escape, for Hideyoshi strictly forbade any peasant from abandoning the land, specifying that, 'If any man leaves his fields to become either a tradesman or a labourer, not only he but also his entire village will be punished'. Those who had already made the switch to serve as ashigaru warriors were forced to stick with their choice and were thereafter considered to belong to the samurai caste.

Seeking to complete the task of reuniting the nation that Nobunaga had begun, Hideyoshi fought long and hard to bring powerful daimyo in distant parts of the country to heel. He sent a successful expedition against the daimyo of Satsuma province on the southern island of Kyushu, and led a force of 200,000 men against another whose base lay on the Kanto plain around the modern city of Tokyo. Reckoning on a long siege, he allowed his troops to bring their wives and laid on entertainments to keep them happy. When his adversary finally yielded in 1590, Hideyoshi assumed undisputed rule over all Japan.

The invasion of Korea

Hideyoshi overreached himself in his later years, when he drew up a grandiose plan to conquer Korea. In 1592 a huge Japanese fleet set sail for the peninsula, landing an invasion force of 160,000 men that advanced rapidly towards the Chinese border. Once the Koreans had recovered from their initial shock, they fought back ferociously. When

Everyday elegance
A silk painting shows an elegant female courtier in the rather inelegant occupation of swatting flies. At night she may have rested her head and elaborate hairstyle on a headrest like this lacquered example, made by one of Japan's many skilled craftsmen. The tea bowl (bottom) is karatsu-ware. The imperial household fell on hard times in the 15th century, and one emperor who was a master of calligraphy was even reduced to selling his works.

a Chinese army also came to their aid, the Japanese had to retreat. Five years later Hideyoshi renewed the assault, again without success. Nothing was gained and tens of thousands of lives were lost.

Like Nobunaga before him, Hideyoshi was well-disposed towards the Christian missionaries, regarding them as a useful counterweight to the Buddhist monks. At one time he even toyed with the idea of converting to Christianity himself. Then, perhaps fearing that Japan's Christians might one day ally with the Europeans against him, he had an abrupt change of heart. In 1587 he issued an edict expelling all Christian missionaries, but the ban was not strictly enforced, and for the next decade Kyushu's Jesuits continued to make converts in secret. In 1597, however, Hideyoshi personally ordered the execution of a number of Portuguese and Spanish missionaries along with their converts, all of whom were crucified with their heads pointing down to the ground.

Hideyoshi died in 1598, having failed to bring the war in Korea to a successful conclusion. The Japanese forces were at once withdrawn from the peninsula. At home Hideyoshi's most powerful vassal, Tokugawa Ieyasu, came to the fore. The two men had long been close. One story told how, when they were riding together one day along the shores of Edo Bay near present-day Tokyo, Hideyoshi had suddenly handed his friend his own sword as a token of trust, advising him to build a castle on the spot. Hideyoshi no doubt sensed that Ieyasu was the man who would one day continue his life's work.

Tokugawa triumph

As the most influential member of the ruling council that Hideyoshi had put in place, Ieyasu was anxious above all to preserve the unity of the nation. He had a dangerous adversary, however, in Ishida Mitsunari, a powerful daimyo who bent all his efforts to breaking Ieyasu's power. In 1600, the forces of the two commanders met at Sekigahara in central Honshu in the last great set-piece battle to take place on Japanese soil. Ieyasu's forces emerged victorious, and three years later he was appointed shogun by the emperor.

Art imitates life (background)
A screen painting depicts scenes from a Noh play concerning the vengeance of the Sogo brothers.

Downfall of the Toyotomi
A detail from a screen painting shows the forces of Tokugawa Ieyasu capturing Osaka Castle in 1615. The fall of the stronghold enabled Ieyasu to eliminate his final rivals – Hideyoshi's son Hideyori and other retainers of the Toyotomi clan.

Hideyoshi had named Ieyasu as the guardian of his young son Hideyori. For more than a decade Ieyasu dutifully fulfilled his obligations, but fearing the young man was a focus for dissension against his rule, he finally struck in 1615. Soldiers under the command of his own son Hidetada stormed Hideyori's stronghold, Osaka Castle. Hideyori himself committed suicide, leaving Ieyasu as the undisputed ruler of Japan.

He had barely a year to live to enjoy his triumph, but in that time he took further measures to curtail the daimyos' power. He was also unsettled by the growing European influence in Japan, swayed by reports, reaching him through Dutch merchants, of Spanish and Portuguese colonial aggression in other parts of the world. He responded by extending Hideyoshi's measures to prevent conversion to Christianity.

A brutal persecution

Ieyasu's son, Hidetada, took power on his father's death in 1616. During his reign the prohibition of Christianity took a violent turn. More than 100 individuals, both Japanese and European, died for their faith, often in horrible ways.

The last act of the tragedy was played out on the Shimabara Peninsula on the south coast of Kyushu. There, in the reign of Iemitsu, the third Tokugawa shogun, local peasants, many of them Christian, rose up under the leadership of masterless samurai in protest against religious oppression and heavy taxation. They were defeated after a prolonged siege by a force of over 100,000 men. The victorious troops showed no mercy, and some 20,000 rebels were killed.

In the wake of the Shimabara Rebellion all foreign nationals were expelled from Japan with the sole exception of a handful of Dutch merchants. Even this tiny trading community had its activities restricted to the artificial island of Deshima, a small, walled enclave in Nagasaki Bay.

Japan had effectively cut itself off from the outside world. It now entered upon a period of voluntary isolation that would last for 200 years.

Palace of the shoguns
Painted landscapes adorn the walls of Nijo Castle in Kyoto. Ieyasu built the stronghold as the Tokugawa residence in the imperial capital following his victory over a rival warlord, Ishida Mitsunari, at Sekigahara in 1600. The interior decorations were commissioned in preparation for a visit by the emperor in 1626.

Portugal's eastern trading empire

Over the course of a few decades the Portuguese established one of the world's great mercantile empires in Asia.

Admiral of India
The son of a Portuguese provincial governor, Vasco da Gama made his reputation as a soldier before being given command of the seafaring expedition to India. This portrait of the 16th-century Spanish school shows him in later life.

On July 8, 1497, four sea captains and their 170 crew members boarded the four ships that made up their little fleet. They set off under the command of Vasco da Gama on a voyage that would open a new chapter in the history of exploration.

Da Gama's flagship, the *São Gabriel*, was a sturdy, square-rigged vessel of a new model, known as a *nao*. His brother Paolo commanded its sister ship, the *São Raphael*. The other two boats were a light, 50-tonne caravel, the *Berrio*, under the command of the experienced Captain Nicolau Coelho, which was suitable for inshore scouting, and a vast, 300-tonne storeship skippered by Gonçalo Nunes. Together, the four ships had supplies for three years on board.

The long road to India
The expedition marked the culmination of almost a century of exploration under the aegis of the Portuguese kings. Backed by royal patronage, caravels had been probing ever further down Africa's west coast. In 1487, a fleet commanded by Bartolomeu Dias had made the major breakthrough, successfully rounding the Cape of Good Hope and proving that it was possible to sail from the Atlantic to the Indian Ocean. Da Gama's mission was to reach India itself.

Ever since the time of Alexander the Great, Europeans had been fascinated by India. As the 16th century approached, the desire for a sea route to its riches had never been greater. The overland passage had been disrupted by the expansion of the Ottoman Empire, so the oriental spices that Europeans craved had to reach the Continent via Arab merchants, passed on by Venetian and Genoese middlemen. Portugal's ambition had long been to break the Muslim monopoly.

In the wake of Dias's voyage, the ruling monarch, João II, had sent an adventurer called Pedro de Covilhão on a perilous spying mission to India. Making his way south from Egypt disguised as an Arab merchant, Covilhão boarded an Arab dhow in Aden and crossed the Indian Ocean to the port of Calicut. For the next three years he travelled from port to port up India's western coast, before recrossing the ocean to reconnoitre the Arab trading posts of East Africa. Back in Cairo in 1490, he passed on what he had learned to emissaries of the King. No copy of his report has survived, but he must have given some account of the opportunities that awaited intrepid merchants, as well as of the monsoon wind system that dictated Indian Ocean traffic.

Commander of the fleet

A new Portuguese king, Manuel I, came to the throne and pressed on with his predecessor's plans. He chose Vasco da Gama to head the expedition to India. Then in his 30s, da Gama was well qualified for the job. He was nobly born and his father, a provincial governor, had brought him up in a tradition of public service. He was well educated, schooled by a Jewish tutor in the arts of mathematics, astronomy and navigation. And he had served his country with distinction as a soldier in Portugal's campaign against neighbouring Castile.

Contemporary portraits show a fearsome-looking individual with hawk eyes and a pirate's black beard. According to tradition, at times his behaviour was arrogant and cruel, but his leadership qualities were never in doubt.

The journey round Africa

Da Gama first set course for the Cape Verde islands off the coast of West Africa, then swung far to the west to catch the prevailing winds. For almost nine weeks the ships travelled through uncharted Atlantic waters out of sight of land. Then by a brilliant feat of navigation, da Gama brought them back to the African coast within one degree of latitude of his target: the Cape of Good Hope.

The little fleet rounded the cape on November 22, dropping anchor a week later in Mossel Bay. At that point da Gama decided to jettison the cumbersome supply ship, burning it after first transferring the remaining stores to the three surviving vessels. The crews celebrated Christmas off the present-day city of Durban, giving the surrounding region the name of Natal, the Portuguese term for the festival.

Da Gama's men first encountered Arab traders in Mozambique, the southernmost of the string of independent Muslim city-states that dotted Africa's Indian Ocean coast. The sultan received the strangers politely, but was less than impressed with the glass beads and tin ornaments that they had brought with them as trading goods and sent them on their way.

They had better luck in the northern port of Malindi, where the ruler made them welcome, supplying them with fresh water and food and placing an Arab pilot at their disposal to guide them across the Indian Ocean. With this man's help the Portuguese ships made the crossing safely, covering the 3700km (2300 miles) from Malindi to the port of Calicut in less than a month.

A seafaring people
A 16th-century painting shows the harbour in Lisbon, from which da Gama's small fleet set sail for India in 1497.

Long-distance ships (background)
For voyages across the Indian Ocean, the Portuguese favoured small lateen-rigged caravels, or the square-rigged three-masters known as *naos*.

At the court of the zamorin
A 16th-century Flemish tapestry depicts the arrival of Vasco da Gama in Calicut and his reception at the court of the local ruler, the zamorin.

Da Gama in India

On May 28, 1498, da Gama and his crew became the first Europeans to reach India by the sea route round Africa. Yet their stay in Calicut was not a happy one. Things began well enough. The local ruler, or zamorin, had da Gama and 13 of his officers carried through the streets to his palace on litters, receiving them while reclining on a green velvet couch, chewing betel nuts and holding a golden spittoon. But relations soured when da Gama presented gifts to his host. According to the expedition's chronicler, palace aides laughed at his offering, saying that it 'was not a thing to present to a king, and that the poorest merchant from Mecca or from any other part of India gave more, and that if he wanted to make a present it should be in gold'. Failing to forge a trading alliance with the ruler, da Gama and his men spent three months in the port, finding little demand for their goods and dogged by the hostility of their Arab competitors.

Return to Portugal

Deciding eventually to cut his losses, da Gama weighed anchor on August 29, 1498. He no longer had the services of his Arab pilot, who had disappeared during their stay, and he soon learned that he had delayed his departure too long to take advantage of the prevailing monsoon winds. The return journey across the Indian Ocean turned into a three-month epic of endurance, and by the time the unprepared fleet limped back into Malindi, scurvy had claimed the lives of 30 sailors. The rest were only saved by the fresh fruit promptly supplied by the friendly local ruler.

Key to the Red Sea
In 1507 a Portuguese force under the command of Afonso de Albuquerque captured Hormuz at the mouth of the Persian Gulf, gaining a base for trade with Persia. Six years later an attempt to take Aden (right) failed, leaving the entrance to the Red Sea in the hands of Portugal's Arab rivals.

Left with only enough crew to man two ships, da Gama scuppered the *São Raphael* soon after leaving Malindi. There were more deaths on the return journey, including that of his own brother Paolo, who was buried on the Azores. The two remaining ships limped back to Lisbon in the late summer of 1499.

Although only 54 of the original crew of 170 returned to Portugal, and they had little in the way of merchandise to show for all their efforts, they were given a hero's welcome. The journey was seen as a national triumph. The fleet had spent two years at sea, sailed a total of 43,000km (26,700 miles) and pioneered the elusive sea route to India.

A second fleet

King Manuel immediately prepared a much larger expedition, which set sail in the following year. Its leader, Pedro Alvares Cabral, had 13 ships under his command and a complement of over 1000 men.

Cabral followed da Gama's lead, swinging far westward across the Atlantic Ocean – so far, in his case, that he reached the coast of Brazil, which he claimed for the Portuguese crown.

Resuming his journey southward, Cabral rounded the Cape of Good Hope and set course for Calicut. He was initially welcomed by the zamorin, who allowed him to establish a fortified trading post, but, following disputes with the Muslim trading community, the post was attacked and most of the Portuguese garrison killed. Cabral bombarded the town in retaliation before sailing north to receive a less hostile reception at the ports of Cochin and Cannanore. In July 1501 he returned to Portugal with only half his

Building a trading empire
Afonso de Albuquerque (above), the second man to be appointed Portugal's Viceroy of the Indies, laid the foundations of Portugal's colonial empire during his six-year spell in office from 1509 to his death in 1515. In that time he seized the port of Goa, driving out the Muslim merchants who had previously held it, subdued Calicut, and established a base at Malacca on the Malay Peninsula to serve as a centre for trade with the Spice Islands. This colour engraving of him is taken from a painting.

Goa – Portugal's Asian trading centre

Goa was the heart of Portugal's commercial empire in India, and the settlers who made their home there lived comfortably. Opulently dressed, they passed through the busy streets shaded by parasols carried by servants. The climate was good all-year-round, and one observer noted that there were 'many pleasant gardens in which they dally'. The races mixed freely, and marriages between Indians and Europeans were common. Favoured entertainments included picnics, dances and boating expeditions.

Mingling on market day
A 16th-century copperplate engraving shows the bustling commercial activity in Goa's streets.

men, having lost six ships, but this time, the surviving vessels were laden with treasures – spices, Chinese porcelain, fine fabrics, precious woods – that amply repaid the costs of the voyage.

Admiral of the Indian Ocean

A new fleet was made ready for the following year, with da Gama, now named 'Admiral of the Indian Ocean', once more in command. Part of his mission was to revenge the attack on Cabral's men, a task he accomplished with ruthless efficiency. He also set up trading posts at the friendly ports of Cochin and Canannore before returning to Portugal in 1503.

Da Gama was to make one final trip to India, in 1524, but died soon after his arrival in Cochin. Twenty-four years later his exploits were immortalised by the poet Luís de Camões in *The Lusiads*, regarded to this day as Portugal's national epic.

The first viceroy

In the years following da Gama's second voyage, a struggle ensued for control of the Indian Ocean trade. The Portuguese quickly got the upper hand over their Muslim competitors, partly thanks to the disunity of their opponents but more to the superior firepower of their ship-board cannons. To coordinate the military effort, King Manuel created a new post, that of Viceroy of the Indies. Its first holder, Francisco de Almeida, followed da Gama's example, both in single-minded determination and in ruthlessness. He sacked Mombasa and seized Sofala and Kilwa on the shores of East Africa, then went on to establish a series of fortified bases on India's Malabar Coast. He also conducted a campaign of terror aimed at driving Muslim traders out. On one occasion he reportedly fired prisoners from his ships' cannons.

Almeida made contact with the ruler of the Kingdom of Kotte on present-day Sri Lanka. The island was strategically situated on the sea route to the Orient and was also rich in cinnamon, a sought-after commodity in Europe. In exchange for an offer of military support, the Portuguese were allowed to establish trading posts to deal in the precious bark.

Albuquerque, empire-builder

In 1509 the post of viceroy passed to Afonso de Albuquerque, a man of huge ambition who did more than anyone else to establish the global Portuguese trading empire. Looking beyond Africa and India, he captured the island of Hormuz off the coast of Persia, opening up trade with that country and also giving the Portuguese a key base at the mouth of the Persian Gulf.

In 1511 he took the port of Malacca on the Malay Peninsula, a conquest of even greater long-term significance. Malacca controlled access from the west to the Spice Islands of Indonesia. Fully realising the strategic importance of the port, its Muslim defenders fought hard to save it; it fell only after two separate assaults that the viceroy personally directed. An eyewitness noted ruefully that 'our soldiers sustained heavy casualties, most of those who were wounded dying from poisoned arrows'.

Albuquerque marched on. In 1510 he seized the port of Goa, midway down India's Malabar Coast, from its Muslim defenders. He built a monastery, a hospital and a new loading dock, as well as stronger fortifications. By the time of his death in 1515, a thriving community of Portuguese merchants was established there.

By that time Portugal had an empire to rival Spain's, extending from Brazil to Southeast Asia. The nation dominated Indian Ocean trade, compelling all foreign merchants to pay dues on entering Portuguese bases. The tariffs levied on the goods they carried generated extra profits to add to the huge sums that Portugal's own merchants made by importing oriental luxury goods into Europe.

To the Spice Islands

To complete their hold on the East Indies trade, the Portuguese still needed to secure the Spice Islands. Their mariners had first arrived on the Moluccas, in what is now central Indonesia, in 1512, but their claim to the islands was challenged by the Spanish government, which maintained that, by the terms of the Treaty of Tordesillas of 1494, they fell within the Spanish sphere of influence.

Oriental spices
An illustration from André Thevet's Universal Cosmography of 1575 shows native people harvesting the bark of cinnamon trees on the Molucca Islands (now in Indonesia).

Eastern trade centre
A map of the fort at Malacca on the Malay Peninsula, dating from shortly after the Portuguese conquest in 1511.

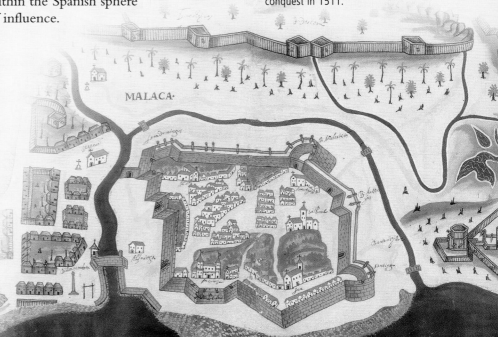

The question was eventually settled by diplomacy. In 1529, strapped for cash for his endless wars with France, Spain's ruler Charles V signed the Treaty of Saragossa, amending the Tordesillas arrangement and ceding the Moluccas to Portugal in exchange for a generous one-off payment. The deal proved a good one for Lisbon; the islands of Ternate and Tidore alone proved to be goldmines.

Portuguese seafarers explored the rest of Southeast Asia in the early decades of the 16th century. They reached Borneo in 1524, the Celebes and New Guinea two years later, and in 1532 landed on Timor in the Lesser Sunda Islands.

Gateway to China
A coloured engraving dating from 1598 shows the port of Macao. The Portuguese established the first European trading base in China there in 1557.

Footholds in the Far East

By mid-century interest was turning to the Far East. The first Portuguese ship to reach Japan made landfall in 1542, and over the next half-century profitable

AMACAO.

trading links were established. In 1557 Portuguese merchants also gained a foothold on the island of Macao off the coast of China, going on to transform this former fishing village into a thriving commercial port.

Unlike the Spanish colonial empire, which took over control of much of mainland Central and South America, Portuguese dominion in Asia was concentrated mainly on trading posts and islands. Within these settlements, however, the colonists introduced their own culture in the form of the Portuguese language and their Christian religion.

As viceroy, Afonso de Albuquerque also established an educational system that featured Portuguese as the key subject of the curriculum. His efforts to establish a permanent colonial presence, however, were hampered by an extreme shortage of European women.

The vast majority of emigrants from the mother country were men, many of whom entered into relationships with native women, with the result that, over time, large mixed-race communities developed. The authorities were quite prepared to sanction marriages in these circumstances, always provided that the bride agreed to adopt the Roman Catholic faith.

Spreading the faith

Catholic missionaries followed in the footsteps of Portuguese seafarers and merchants, and in some countries they had great success. By the end of the 16th century, for example, some 300,000 Japanese had converted to Christianity. The outstanding figure among these wandering evangelists, St Francis Xavier, was actually born in Spain, but he achieved his great success in the service of Portuguese kings, spreading the gospel message throughout East and Southeast Asia from India to Japan. Francis Xavier died of fever in 1552 on an island off the Chinese coast while waiting for a permit to enter the country.

By the late 16th century, Portugal had become the world's foremost commercial power. Its trading dominance in Asia was to last for almost 150 years, and the nation's flag flew over such bases as Goa, Macao and Timor until modern times.

The Safavids – Persia at a peak

After a long period of foreign domination, the Safavid dynasty united Persia, or Iran, bringing political stability to the country and imposing the Shi'ite version of Islam.

Persia had known greatness in the past, first under Cyrus and Darius and the other great Achaemenid kings of antiquity, then again under the Sassanid rulers who reigned from the 3rd century AD, but whose empire was swept away in the 7th century by the tide of Islam. Politically and culturally, Persia's people had been overshadowed by their western neighbours, the Arabs, who were the standard-bearers of the new faith. That situation finally changed in the 16th century with the rise of a new dynasty, the Safavids, who

reunited the land under the banner of the minority Shi'ite branch of Islam, which is the dominant faith of Iran to this day.

The dynasty traced its origins to the Safavid religious order, founded early in the 14th century in the city of Ardabil by

Heavenly dome
Visible from afar, the turquoise dome and minarets of the Royal Mosque of Isfahan tower over the city. Shah Abbas I made Isfahan his capital in 1598, sparing no expense in its development.

Sheikh Safi ad-Din, from whom it took its name. Like his descendants, the sheikh was a Sufi – an adherent of the mystical branch of Islam seeking direct personal communion with God. He and his followers were also Shi'ites, accepting an order of succession from the Prophet Muhammad that differed from that acknowledged by the majority Sunni branch of the faith.

For much of their history the Shi'ites had been a down-trodden minority, but by the mid-15th century the sheikh's successors were becoming involved in politics. The movement attracted a large following among the nomadic Turkmen tribes of the region. Thanks to their characteristic red headgear, these fierce warriors would become known as *kizilbash* ('redheads'). Many of them believed that the 12th and last imam of the Shi'ite line of succession, who had disappeared in mysterious circumstances in the year 874, would reappear one day as the Mahdi, or saviour, signalling the coming of the Last Days and the reign of divine justice on Earth.

Redheads and White Sheep

At the time, Persia was still reeling from the destructive wars of conquest waged by the Mongol ruler Tamerlane toward the end of the 14th century. In his wake, a number of local potentates seized power under the nominal rule of his ever-weaker successors. Northern and central Persia came under the control of two rival tribal groupings, known respectively as the *Ak Koyunlu* ('White Sheep') and the *Kara Koyunlu* ('Black Sheep') Turkmen.

Founder of a dynasty
Ismail I started his rise to power at the age of 7, when he inherited the guardianship of a Sufi holy place at Ardabil, close to the Caspian Sea. His Shi'ite followers subsequently carried him to victory over the 'White Sheep' Turkmen who controlled most of Iran at the time. In 1501, still aged only 14, he was proclaimed the first ruler of the Safavid dynasty.

Initially, the White Sheep rulers lent their support to the kizilbash, who were engaged at the time in a struggle with the Christian Georgians and Circassians beyond Persia's northern borders. Toward the end of the 15th century, however, the White Sheep became fearful of the rising power of the mounted tribesmen and turned on the Safavids and their followers, who suffered a crushing defeat. The leader of the Safavids was killed, but his seven-year-old son, Ismail, survived.

The dynasty comes to power

The kizilbash fighters quickly regrouped around their new boy leader. At the turn of the century they revenged themselves on their enemies, driving out the White Sheep forces and overrunning the whole of northwestern Persia.

In 1501 Ismail was proclaimed *shah-in-shah* (king of kings) in the city of Tabriz, becoming the first ruler of the new Safavid dynasty. His Shi'ite followers held absolute power over the predominantly Sunni populace of the region. As a sign of the new regime's puritanical intent, over 300 prostitutes were publicly executed.

Victory and defeat

Over the next decade, Ismail and his kizilbash army conquered the rest of Persia in a series of hard-fought battles. Their greatest triumph came in 1510 at the Battle of Merv, fought against the Uzbeks of Central Asia, which gave the Safavids control over the city of Herat and the northeastern province of Khorasan.

The dynasty's rapid rise alarmed the rulers of the region's other great power, the Ottoman Empire, as the Ottomans regarded themselves as champions of Sunni orthodoxy. In 1514 Sultan Selim I, 'the Grim', dispatched a huge army to confront the Safavids. The two forces met outside the town of Chaldiran, now in eastern Turkey. The Turkish army included an artillery contingent and sharpshooters armed with muskets who took up position behind a defensive circle of wagons to await the onslaught of the kizilbash cavalry. At that time the Safavid armies shunned the use of firearms, regarding them as weapons fit only for cowards who were unwilling to fight hand to hand. At Chaldiran they paid a heavy price for their idealism. As soon as the horsemen came within range of the Ottoman guns, they were cut down. Ismail himself was wounded and nearly captured in the ensuing rout, and his forces suffered a devastating defeat.

After the victory, the Ottomans took Ismail's capital of Tabriz, but a mutiny forced Selim to withdraw. Ismail was able to reassert control over his realm, even though his own authority had been severely shaken by the defeat.

Keeping control

Ismail's kizilbash backers had more reasons than military defeat to make them restive. Ismail had been in the custom of rewarding trusted lieutenants for their services by granting them estates. In theory, the grants were given at the shah's discretion and were not hereditary, but in practice, powerful subjects treated them as theirs by right. In time, a number of kizilbash leaders managed to set themselves up as local rulers, threatening the central authority of the shah.

To counterbalance the power of the kizilbash, Ismail appointed large numbers of ethnic Persians to high administrative posts. Increasingly, the dynasty was turning away from its former key supporters.

Astrological symbols
A glazed tile, made in about 1563, depicting the 12 signs of the zodiac. The Safavid rulers of Persia employed court astrologers to study the course of the stars and to predict propitious times for military campaigns and other major events.

History in art
A ceiling fresco from the Chehel Sotun palace in Isfahan depicts a Persian military conquest. The early Safavids relied on Turkmen cavalry as their shock troops, but Shah Abbas introduced a standing army and imported cannons and muskets from Europe.

Scenes from a bath-house
A miniature by Bihzad of Herat, or one of his pupils, depicts the Abbasid caliph Harun ar-Rashid having his hair trimmed. Although Harun – the idealised ruler of the *1001 Nights* – actually reigned in the 8th century AD, the hamam or bath-house is shown as it would have looked in Safavid times.

The situation would become familiar to Tahmasp in his 52-year reign, as he had to put down many uprisings and revolts fomented by his family's former backers. Danger also loomed constantly on his borders, as the Ottomans in the west and the Uzbeks in the east both tried to profit from divisions within the Safavid ranks.

Most contemporary records paint an unfavourable picture of Tahmasp, accusing him of stinginess – always a discreditable trait in an oriental monarch. It was said, for example, that he was so mean he sent his secondhand clothes to be sold in the bazaar. The bad press no doubt reflected his chequered military record, for Ottoman troops invaded Persia three times during his reign, capturing sizeable amounts of territory. He had greater success against the Christian kingdoms of the Caucasus region, launching four successive campaigns against Georgia and Armenia that saw many richly appointed churches sacked and thousands of people taken prisoner.

In 1568 Tahmasp transferred his capital from Tabriz to Qazvin, south of the Caspian Sea. The move was a security measure – the new site lay further from the dangerous Ottoman frontier.

As the lawful representative of the Hidden Imam, the shah remained Shia's highest religious authority, combining in his person supreme secular and sacred power. Seeking to buttress his position in the territories he had conquered, he summoned Shi'ite religious scholars from abroad to help to convert the local Sunni population to his own branch of the faith. Ismail lavished generous gifts on these religious dignitaries, making them, too, an important prop of Safavid power.

Ismail was only 37 when he died, in 1524, leaving the throne to his 10-year-old son Tahmasp. The succession of a minor immediately triggered unrest among the discontented kizilbash leaders.

Abbas mounts the throne

Tahmasp's death set off a fresh round of infighting over the succession, from which his grandson Abbas I emerged victorious in 1587. With the accession of this dynamic new shah, Persia's rise to greatness got under way once more. In Abbas's 42-year reign, the Safavids proved themselves militarily and culturally equal to their all-powerful Ottoman neighbours.

Few could have foreseen such an outcome when the young shah first ascended the throne. Just 16 years old,

Abbas soon realised that he needed to shore up his position at home before embarking on campaigns against his enemies abroad. To gain time, he concluded a peace treaty with the Ottomans on very unfavourable terms, agreeing to cede Iraq, Georgia and most of Azerbaijan to the old enemy. At a stroke, the Safavid realm lost some of its wealthiest provinces.

Rebuilding the army

Abbas put his dearly-bought freedom of action to good use. He promptly set about freeing himself once and for all from the grip of the kizilbash, taking them on in their power base, the army. Taking a leaf from the Ottoman book, Abbas started recruiting slave-soldiers from the Christian lands of the Caucasus. Soon regiments of Georgians, Armenians and Circassians were complementing the old tribal levies, while the shah's personal safety was guaranteed by a bodyguard of 3000 foreign-born warriors whose loyalty was

to himself alone. In time the shah built up a standing army 37,000 strong, including in its ranks an elite Circassian cavalry unit of 10,000 men. He also recruited an infantry force mostly staffed by ethnic Persians armed with muskets. Their firepower was complemented by a powerful artillery detachment. The changes caused discontent in the kizilbash ranks, but Abbas put the unrest down decisively.

By 1598 he felt sure enough of his position to turn his attentions to the Uzbeks who were threatening the north-eastern borders of his realm, and seized the city of Herat from their control.

At about the same time Abbas took the decision to move his capital from Qazvin to Isfahan, right in the heart of his empire. To beautify the city he gathered craftsmen and architects from all the corners of his realm. Magnificent buildings, covered inside and out with glazed tiles, rose to

BACKGROUND

Carpets as woven gardens

In the dry uplands of Iran, heaven has traditionally been visualised as a well-watered garden bursting with trees and flowers. Unsurprisingly then, horticultural imagery found its way into the rich stock of motifs employed by the nation's carpet-weavers, who delighted in filling their works with vividly detailed flora and fauna in many different forms and colours. Verses woven into the borders compared the carpets to paradise gardens offering an earthly foretaste of the joys awaiting the faithful in the world to come.

The tradition of carpet-making in Persia dates back to at least the late 15th century. Centres developed at Tabriz, Kashan, Isfahan, Kerman and Herat, each with its own individual style of manufacture.

The Great Shah
Seen above in a detail from a mural painting, Shah Abbas I was less than average height and dressed modestly. He was the most successful Persian ruler since antiquity.

Carpet craft (background)
The finest carpets of the Safavid period came from Kashan in central Iran. They were made partly of silk, and the most valuable examples had more than one million knots to the square metre.

The art of imitation
Safavid potters developed a range of blue-and-white ware in imitation of Chinese porcelain, in part aimed at the export market; European buyers at first had difficulty distinguishing their imitations from the real thing.

Culture in clothing
The Safavid period was a time of achievement in arts as diverse as fabric design and architecture. A Russian tsar gave the Persian velvet brocade coat (above) as a gift to the queen of Sweden in 1644.

adorn Isfahan's streets and open spaces. At the town's heart was the Maidan-i-Shah, a rectangular space 510m long by 160m wide (1675ft by 525ft) that was the focus of the city's public life. Two mosques dominated the Maidan. One, that of Sheikh Lutfullah, was the ruler's personal place of worship. The other, the larger Royal Mosque, was dedicated to the twelfth Shi'ite imam, the Mahdi of the End of Days.

By day, the Maidan was covered with market stalls, but at night it played host to a fun fair. It also served as a parade ground for the shah's armies and as a venue for polo matches, horse races, archery tournaments and wrestling contests, as well as for public executions. The city's enormous covered bazaar led off it to the north – a scene of bustling commercial activity, attracting merchants from many parts of the world including the Dutch, Portuguese, English and Indians.

Arts and crafts enjoyed a heyday in Abbas's reign. Persian carpets and porcelain were particularly highly prized, and the nation's sword-makers were said to manufacture damascened blades to a higher standard than any produced at the time in Europe.

Abbas laid out extensive gardens adorned with pavilions where he staged splendid festivities. An English courtier described one such festival that lasted for 30 days. Marquees stood among babbling streams spread over a distance of 3km (2 miles). Guests were directed to the tent that was appropriate to their rank, where they were plied to bursting point with meats, fruit and wine. Impressed, the Englishman noted that he had never seen such royal magnificence before and never expected to again as long as he lived.

A magnet for foreigners

Foreign visitors were common at Isfahan, for the shah took care to maintain friendly relations with most of the European powers. Many envoys found their way to the capital at his invitation, among them diplomats, merchants and even Christian priests. Several of the visitors wrote admiringly of the shah's attitudes and accomplishments, one German traveller noting that he 'did not deck himself out in royal purple, but rather showed by his deportment that a ruler's true glory lies not in finery but in the obedience and love of his subjects'. Abbas even sanctioned the construction of a church for his guests' use, although they were forbidden to make converts among the native Muslim population.

Built to last
The Khadjoo Bridge was one of ten that spanned the river running through Shah Abbas's capital of Isfahan.

Following in the tradition of Caliph Harun ar-Rashid in the *1001 Nights*, the shah liked to wander the streets of his capital incognito, mingling with the crowds in the evening to overhear people's conversations. He also carried out spot checks on the honesty of street traders. Sometimes he would take purchases of bread or meat back to the palace and weigh them on kitchen scales. Any trader who had swindled him could expect to face harsh penalties.

Promoting trade

Trade was especially important to Abbas and he took pains to improve the roads throughout his realm and to provide *caravanserais* where travelling merchants could stay in safety overnight. Wanting to establish a centre for the silk trade in Isfahan, he built a new suburb and enticed Christian silk merchants from the Armenian city of Dzhulfa to move there, granting them freedom of worship, reduced taxation and a free hand to organise their affairs. Muslims were not permitted to live in the neighbourhood.

Taking on the Ottomans

Having put his own house in order, Abbas turned his attention back to his greatest foes, the Ottoman sultans. His aim was to win back the western provinces he had been forced to cede when he came to power. In an energetic campaign launched in 1603, he recaptured the one-time Safavid capital of Tabriz and drove the Turks out of Armenia and northwestern Persia. When the Ottoman army tried to regain the city two years later, it was roundly defeated at the Battle of Sufiyan.

In 1612 the two sides agreed to a peace treaty that restored the frontier between their lands to where it had been in the mid 16th century. Ten years later, the conflict resumed after the Ottoman governor of Baghdad rebelled against his political masters in Istanbul. Abbas took advantage of the situation to invade Iraq, capturing Baghdad in 1624 and

succeeding in holding it in face of a brutal siege. It was his greatest victory, prompting the Safavid historian Iskandar Beg Mundzhi to exclaim patriotically, 'May Baghdad remain in Safavid hands until the end of time!'

The victorious Persian army then pressed on into northern Iraq, reducing the Turkish overlords there to dire straits; one observer noted that 'elegant gentlemen who once disdained to wear a shirt of Egyptian cotton are now glad if they can get their hands on a simple shift made of tent canvas'.

The Safavid decline

When Abbas died in 1629, the Safavid Empire was at its peak, but his successors soon squandered his legacy. Abbas was partly responsible for the decline, as he failed to provide adequately for the succession: fearing conspiracy, he had had his own sons assassinated or blinded, so the throne passed to his eldest grandson, Safi I. The young ruler was unable to build on the successes of his predecessor, losing Baghdad to the Ottomans and Kandahar to the Indian Mughal Empire.

After Safi's death in 1642, the decline accelerated. Even so, the strength of the institutions that Abbas had put in place kept the Safavids in power for another 80 years. The dynasty finally collapsed in 1722, when Isfahan fell to a former vassal ruler from Afghanistan. Persia remained Shi'ite following the change of regime, but once more the nation found itself under foreign rule.

Gift for a tsar
The Safavids demonstrated their magnificence by lavishing splendid gifts on foreign rulers. This golden throne, studded with precious stones, was presented to Russia's Tsar Boris Godunov.

Decline and fall of China's Ming dynasty

After almost 300 years in power, China's mighty Ming dynasty was brought down by a mixture of incompetence and corruption. Yet its latter years were a time of great cultural achievement and renewed contact with Europe.

End of the line (background)
The tombs of the Ming emperors were preserved in the imperial necropolis 50km (30 miles) north of Beijing. Visitors could only gain admission on foot and passed down a highway lined with colossal statuary, known as the Spirit Road.

A queen's crown
Decorated with guilded feathers and precious stones, this filigree-work crown of silver-gilt would probably have been worn by one of the wives of a Ming emperor.

In 1516, the Zhengde emperor – the tenth of the Ming dynasty that had been ruling China for the past 148 years – decided to abandon his frustrating existence in the Forbidden City and take up residence in a garrison town 150km (95 miles) away. He was sick of the responsibilities of government, especially as the state was chronically short of funds, and the unending palace intrigues of the court eunuchs who surrounded him. To make matters worse, the steppe nomads who were an ever-present threat on the nation's northern frontiers had begun causing trouble again.

The Emperor's departure was just what the court eunuchs wished, since his absence from the seat of government gave them complete control of the state apparatus. Since his early childhood, they had been diverting him from his duties, encouraging him to devote his time to sport, music, dancing, hunting parties, mock battles and daring visits to the streets of Beijing disguised in commoner's dress – anything, in fact, rather than the day-to-day business of governing. Now, in his new home, he played at being a general – a role for which his military inexperience and the weak state of the armed forces hardly prepared him. From that time on he rarely bothered to read the official correspondence that reached him from Beijing, and the empire was left without an effective head.

The coming of the Europeans

The Emperor might have acted differently if he had understood the significance of events that were taking place in the south of his vast realm. The arrival of Vasco da Gama's fleet on the coast of India in 1498 signalled the opening of a direct sea link between Europe and Asia around the Cape of Good Hope. Sixteen years later, while the Emperor was recuperating from injuries sustained on one of his hunting escapades, the first Europeans appeared off southern China.

In 1511, Portuguese forces had overrun Malacca (now in Malaysia), a vital trade centre that had once paid tribute to the Ming. Two years later, the traders who set up shop there sent a ship commanded by Jorge Alvares to the Bay of Guangzhou on China's south coast, where there was a trading station specially designated for the use of foreigners. A year later an Italian seaman, Rafael Perestrello, sailing on behalf of the Portuguese crown, also reached Guangzhou.

A cultural flowering

In Guangzhou the Europeans were impressed by the exquisite craftsmanship of Chinese porcelain, typically white and cobalt blue in colour and decorated with landscapes and human figures. They were also intrigued by lacquerwork, featuring buildings, rivers, mountains and people carved into a hundred layers or more of resin exuded from the lac tree. Such arts and crafts were only one aspect of a general cultural upsurge in China stimulated by the continuing prosperity of its cities. Craftsmen were absolved from the requirement to do compulsory labour for the crown, and within the cities' crowded streets they rubbed shoulders with wealthy businessmen and civil servants. These were the people who made up the audience for a new, more realistic type of literature that emerged in the late Ming years. Written in a vernacular style, it portrayed the mores of the age, often with a marked erotic content.

Painters also had a new self-confidence. The work of the established masters was characterised by fluid execution, rich ornamentation and a bold use of line and two-dimensional form. The Ma Xia school, in contrast, employed vigorous brushstrokes said to resemble 'the blows of an axe'. Shen Zhou, one of the so-called Four Great Masters of the Ming period, was the leading figure of another school, the Wu, whose scholar-artists took their inspiration from literature. Shen Zhou himself excelled at poetry and calligraphy as well as painting, creating elegant studies of trees and misty mountain landscapes

Obstacles to trade

The first European visitors whetted the appetites of the authorities in Malacca for the lucrative opportunities that trade with China might bring. In 1517, a fleet of eight ships carrying a royal envoy from Lisbon reached the Chinese coast, and three more vessels followed two years later. These early encounters were not a success. The Portuguese had built their Asian trading empire on firepower and the use of force, and stories of their behaviour in Malacca, where they had engineered a coup against the native ruler, worked against them. Their Chinese hosts found them disrespectful and aggressive.

As a result, one faction at the Ming court strongly opposed further trade relations. Their chance came with the death of Zhengde in April 1521. The day after his demise, all contact with the Portuguese was forbidden. The authorities set about imposing the edict by force, sending warships to expel the intruders. Thereafter all foreigners were temporarily banned from trading in Guangzhou, and even when the embargo was partially lifted in 1530, the Portuguese were still excluded.

The merchants eventually found a way around the problem through bribery. A trader named Leonel de Sousa reached an agreement with a corrupt government official, who agreed to overlook the nationality of the foreigners with whom he was dealing. The Portuguese duly established themselves at Macao, a walled-off peninsula on the coast of southern

Classic style
No Chinese artworks attracted greater admiration abroad than Ming ceramics, particularly the almost translucent china known as porcelain. Objects like this early-16th-century jar were the nation's main luxury export.

Priceless paperweight
Ming craftsmen applied their skills to many everyday objects – this enamel ruler decorated with a gilt-bronze dragon is actually a paperweight. It was made by the cloisonné technique, which involves filling in a raised-wire outline with coloured enamel.

Blending in
The first Jesuits in China adopted local dress to win acceptance. Matteo Ricci (above) learned to speak and write Chinese well enough to win the commendation of Confucian scholars. Adam Schall von Bell (right) so impressed the emperor by predicting a solar eclipse that he was appointed head of the Imperial Board of Astronomy.

China just west of the Pearl River estuary. In return for lavish pay-offs and the payment of duties on at least some of the goods that the merchants shipped, the authorities were content to turn a blind eye.

By 1562, some 900 Portuguese nationals were living in Macao. Their status improved a decade later, when the state treasury agreed to accept a ground rent for the territory, in practice legitimising a presence that was to endure up to the late 20th century. Thanks to its biannual trade fairs, Macao soon became the hub of Portuguese trade with China.

One reason why the Chinese tolerated the European presence on their shores was the state's ongoing need for imported silver. Unminted, this precious metal was widely used as a currency both for the payment of taxes and for large commercial transactions. Before the Portuguese colony was established in Macao, the main source had been Japan, which also provided copper, swords, sulphur and sappanwood in exchange for sought-after Chinese silk. The supply was never large enough to satisfy demand, however. It was only the arrival of New World silver, shipped

in by Spanish and Portuguese merchants, that saved the Chinese economy from collapse.

The main trans-shipment centre for the bullion was Manila, captured in 1570 by the Spanish, who soon made the Filipino port their principal trading base in Asia. Two years later Chinese merchants brought a first shipload of silk there, and in the following year the cargo made its way across the Pacific, bound for Acapulco in New Spain. Vast quantities of silver were soon flowing in the opposite direction. By 1598 some 345 tonnes were reaching China annually.

Bullion reached China not just from Spain and Portugal but also from London and Amsterdam. The first Dutch ships entered Chinese waters in 1601, but were driven off by the Portuguese. In 1604 and again in 1607 the Dutch East India Company, which had been founded specifically to promote eastern trade, approached the Ming authorities for permission to operate in China, but on each occasion the request was turned down. An attempt to seize the port of Macao in 1622 also met with failure.

The Dutch on Taiwan

The Dutch responded to this last rebuff by seizing some small islets in the Taiwan Strait. The Chinese soon drove them off, so they moved instead to Taiwan itself, which was not at the time a part of China. Company employees used this island base from 1624 onwards to extract the same healthy profits from the Asian market that their Portuguese and Spanish counterparts had been enjoying for more than half a century.

Trade blossomed. Silk in all its forms was exported, along with cotton textiles and the products of local craftsmen. This stimulated a fashion for all things Chinese in Europe and the New World. Well-to-do families in Amsterdam, Lisbon, Antwerp, Mexico City and Lima were soon wearing silk garments and sitting on silken brocade cushions, sipping tea from porcelain cups that, like the drink itself, came to them all the way from the Middle Kingdom.

The Jesuit mission

As Europe's mercantile contacts with China grew, missionaries followed in the wake of the traders. A Catholic enclave was established in Macao under the spiritual leadership of the Jesuit order. The priests prepared themselves well for the challenges that lay ahead, learning to speak Chinese and translating key Christian texts into the language, while also taking care to familiarise themselves with the complex etiquette of the host nation.

The first to make his mark was an Italian, Father Matteo Ricci, who arrived in Beijing in 1583 as part of an embassy of high officials. Presenting himself in the humble guise of an admiring envoy of a tributary nation, he gained acceptance at the Ming court and eventually was given official permission to settle in Beijing. Over time, Ricci and his colleagues enjoyed a lively exchange of ideas with high officials and literary figures in the capital, sending valuable accounts of China and its culture back to Europe. For the most part, though, the Chinese scholars who conversed with them were more interested in their artistic, mathematical, technical and scientific knowledge than in their religious beliefs.

The Jesuits made a few high-ranking converts, but the majority still regarded the foreigners with deep suspicion. European merchants and seamen were for the most part viewed as pirates, on account of their aggressive trading tactics and their involvement in black-market transactions and smuggling.

The pirate threat

Piracy was a major issue along the coast of China in the late 16th century. The growth in maritime commerce, combined with a ban on Japanese trade with China, imposed from 1530 onwards, brought with it a corresponding rise in lawlessness. The coastal population in particular suffered as never before from seaborne assaults. Bandits based on islands off China's coasts or in the southern Japanese archipelago conducted campaigns of pillage that sometimes expanded into full-blown invasions. The raiders would land unannounced on the mainland and sack towns and villages up to 100km (60 miles) inland, then quickly head back to their boats with their spoils.

The pirates themselves were an ill-assorted bunch, comprising both landless Chinese peasants and Japanese freebooters who had the tacit support of their home government. Desperate to counter the threat but uncertain how best to do so, the Ming authorities took to relocating some coastal settlements far inland to make them less accessible to attack. The heyday of the raiders only came to an end after the reunification of Japan in the 1590s, which restored the rule of law and economic prosperity to the island kingdom.

Even so, a newly united Japan soon offered an even greater and more direct threat to its mainland neighbour. Hideyoshi, the nation's military leader,

Pictures from the loom
A fragment of silk fabric from the Ming dynasty period. It was made by the kesi or slit-weaving technique, in which the warp (lengthways) threads form a continuous background, and the images are woven in using separate weft (crossways) threads for each colour.

A taste for caricature
The very large brain of this Daoist sage, seated beside a deer, shows that Ming ceramicists had a sense of humour as well as refined aesthetic sensibilities. The glazed earthenware piece is now in the collection of London's Victoria and Albert Museum.

Imperial splendour
The throne room in the imperial Forbidden City in Beijing suggests something of the sumptuous opulence that surrounded the Ming emperors. In time, such magnificence cut them off from their subjects, contributing to the dynasty's downfall.

launched a full-scale invasion of Korea, China's tributary state, intending the assault as a preliminary to an attack on the Ming empire itself. The first incursion into Korea, in 1592, was repelled with the help of 200,000 Chinese troops. In 1597 a fresh wave of invaders arrived, but was called back on Hideyoshi's death the following year.

Although China retained its territorial integrity, the costs of defending it drained the state coffers, which were already depleted thanks to extravagant emperors and greedy court eunuchs.

The rise of the Manchus

The need to defend the vulnerable northern borders was a further, permanent, drain on the treasury. A new threat now came from Liaodong, in the southernmost part of Manchuria, where a nomadic people named the Jurchen had for centuries past lived peaceably. From 1583 on, however, an ambitious leader named Nurhachi appeared, united the tribes and, in 1616, proclaimed himself emperor of a new northern dynasty.

During the next six years Nurhachi won two overwhelming victories over Ming forces. Earlier, the Chinese had, in the words of a contemporary chronicler, erected 'solid walls of willow trees along their frontiers' to repel the cavalry of the northern nomads. Without too much trouble, Nurhachi's warriors swept through this Willow Palisade and seized a substantial area of northern China.

Nurhachi died in 1626, but his demise did not halt the progress of his troops. Over the next decade the Manchus, as the Jurchen now styled themselves, made repeated incursions south of the Great Wall, on two occasions even threatening Beijing itself. In 1636 they took the dynasty name of Qing, meaning 'Pure', in contrast to the corruption associated with the Ming name. Six years later, all the lands north of the Great Wall were in their hands, and they were threatening the Ming survival.

Decline and fall

The Ming state was undermined by financial mismanagement, inefficiency and corruption in the imperial court. To add to the government's woes a series of natural disasters had also afflicted the empire. An earthquake that hit Shansi and Shensi provinces in 1556 had caused 800,000 deaths in the Wei Valley alone. Subsequently, there had been epidemics claiming up to 10,000 lives in a single day, inundations, droughts, plagues of locusts and failed harvests, which all took their toll, leaving the populace close to despair. Homeless beggars roamed the countryside, barely surviving by eating seeds, tree bark, animal dung and even human flesh. The population of the Middle Kingdom, which had reached an estimated 175 million at the end of the 16th century, went into steep decline.

In 1627 the storm broke and civil war engulfed the nation. Order broke down, and the imperial army fell apart in face of mass desertions. In 1644, a rebel leader named Zhang Xianzhong founded the breakaway Great Western Empire in Sichuan province, while Li Zucheng, a one-time shepherd and postal employee, conquered large parts of the north.

When Li's troops entered Beijing on April 25, 1644, the last Ming emperor retreated into the grounds of the Forbidden City and hanged himself. Li proclaimed himself emperor, but the rabble he commanded was no match

for the disciplined Manchu forces, who seized the opportunity to make themselves masters of all China.

Two days after Li's proclamation the Manchus entered the capital, putting the would-be ruler to flight; he was murdered soon after by peasants. His rival, Zhang, was captured by Manchu troops and also met a violent end. The Ming dynasty was no more, and China found itself once again under foreign rule.

Working in a coalmine
A 17th-century print shows men at work in a colliery in southern China. Below ground, one miner inserts a prop to support a tunnel roof while another labours at the coalface with a pickaxe. On the surface, a worker operates a hoist bringing up the loose coal with the aid of a cable winch, while his companion holds bamboo tubing that served to draw out and disperse gases that built up underground.

The Mughals in India

A new Muslim leader, descended from the Mongols, swept out of the north to conquer northern India. Babur founded the Mughal dynasty, and his grandson Akbar would spread its grip over much of the subcontinent.

Founder of the empire
Babur came to power in Ferghana after his father was killed when a balcony collapsed beneath him. By the age of 14, the young ruler had conquered neighbouring Samarkand, but he proved unable to hold on to the city. Here he is shown invading Persia.

On April 21, 1526, India's fate was decided outside the city of Panipat, 80km (50 miles) north of Delhi. The victorious general, Babur, later wrote of the battle: 'The sun stood only a lance's height above the horizon when battle commenced; by midday the enemy was vanquished and fully subdued. In just half a day, we had annihilated a mighty army… Later, when we reached Agra, we learned that between forty and fifty thousand men had perished on the battlefield.'

Babur's triumph repeated a familiar pattern in northern India – that of a Muslim army invading the subcontinent from the north to defeat local forces. Babur's home was the small central Asian kingdom of Ferghana, in what is now eastern Uzbekistan. It had once been part of the empire of Timur Lenk, or Tamerlane, and Babur himself was a great-great-great-grandson of the famous conqueror. Inheriting the throne at the age of 10, he struggled to hold on to his patrimony. Ten years of strife culminated in him being driven out of his kingdom by the powerful Turkic Uzbeks. Temporarily homeless, he led a band of retainers to seize Kabul in Afghanistan. From this new base he launched raids into northern India that exposed the region's wealth and vulnerability. At the time, the North Indian Plain was ruled by the Afghan Lodi dynasty – all that was left of the once-mighty Sultanate of Delhi. Even though the realm was much reduced from its glory days in the 13th and 14th centuries, it could still put a huge army in the field, and its ruler, Ibrahim, expected little difficulty in destroying Babur's small invasion force. But he had not reckoned on Babur's tactical skills as a military strategist, inherited from the forebears whose name would ultimately be borne by the dynasty he founded: 'Mughal' was an Indo-Persian word for 'Mongol'.

Victory at Panipat

Babur owed his victory over the much larger force largely to the use of muskets and field artillery, which he had recently acquired from the Ottomans. He placed his cannons under the command of an Ottoman officer behind a protective barrier of wagons linked together by chains. When Ibrahim tried a frontal assault, his troops were mowed down by Babur's firepower, and the sultan himself fell on the field of battle.

The victorious Babur occupied Delhi and Agra, but his hold on northern India was at best fragile; in those early days he was surrounded by enemies eager to contest his position. To secure his gains, he sought first to ensure the loyalty of his own retainers through a generous distribution of booty. The move was wise, for many of his men were already pining for the cool uplands of Afghanistan, wanting nothing more than to escape the searing heat of the Indian summer.

An unenthusiastic conqueror

Babur himself had other goals in mind: he intended to establish a lasting empire on Indian soil. In his memoirs, *The Baburnama*, now considered a classic of autobiography, he revealed an ambivalent attitude towards his adopted homeland, painting a less than flattering picture of the land he had invaded. 'India holds few attractions and offers scant pleasures,' he wrote. 'One looks in vain among the populace for signs of grace and beauty. No trade is conducted here, and people do not visit one another or have any other form of social life…They have no decent horses, no hunting dogs, no good grapes, melons or tree fruits, and they are unfamiliar with ice or fresh water. There is no palatable food or good bread to be found in the bazaars.'

But there were other enticements. He noted that the land had 'gold and silver in abundance…and the advantage of having at its disposal an unlimited supply of craftsmen and labourers'. One of his first acts on seizing power was to lay out gardens in Agra and have large cisterns and bath-houses erected.

Taming the sons of kings

The most formidable of the enemies arrayed against Babur were the Rajputs, literally 'sons of kings', an interrelated group of Hindu princes whose power base was in Rajasthan, southwest of Delhi. Fierce warriors, they had been fighting Muslim rulers for 500 years and they saw no reason to stop now: this, surely, was their chance to consolidate their power on the ruins of the Sultanate of Delhi.

Other forces, too, were vying for power in northern India, including rival Muslim potentates governing territories that had once been under Delhi's control. Other independent Muslim states flourished further south on the Deccan Plateau, where centres of Islamic culture had grown up that kept in contact with the wider Muslim world through the seaports of India's west coast. The southern part of the subcontinent remained Hindu, much of it under the control of the powerful Vijayanagar dynasty.

The Rajputs were the first to strike against Babur. Within a year of the Battle of Panipat, they mobilised a huge army

The art of weaponry
Magnificently crafted daggers like this *khanjar* were prized by Mughal noblemen. Emperor Akbar's son Jahangir wrote of one that 'it is so delicate that I never want to be separated from it even for a moment'.

Stronghold of the Rajputs
The fortress of Gwalior was built by Rajah Man Singh early in the 16th century, and fell to the Mughal Emperor Akbar in 1559. The Rajputs were independent Hindu rulers of northern India, who fought off a succession of Muslim challengers from the 9th century on. They finally succumbed to the Mughals, won over by a combination of military strength and diplomacy.

Akbar the Great
According to one contemporary account, Akbar was of middling height but thick-set, with broad shoulders and narrow hips. He sported a moustache in the Turkish manner and had a sonorous, powerful voice. This portrait, on ivory, is painted in gouache.

Mughal mausoleum (background)
The mausoleum of Humayun, Babur's successor, was built in Delhi on the orders of the emperor's second wife, Hamida. It is regarded as an architectural precursor of the Taj Mahal.

Yet the realm he ruled was, at best, a loose confederation of regions rather than a united empire, and Babur himself did not live long enough to impose an effective centralised administration. A man of unusual gifts, he might well have made an excellent peace-time ruler. He had a passion for books, and was himself a prolific author who wrote poems in both Turkish and Persian. There was no trace of religious fanaticism in his nature, and he showed a deep desire to conciliate his new subjects and to respect their lifestyle. Sadly, his life was given over to war; he died barely 18 months after his victory at the Ghaghara River, aged just 47.

Losing an empire

Babur's legacy was almost squandered by his son and heir, Humayun, one of very few rulers in world history to have inherited an empire, lost it and then won it back again. Intelligent and capable, Humayun was also careless by nature and given to spells of lethargy between bouts of intense concentration. His lack of focus brought the Mughal dynasty to the brink of disaster at a time when only the strongest survived in India.

At his accession in 1530, the dynasty's grip on northern India was still far from secure. Mughal rule was threatened from the west by Bahadur Shah of Gujarat and from the east by an Afghan warlord, Sher Khan, who had a power base in Bengal. There was trouble, too, in the Emperor's own family. Three of his half-brothers plotted against him, and one, Kamran, who ruled over the Afghan component of the empire from Kabul, was to prove a persistent thorn in Humayun's side.

Having dealt successfully with Bahadur, who was forced to seek sanctuary with the Portuguese in the port of Diu, Humayun turned to Sher Khan. However, he was defeated by the Afghan warlord, who overwhelmed his forces in two decisive battles fought on the banks of the River Ganges, at Chausa in 1539 and at Kanauj in the following year.

under the command of Rana Sanga of Mewar, a formidable warrior whose body was said to bear 80 scars sustained in a lifetime of combat. Even so, his forces were no match for Babur's firepower, which won the day at Khanua after a desperate 10-hour battle. Two years later, in 1529, Babur's men won another victory, this time beside the Ghaghara River over remnant forces of the Delhi Sultanate that had rallied under the command of Ibrahim's brother.

The death of Babur

With this third triumph, Babur established his hold over a vast area stretching from Afghanistan across the Punjab and the Ganges Plain to the borders of Bengal.

Having lost his empire, Humayun was now homeless, just as Babur had been after the loss of Ferghana. His brother Kamran refused to offer him sanctuary in Afghanistan, so he took his small remaining band of followers first to the wilderness of Sind in western India and then to Persia, whose Shah Tahmasp agreed to give him refuge. The Mughals appeared to have lost control of India for good.

The victorious Sher Khan set about establishing the effective, tolerant government in northern India that Babur might have installed if he had had time. He divided the empire up into individual administrative districts, each controlled by an official appointed by and directly responsible to the shah. A uniform tax system was created on the basis of a freshly commissioned land survey. Yet Sher Khan was not able to enjoy the fruits of his labours for long. He died from wounds sustained while besieging a Rajput fortress in 1545.

Humayun's return

Meanwhile, Humayun was plotting a comeback. He persuaded Tahmasp to give him an army, then led it against the Persians' Uzbek enemies as well as against his own brother. After eight years of campaigning he won back Afghanistan, sealing his hold on the country by having the disloyal Kamran blinded.

Once more Humayun was the leader of the Mughal forces, and he had set his sights on regaining his father's Indian empire. Taking advantage of a civil war between Sher Khan's successors, he invaded from the north just as Babur had done before him. He defeated the Afghan forces at Sirhind in 1555, then went on to reoccupy Delhi and Agra.

Yet Humayun, too, had little time to enjoy his victory. Five months later, he fell down a flight of steps while descending from the roof of his library, where he had gone to observe the rising of Venus. He died of his injuries a few days later.

His son Akbar was only 13 years old at the time. Born while his father was on the run, he had been exposed to dangers from his earliest childhood. He had grown up loving sports and combat, but had resisted all attempts to teach him to read or write, perhaps as a result of dyslexia. Even without the benefit of book learning, though, he was an avid student of human nature and would later become a keen patron of the arts and sciences. When Humayun died, the future of the Mughal dynasty was far from assured, however. Akbar's own hold on power was shaky. He survived to rule largely thanks to the efforts of his guardian and protector, a Mughal general called Bairam Khan. Bairam steered the ship of state through difficult times, preserving the empire for Akbar and also winning back a number of lost provinces.

When he turned 18, Akbar dispensed with the services of a guardian. His impulsiveness and energy were demonstrated soon after, when a palace conspiracy came to light. The emperor laid out the ring-leader with a blow of his fist and then ordered him to be

Fatehpur Sikri – seat of power
Akbar's throne rested against this pillar in the private audience hall of his palace at Fatehpur Sikri, the 'City of Victory'. Like the decoration in Akbar's throne-room, the intricate filigree work on the stone screens of Fatehpur Sikri's mosque (background) testifies to the craftsmanship of the stonemasons who worked on the new city. The new capital was built to commemorate the birth of an heir in 1569, but it was occupied for less than two decades.

flung from the ramparts; when a first attempt left the conspirator still breathing, he had him thrown down a second time.

As a warrior, Akbar followed the tradition of his ancestors, convinced that it was his duty to enlarge the empire they had bequeathed him. It was not long before he was leading his first campaigns against rebellious Rajput princes in their mountain fortresses.

In 1568 Akbar and his army attacked Mewar, one of the most troublesome Rajput states. He used heavy artillery and mines to breach the walls of its principal stronghold, the hilltop fortress of Chitor near present-day Udaipur. After Akbar had personally dispatched the Rajput leader with a well-aimed shot from his musket, the defenders set the fort on fire and proceeded to slaughter their own women and children to prevent them from falling into enemy hands. The survivors were massacred when Akbar's forces finally overwhelmed the bastion. In total, 30,000 people are said to have died in the course of the siege.

A few months later, the fortress of Ranthambore avoided a similar fate when its commander agreed to negotiate a surrender. Magnanimous in victory, Akbar proved only too happy to accommodate Rajput rulers who were willing to acknowledge his rule. He realised from the start that Mughal authority could not be upheld through brute force alone.

He also inherited his grandfather's tolerant attitude to other people's religious beliefs, and had no ambitions to convert the Hindu population en masse to Islam.

Winning over the Rajputs

Akbar tried to win over the Rajputs by offering them places at court and posts in his administration. Rajput princes were appointed as provincial governors and were given positions of command in the army; some even secured seats on the imperial council that advised the Emperor on matters of state. In addition, they were largely allowed to administer their own realms as they wished, so long as they accepted overall Mughal sovereignty. In terms of court protocol they were granted the same privileges as Muslim office-holders, meaning that they could ride up to the palace to the sound of drums and were permitted to bear arms into the public audience chamber as a symbol of the trust the ruler put in their loyalty.

To cement the alliance Akbar took several Rajput princesses as wives, allowing them to practice their Hindu faith within the palace harem. In 1569 the first of these gave birth to a son, the future Emperor Jahangir. To celebrate the happy event Akbar planned to build a new capital on the spot where the boy had been born. This was the village of Sikri, 37km (23 miles) from Agra. It was home to a Muslim saint who had predicted that Akbar's wife would bear him three boys; on hearing of the prophecy, the Emperor had made her take up residence there to hasten its fulfilment.

Built on a high sandstone ridge, the new city became known as Fatehpur Sikri, or 'City of Victory', a name that celebrated the Emperor's triumphant

BACKGROUND

The Sikhs

The Sikh religious community was founded in the Punjab by its first *guru* (teacher), Nanak, in the late 15th century. Nanak combined elements of both Hinduism and Islam in his teachings – for example, combining a belief in the transmigration of souls with an interdiction on worshipping graven images, or indeed against depicting God visually in any way.

Nanak's original vision embraced pacifism, but Mughal persecution at the beginning of the 17th century forced his followers to develop warrior traditions.

campaign of reconquest in Gujarat in 1573. The airy, filigree decoration of its pavilions and palaces showed exceptional grace and delicacy, while the design of many of the buildings, left open to the elements, distantly recalled the lavish ceremonial tents of the Mongol rulers of the Central Asian steppes.

But the site had a fundamental flaw: its hilltop location made it impossible to guarantee an adequate water supply. As a result the city was all but abandoned within 20 years of its construction. Even so, Akbar liked to retire there to get away from the business of government and to devote long hours to prayer.

Founding a new religion

An original religious thinker, Akbar increasingly distanced himself from Islamic orthodoxy. He took to summoning adherents of all the major religions to his court to discuss matters of faith. Muslim theologians mixed there with Hindu Brahmans, Persian Zoroastrians and even Christian Jesuit priests from Goa, gathering for lengthy seminars in which they would argue the merits of their respective faiths in the presence of the Emperor.

In time, Akbar devised a new religion of his own, that combined elements of all these belief systems. Known simply as the Divine Faith, his creed accorded a central place to worship of the Sun as a symbol of divine power. Regarding himself as the executor of God's will on Earth, Akbar assumed a semi-divine aura that reflected ancient Indian traditions of god-kings. The Emperor made no attempt to force the cult on his subjects, and only a tiny circle of court acolytes ever professed it. Even so, the godlike glow that came to surround the Emperor and his successors helped to cement the loyalty of their Hindu subjects, who came to see any form of attack on the Mughals as tantamount to blasphemy.

Splendour in sandstone
Completed under Akbar's successors in 1648, the Red Fort at Delhi lies within a curtain wall 1000m long and 500m wide (3300ft by 1650ft). The main entrance to the complex is through the Lahore Gate.

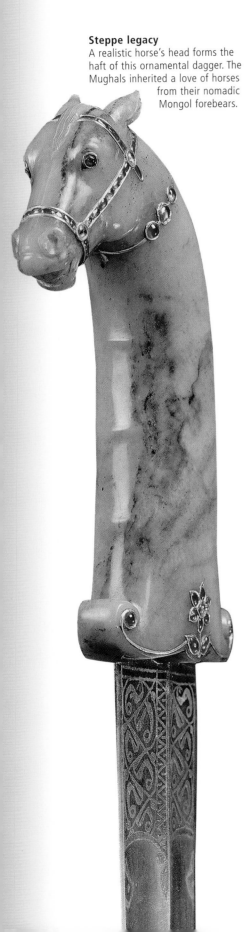

Steppe legacy
A realistic horse's head forms the haft of this ornamental dagger. The Mughals inherited a love of horses from their nomadic Mongol forebears.

A firm grip on power

It was a sign of Akbar's power in the latter years of his reign that he was able to challenge Muslim orthodoxy so directly without stirring up revolt among his followers. Even so, his heterodoxy caused hostile mutterings, as did his decision to abolish the *jiziya* (poll tax) on non-Muslims that was customary in Islamic countries. Some Islamic clerics accused him of polytheism, and there were ripples of discontent among the community of the faithful, but no serious challenge to his authority emerged.

The Emperor owed his success partly to constant political vigilance, but also to the adoption and expansion of the highly effective system of government instituted by Sher Khan. Under Akbar the empire was split for administrative purposes into a dozen provinces, which were themselves subdivided into districts and subdistricts. Taxes were raised in the emperor's name on the basis of Sher Khan's land survey, with farmers generally handing over a third of their crop, or its equivalent in cash, to the state. A minister known as the *diwan* had responsibility for supervising revenue collection.

Reorganising society

At the same time Akbar set about reorganising the upper echelons of society on military lines. He created 33 separate ranks for noblemen and government officials, each linked to the number of cavalrymen the individual could command in the field. The lowest-ranking officers were responsible for 10 men and their mounts, while the highest commanded 5000; Mughal princes were assigned even more. The *mansabdars*, or officers, were paid by the state, either in cash or by lands from which they could collect revenue. To prevent powerful individuals from building up power bases, the estates were frequently transferred from one officer to another.

The backbone of the armed forces continued to be the mounted archers who had served the Mongol conquerors so well in earlier centuries. They were now supplemented by infantry armed with bows and spears, and by the musketeers and artillerymen that Babur had used to such good effect.

War elephants – long a distinctive feature of warfare on the subcontinent – no longer played a major role. They were used primarily as draught animals or mobile command posts for army commanders in the field. Nevertheless, a special aura surrounded the mighty creatures. One observer noted that 'these amazing beasts are as huge and as strong as mountains, while their wildness and courage match that of the lion… Those in the know in India say that one good elephant is worth 500 horses'.

On the march

A Mughal army on the march was an impressive sight. The heavy weapons travelled in the vanguard, followed by a huge baggage train. The cavalry rode at the head of the main column, followed by the emperor himself, guarded by the infantry. Heralds rode ahead to warn the rulers of petty states in the army's path of the emperor's imminent arrival, while specially picked pioneer detachments went ahead to clear obstacles and to repair damaged bridges. Akbar took a personal interest in the artillery, which he kept firmly under imperial control: it played a major role in the many sieges that he conducted.

An expanding realm

While Akbar always appeared happy to conciliate rivals who were willing to seek an accommodation with him, he never doubted that Mughal power rested on a base of military force. 'A ruler should always be intent on conquest,' he claimed, 'otherwise his neighbours will rise up against him.' After securing his hold on Gujarat in 1573, he echoed the practice of his Mongol forebears by constructing a pyramid of 2000 human skulls to strike terror into would-be opponents.

Akbar continued to expand his empire for the next 30 years, widening its frontiers to include Bengal, Kashmir, Orissa and Sind. In the last years of his reign he advanced into the Deccan Plateau of central India, subjugating the Muslim sultanates of Berar and Khandesh and part of Ahmednagar. By the dawn of the 17th century, the Mughal realm, stretching from northern Afghanistan to central India, had joined the Ottomans and Persians as one of the three great empires of the Islamic world.

Trade flourished within Akbar's lands, thanks to improved transport links, which benefited travelling merchants while also facilitating the transfer of troops. Ships from Arabia, Egypt and the Persian Gulf came to the port of Surat on India's west coast to load cargoes of rice, cotton, indigo, silk, spices, steel and many other commodities. In Mughal times, the volume of goods shipped by sea outstripped the amount carried by land through the northwest frontier passes. Yet Akbar also encouraged horse breeding on the subcontinent, even though most of the best mounts for his cavalry still came from Iran and Central Asia.

The Mughal achievement

The empire's growing prosperity was expressed in a profusion of mosques, palaces, fortresses, gardens and mausoleums, all blending Islamic with native Indian stylistic features. Persian culture was also very influential at the Mughal court, and many poets chose to compose works in the Persian language. Poetry contests in which rival bards vied to show off their skills were a regular feature of court life. Persian also served as the official language of diplomacy and the civil service, and educated Hindus and Muslims employed it throughout the empire. The Persian influence also made itself felt in miniature painting. Some of the finest examples of this art adorned the *Book of Akbar*, commissioned by the Emperor to provide a visual record of his life and achievements.

Akbar was the first of the Mughals to open up relations with the Portuguese, who had established a foothold on India's west coast. He invited government representatives and Jesuit missionaries to visit his new capital of Fatehpur Sikri, and then reciprocated by sending officials and craftsmen to the Portuguese trading base at Goa. He resisted the temptation to attack the port and chose instead to cultivate good relations with the wealthy trading community based there.

Akbar remained actively involved in affairs of state up to his death at the age of 63 in 1605. He bequeathed to his heirs an empire on a sound foundation that would survive, albeit in weakened form, for another two and a half centuries.

Imperial memento
A gold medallion embossed with an image of Akbar the Great (left) was coined in the reign of his son and successor Jahangir, who distributed the images as keepsakes to members of his retinue who had rendered outstanding service. High-ranking individuals were fond of gold jewellery, like this bird-shaped pendant (background), that would have been worn around the neck or as a turban decoration.

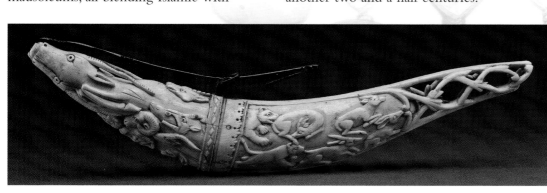

Hunting scenes
An intricately carved Mughal powder flask that would have been part of a nobleman's hunting equipment.

Russia expands across Siberia

In the space of a few decades, Cossack adventurers moved Russia's border 5000km (3000 miles) eastwards from the Ural Mountains to the Sea of Okhotsk.

Scourge of the Tartars
A bust by the 20th-century Russian sculptor, Mikhail Gerasimov, of Tsar Ivan IV, 'Ivan the Terrible'. The feared 16th-century ruler set the conquest of Siberia in motion when he overran the Tatar khanates of Kazan and Astrakhan, opening a path to the east.

One of the great untold epics of world history took place far from the world's view in the late 16th and early 17th centuries. The conquest of Siberia carried Russian sovereignty from the Ural mountains on the eastern borders of Europe all the way to the Arctic Ocean and the Sea of Okhotsk, an inlet of the Pacific 5000km (3000 miles) to the east. In its way just as dramatic and significant as the winning of the American West in the 19th century, Russia's annexation of its own 'wild east' was less well chronicled at the time, and even today is relatively little studied. Yet its implications were enormous. Although the wastes of Siberia remained thinly settled, especially before the opening of the Trans-Siberian Railway at the end of the 19th century, their acquisition quadrupled the amount of land under Russian rule, and turned Russia into an Asiatic power as well as a European one.

One reason for the lack of attention paid to the great Siberian venture lay in the nature of the individuals who undertook it. They were, in the main, rough adventurers making a living from the fur trade, and they left no written record of their exploits. Most were Cossacks, descendants of Russian and Ukrainian serfs who had fled from servitude. The indigenous peoples whose lands they invaded had no writing either, so the European encroachment went virtually unrecorded.

Unknown lands of Tartary

Before the incursions, very little was known about the land beyond the Urals. Maps called it 'Great Tartary' – a term that covered Mongolia and what are now the Central Asian republics – but provided few other details. For Russians, the River Ob on the Asian side of the Ural range represented the far edge of the known world. People had no inkling of the fact that Siberia stretched for thousands of

Feared horsemen
Originally serfs who had escaped from their masters, the Cossacks blazed a trail into the Siberian interior, raiding the villages of the region's indigenous inhabitants and also guarding isolated Russian settlements of merchants and fur trappers.

miles to the east, nor that this vast land covered such varied and extreme climates. The Yenisei and Lena rivers, the Altai mountains, the Yablonovy and Verkhoyanski ranges, the volcanoes of the Kamchatka peninsula – all were unknown, as was the existence of some 140 separate ethnic groups of indigenous peoples.

Until the 1550s, the route to the eastern lands had been blocked by the Mongol Golden Horde. Gradually, the rulers of Muscovy drove the Tartars back, and between 1552 and 1556 Tsar Ivan IV, the Terrible, finally opened the door to expansion when his forces overcame the khanates of Kazan and Astrakhan.

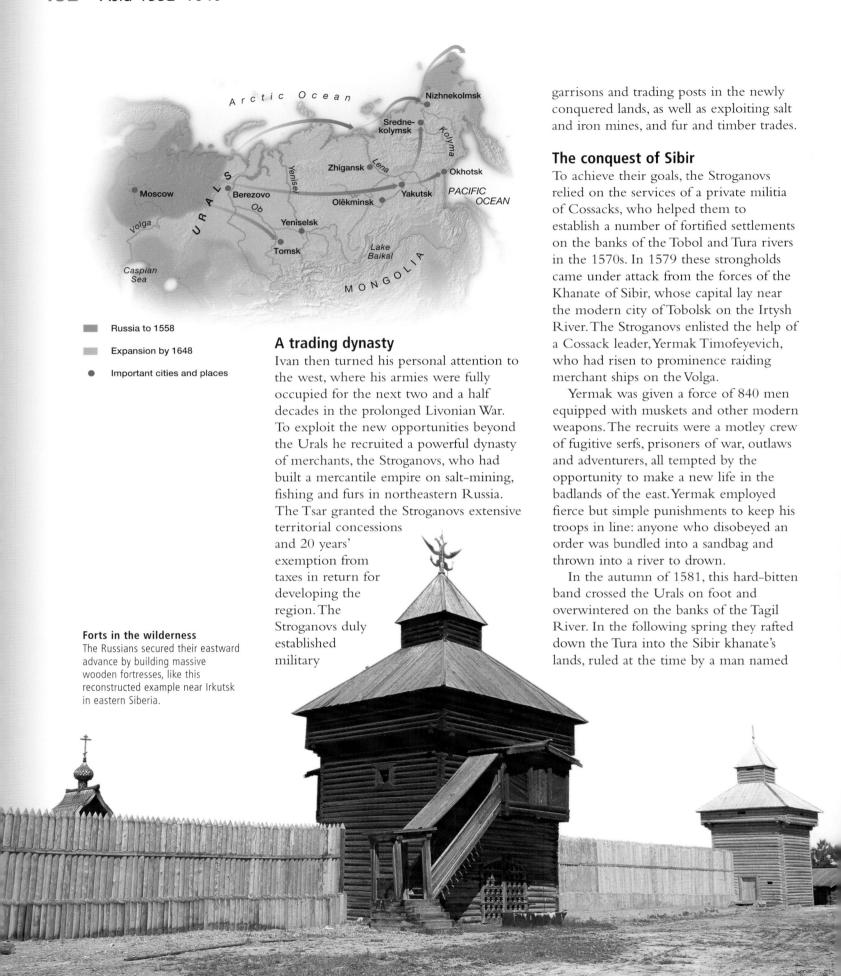

Arctic Ocean

Nizhnekolymsk

Sredne-
kolymsk

Kolyma

Zhigansk

Lena

Okhotsk

Moscow

Urals

Berezovo

Yenisei

Yakutsk

PACIFIC
OCEAN

Ob

Olëkminsk

Volga

Yeniselsk

Lake
Baikal

Tomsk

Caspian
Sea

MONGOLIA

■ Russia to 1558

■ Expansion by 1648

● Important cities and places

Forts in the wilderness
The Russians secured their eastward
advance by building massive
wooden fortresses, like this
reconstructed example near Irkutsk
in eastern Siberia.

A trading dynasty

Ivan then turned his personal attention to
the west, where his armies were fully
occupied for the next two and a half
decades in the prolonged Livonian War.
To exploit the new opportunities beyond
the Urals he recruited a powerful dynasty
of merchants, the Stroganovs, who had
built a mercantile empire on salt-mining,
fishing and furs in northeastern Russia.
The Tsar granted the Stroganovs extensive
territorial concessions
and 20 years'
exemption from
taxes in return for
developing the
region. The
Stroganovs duly
established
military

garrisons and trading posts in the newly
conquered lands, as well as exploiting salt
and iron mines, and fur and timber trades.

The conquest of Sibir

To achieve their goals, the Stroganovs
relied on the services of a private militia
of Cossacks, who helped them to
establish a number of fortified settlements
on the banks of the Tobol and Tura rivers
in the 1570s. In 1579 these strongholds
came under attack from the forces of the
Khanate of Sibir, whose capital lay near
the modern city of Tobolsk on the Irtysh
River. The Stroganovs enlisted the help of
a Cossack leader, Yermak Timofeyevich,
who had risen to prominence raiding
merchant ships on the Volga.

Yermak was given a force of 840 men
equipped with muskets and other modern
weapons. The recruits were a motley crew
of fugitive serfs, prisoners of war, outlaws
and adventurers, all tempted by the
opportunity to make a new life in the
badlands of the east. Yermak employed
fierce but simple punishments to keep his
troops in line: anyone who disobeyed an
order was bundled into a sandbag and
thrown into a river to drown.

In the autumn of 1581, this hard–bitten
band crossed the Urals on foot and
overwintered on the banks of the Tagil
River. In the following spring they rafted
down the Tura into the Sibir khanate's
lands, ruled at the time by a man named

Kutschum. The invaders encountered stiff resistance in a series of clashes with the khan's men, but eventually their guns enabled them to triumph. They captured the khan's capital in 1582, Kutschum was forced to flee, and they sent substantial spoils back to Moscow. Sibir would eventually give its name to the whole of the vast region opened up by their victory.

In the war that followed, Yermak succeeded in extending Russian power to the banks of the River Ob. Then one night, in August 1585, he was taken by surprise by Tartars while camped with his band on a river island. He jumped into the river to escape, but was dragged down by his coat of chain mail, sent to him as a gift from the Tsar, and he drowned.

The eastward drive

Yermak's death proved to be only the prelude to a fresh wave of Cossack incursions. In the next two decades most of western Siberia came under Russian rule. Local Turkic and Mongol groups put up occasional fierce resistance, but they had no weapons to match the Cossacks' guns. The invaders marked the stages of their progress by constructing wooden fortresses at strategically important river crossings such as at Tomsk and Mangaseya, which grew into significant towns.

Beguiled by the riches to be had in Mangaseya, in 1632 Tsar Mikhail Romanov gave the signal for a fresh exodus to the land he called 'east of the Sun' – the basin of the Lena River, which lay some 4000km (2500 miles) east of the Urals. The first scouting parties had reached the region by travelling up eastern tributaries of the Yenisei. The adventurers

who responded to the Tsar's call had to confront difficult terrain and an extreme climate, as well as fierce resistance from the local Yakut people. In spite of all the obstacles, they succeeded in establishing

the future city of Yakutsk as a fortified settlement on the Lena's middle reaches. The outpost soon became an important launching pad for further expeditions to the Arctic Ocean and the Sea of Okhotsk – Siberia's outlet to the Pacific.

The indigenous peoples were forced to submit to Russian rule and to pay tribute to the distant tsar, who not only gained a huge new expanse of territory but also vast untapped wealth in pelts and mineral resources.

Siberians versus Cossacks
The aboriginal inhabitants of Siberia – like this family from the Kamchatka peninsula (above), sketched by a Russian naval officer – put up stiff but ultimately unsuccessful resistance to the Russian invaders. The Cossack leader Yermak Timofeyevich (left) conquered the khanate of Sibir in the drive to the east, opening the way to the European penetration of Siberia.

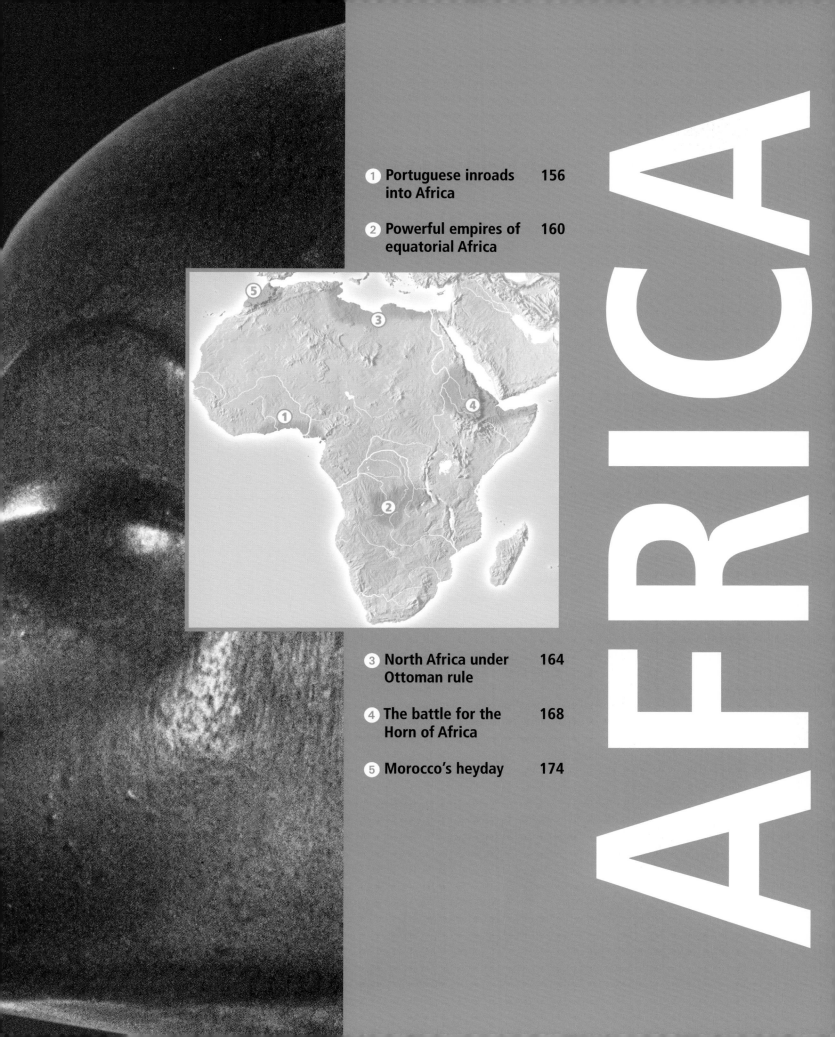

AFRICA

Portuguese inroads into Africa

The Portuguese established a number of fortified bases along the coasts of Africa and maintained close trading contacts with several African kingdoms.

By the time Columbus embarked on his westward voyage of discovery, in 1492, the Portuguese had already sailed south down the west coast of Africa in search of the sea route to India. Their mariners learned with some astonishment that there were powerful kingdoms in the interior of the continent that had spread their influence to the tribes living on the coast. Furthermore, these kingdoms offered enticing trading opportunities.

In West Africa, Portuguese traders were active in the region between the mouths of the Senegal and Congo rivers. By 1506 they were bartering more than 3500 slaves annually from the area between the Senegal River and Sierra Leone alone, along with ivory, gold and cotton fabrics. In exchange they offered salt, textiles, glassware, tools and other metal goods – such as firearms.

They negotiated with native rulers to construct a number of forts at strategic points along the coast in return for agreeing to pay ground rent for the sites. The first such was Elmina, built in 1482 on the coast of present-day Ghana. Initially the Portuguese requested permission to build a warehouse for the storage of goods. The local ruler began to have second thoughts when a fortified settlement rose up in place of the single building he had expected. Worse, the newcomers used stones that the native people regarded as sacred. Conflict threatened, but the Portuguese bought their way out of trouble with a cash payment. Thereafter, they pressed on so

Portugal's West African bastion
The stone-built fortress of Elmina, on the coast of what is now Ghana, was a vital base for Portuguese merchants. It provided secure warehousing for goods stored for trans-shipment, and later became a centre for the trans-Atlantic slave trade.

quickly that the expedition leader was later able to claim that 'within 20 days, the walls of the fortress had reached their full height and the tower was also complete'.

Mutual respect

In those early days, the foreign trading community was dependent for its survival on the goodwill of local African rulers. Portugal was a small nation whose resources were already stretched by commitments in Brazil, India and the East Indies as well as in Africa. The tiny presence its merchants maintained on the African coast could easily have been swept away by native armies that vastly outnumbered their own forces.

Portugal kept up close relations with Benin, then the largest of the West African kingdoms, throughout the 16th century. The kings of the two nations maintained diplomatic contact, and some Beninese traders even learned Portuguese. The king himself mastered the language.

Development aid

The kingdom where the Portuguese came to exercise the greatest influence, however, lay well to the south of Benin. This was the realm of Kongo, located in the coastal lands south of the Congo River.

Shortly after contact was first made by the explorer Diogo Cão in 1483, the ruler of the kingdom, Nzinga, converted to Christianity, taking the European name of John I. Thereafter, Kongo received important aid from Portugal in the form of the services of artisans and soldiers.

In return the Portuguese wanted ivory and, above all, slaves, which they needed to supply the plantation economies they had established in Madeira and the Cape Verde Islands – both Portuguese possessions. From the 1520s onwards, demand rocketed to supply Brazil and Spanish America, too.

The lust for guns
A Portuguese soldier holding a firearm, depicted on a bronze plaque from Benin. Guns soon became sought-after imports in the African kingdoms.

Strangers on the shore
An ivory salt cellar from Benin shows a Portuguese soldier clutching a sword and a pike beneath a model of the boat he and his comrades arrived in (right). African artists were fascinated by Europeans and enjoyed portraying the details of their dress and accoutrements.

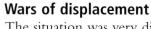

King of Kongo
A 19th-century French print shows a ruler of Kongo on his throne. Lying to the south of the River Congo in what is now Angola, Kongo was the first African kingdom to seek to take on European ways. Yet its rulers' adoption of Christianity did not save the kingdom from the activities of Portuguese slavers.

One result of the burgeoning trade contacts was a growing Portuguese involvement in the internal politics of Central Africa. Traders based on the island of São Tomé off the African coast were convinced that there were substantial silver deposits in Ndongo, a tributary kingdom on Kongo's southern borders. They tried to gain influence there, initially by peaceful means, but when these overtures failed, they urged King Diego I of Kongo to declare war.

The campaign was an abject failure. In response, Ndongo warriors advanced far into Kongo territory and the warlike Jaga people of northern Angola took advantage of the situation to launch an invasion of their own. They sacked Kongo's capital, São Salvador, and the king had to take refuge on an island in the Congo estuary. In 1570, King Sebastian of Portugal sent a fighting force of 600 men in support, and with their help the Jaga were driven back to their own lands.

These conflicts enabled the Portuguese to entrench their own position, notably as suppliers of firearms, which came to play an increasingly important part in African warfare. Local rulers needed as many guns as they could lay their hands on to maintain their own positions; in return, the Portuguese were able to obtain all the slaves they desired.

Wars of displacement

The situation was very different on the East African coast. There, a long-established network of important trading ports included Kilwa in what is now Tanzania and Malindi and Mombasa (both in modern-day Kenya). The explorer Vasco da Gama and his crew were the first Portuguese to see these cities, and they brought back glowing reports of stone-built dwellings and luxuriant gardens, as well as of the wealthy citizens. Arab, Persian and Indian merchants had been established in the ports for centuries, conducting a lively trade in gold, ivory and textiles. Attracted by such accounts of wealth in the east coast ports, the Portuguese government decided to drive out the competition and monopolise the lucrative Indian Ocean trade.

In 1505, a fleet under the command of Francisco de Almeida appeared off Kilwa. Almeida was on his way to India to be the first Portuguese viceroy, but took time out to attack the town. After a brief skirmish, Kilwa was captured and pillaged, and the sultan agreed to pay tribute. Mombasa, to the north, suffered a similar fate. One sailor described the operation there with these words: 'Almeida issued an order for the town to be sacked and for everyone to take anything of value he could lay his hands on back to his ship'. The ports of the Somali coast to the north also soon fell to Portuguese attackers, who forced the local people to erect stone forts from which they could control the coast.

As the century progressed, the European settlers became increasingly interested in a powerful ruler known as the Mwene Mutapa, or Monomatapa, who was said to control a wealthy inland kingdom in southern Africa. By the 1530s Portuguese explorers had ventured up the Zambezi to the borders of his lands, founding the river ports of Sena and Tete. Soon after, Portuguese missionaries arrived at the court of the Mwene Mutapa himself with the intention of converting him. They paid for their zeal with their lives.

When Portugal's young King Sebastian reached his majority in 1568, the pace of exploration stepped up a gear. In 1570 a major expedition set out from Lisbon under the command of Francisco Barreto to make contact with the African ruler, whose title meant 'King of the Mines'. The venture was a disaster; illness and constant attacks took their toll, and Barreto himself died on the campaign. The survivors turned back after torturing to death a dozen Muslim merchants who had initially welcomed them to the region. When a later expedition did finally succeed in penetrating the Mwene Mutapa's realm, its members found that the kingdom's riches had been greatly exaggerated. The trade in gold that was eventually established through the port of Sofala barely served to cover the costs of maintaining a presence there.

The end of Portugal's monopoly

From 1550 onwards, attacks by Turkish pirates from the Red Sea threatened the Portuguese position on the East African coast. An Ottoman fleet reached Mombasa in 1585, sparking a popular uprising against the port's European masters. The Portuguese quickly regrouped, consolidating their control in 1593 by constructing Fort Jesus, their largest and best-defended stronghold to date.

Inevitably, the lucrative Swahili coast trade attracted the attentions of English, French and Dutch mariners. In a single trip, two English ships brought 180kg

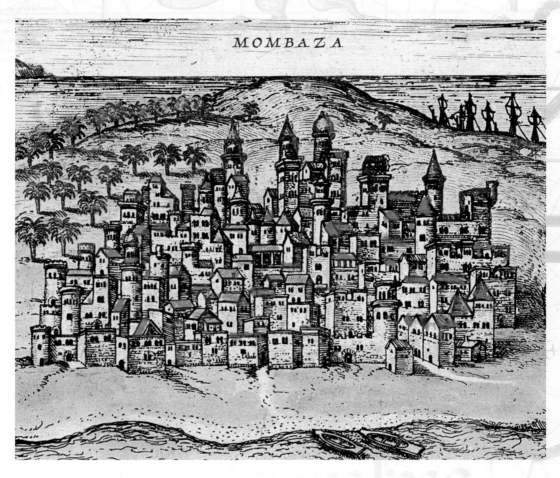

MOMBAZA

(400lb) of gold, 36 barrels of peppercorns and 250 elephants' tusks back to London. By the mid 16th century, clashes were breaking out between rival vessels. One English captain described one of these encounters: 'a ship suddenly appeared on our windward side, a French vessel… which noticed that we had come a long way. He clearly planned to board us… So, we gave him a taste of our wares – bar shot, chain shot and cannonballs, such a hail of fire that their ship's masts and rigging fell about their ears.'

African traders were also well aware by that time that ships of other European nations beside Portugal were plying their waters. Over time, the Dutch came to pose the most serious threat to the Portuguese by concluding treaties of their own with local rulers. By the start of the 17th century the Dutch had succeeded in denying the Portuguese their exclusive position on the continent.

Thriving in Africa
Seen here in a 17th-century engraving, the east coast port of Mombasa had a long history as an important trading centre. Arab merchants had been operating there for at least 400 years before the Portuguese explorer Vasco da Gama and his crew became the first European mariners to reach it in 1498.

Seafarers' secrets (background)
As well as showing the outlines of coasts, the early maritime charts, known as *portolans* from an Italian word meaning 'pilot book', also contained nautical, geographical and ethnological information. They were considered top-secret documents at the time, and it was high treason to pass them on to unauthorised individuals.

Powerful empires of equatorial Africa

Having plentiful resources of iron and salt enabled the Luba and Lunda peoples of the southern Congo region to dominate Central Africa.

The founding of the Luba Empire is steeped in legend. Stories passed down through the generations told how a powerful chief of the Songhai people of the western Sudan pushed southwards sometime around the year 1500. Named Nkongolo, he was a cruel ruler who would have the nose, ears and arms cut off individuals who incurred his displeasure. As a child, he had once watched a column of ants wiping out a termite colony, and the sight had inspired him to use the ants' strategy of destruction to turn himself into a mighty leader. He duly won renown as the founder of the Luba Empire.

The Luba people themselves are thought to have lived in the region to the west of Lake Tanganyika since the 10th century. The land they inhabited was an area of mixed woodland and savannah that is today divided between the Democratic Republic of Congo and Zambia. A Bantu-speaking people, the Luba were divided into many different clans. They cultivated sorghum (a type of millet) and bananas on plots cleared from the jungle using slash-and-burn techniques.

At some stage, a hunter called Mbidi Kiluwe arrived at Nkongolo's capital of Mwibele, which was situated close to the modern city of Katanga. The king welcomed him to his court, taking him in to his palace and giving him two of his sisters as wives. But when Mbidi Kiluwe tried to tell Nkongolo how a chief should behave, the two fell out, and Kiluwe was forced to leave. One of his sons, Kalala Ilunga, 'Ilunga the Warrior', remained behind with his uncle and helped him to expand his empire. In time, the young man became so popular and successful that the ageing king saw him as a rival for power and determined to get rid of him. Kalala Ilunga got wind of his plans, however, and fled. Returning sometime later with an army of his own, he killed Nkongolo and took power in his place.

A stool for a chief
Carved stools like this one from the Democratic Republic of Congo were status symbols as well as practical furnishings. The head of every household had one, but chiefs' seats were more elaborately carved than those of their subjects.

A warrior king

Kalala Ilunga greatly expanded the area under his control, but his authority did not reside simply in the spears of his warriors; it was also based on a rather complicated series of tribute payments. The tributes were delivered primarily in the form of precious commodities, and it was the king's responsibility to distribute them among his subjects. If certain goods were not available in a particular region, then the king's bounty became all the more essential. On the other hand, the king could not countenance missed tribute payments or any other form of resistance to his rule. Anyone who failed to supply an expected contribution could reckon on drastic retribution. A later eyewitness gave a graphic account of the punishments that a subsequent Luba king meted out: 'Across all their villages, there are some 300 to 400 people who are missing either noses, ears or arms.'

Riches from the earth

High court officials supervised the delivery of tribute, and as recompense for their services they were entitled to a share of the goods. Copper ingots weighing as much as 5kg (11lb) came from what is now the border region between the Democratic Republic of Congo and Zambia, while the upper reaches of the Congo River provided fish in abundance.

Salt and high-quality iron ore came from the Lubas' ancestral homeland. They extracted the salt from the soil by packing handfuls of earth into a funnel and then pouring boiling water over it. The resulting brine was collected in vessels placed underneath the spout. The water was then allowed to evaporate, leaving behind blocks of salt weighing as much as 1.5kg (3lb).

Oral tradition also credits Kalala Ilunga with introducing ironworking to the region. As legend has it, a master black-smith from his father's homeland passed on to the Luba the knowledge of how to work the metal.

A secret society

The empire's central location gave its kings control of a long-established network of trade routes. They increased their prosperity by claiming a share of all the goods that passed along these routes, including iron, earthenware and fabrics made from the fibres of the raffia palm.

As the empire grew, so too did the royal court, which eventually played host to a multitude of local chiefs, their families

Aid to oral history
A Luba *lukasa* – a wooden memory board decorated with beads and metal artefacts. The individuals who served as keepers of the tribe's oral history used these boards as mnemonic devices to help them remember details of genealogy and king-lists.

A regional power
Founded early in the 16th century, the Luba Empire extended eastward to the shores of Lake Tanganyika.

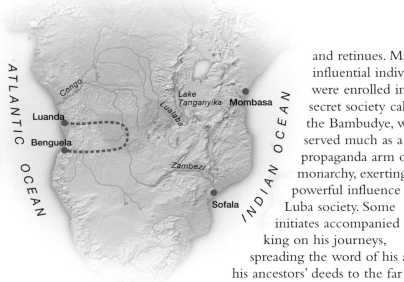

Luba Kingdom

Lunda Kingdom

---- Trade routes

Hard pillows
Wooden headrests like this one were designed to protect the coiffures of women while they slept. The heads of the carved figures suggest how elaborate the hairstyles could be.

and retinues. Many influential individuals were enrolled in a secret society called the Bambudye, which served much as a propaganda arm of the monarchy, exerting a powerful influence on Luba society. Some initiates accompanied the king on his journeys, spreading the word of his and his ancestors' deeds to the far corners of the empire. Others specialised in passing on myths about the gods, accounts of historical events, and legends concerning the origins of the Luba. Secret ceremonies and sacred rites accompanied the initiation of novices into the ranks of the Bambudye.

Kings as gods

Sacrificial ceremonies formed part of the accession celebrations for a new Luba king. A man would be forced to dance in front of a pit lined with rows of spears until, completely exhausted, he finally fell to his death within it. All the eating utensils used by the heir-apparent for eating were destroyed to emphasise the point that he was starting a new life as ruler.

The Luba practiced ancestor worship, venerating the dead as spirit beings who were thought to endow the living with something of their vital power. Deceased kings were given the status of gods, and their personal effects, along with some body parts including the genitals, were kept in a basket in the former royal residence, which was then preserved as a sacred precinct. A female diviner known as a 'watcher' kept guard over the shrine.

Meanwhile, the new king set up his court in a fresh location. Kalala Ilunga's palace was at Makwidi, which lay to the east of Nkongolo's base of Mwibele. The Luba fortified important settlements with earthworks that sometimes ran for several miles, protected by palisades of wooden stakes and deep moats.

A warrior court

Local chiefs, who were almost all blood relations of the royal family, travelled to the king's court from far-flung parts of the realm, bringing women from their home villages with them. The women stayed on as lesser wives in the royal harem, serving as hostages to guarantee the continued good behaviour of their male relatives.

The Luba kings often went to war, either to force neighbouring tribes to pay tribute or else to subjugate fresh territories. Before any such undertaking they sought the advice of their divine ancestors, employing the services of special diviners for this purpose. The Luba army was made up of the king's personal bodyguard, together with contingents provided by individual chiefs. Young men willingly heeded the call to arms, since proving oneself in battle brought not only booty but also the chance of preferment. In time of war the king's whereabouts was kept secret to protect him from the risk of enemy attack. A trusted official would mark the route to his hideaway with a ritual axe, leaving a trail that only the king's messengers could decipher, so aides could seek the ruler out without alerting the surrounding populace to his presence.

The Luba employed terror as a regular part of their battle tactics. One later chronicler reported that: 'Whenever the king went into battle, he would place at the head of his warriors individuals who had had their arms, ears or noses cut off, which had the effect of filling his enemies with dread. There would often be as many as 7000 such disfigured men in the vanguard of his army, and as they marched by, a shudder of fear ran through the onlookers'.

Powerful neighbours

In the southwest, the Luba Empire bordered on the Lunda kingdom, whose ruling hierarchy was organised along similar lines. The Lunda developed into a major nation as early as the 15th century, on lands that now lie in the Democratic Republic of the Congo and Angola.

The foundation myth of the Lunda recounted that a member of the Luba royal house by the name of Kibinda Ilunga arrived in their territory and married their queen. He and his successors then took the title of Mwata Yamvo, or 'Lord of the Snake'. Under their new ruling dynasty, the Lunda realm expanded in the late 16th and early 17th centuries to the shores of the Atlantic Ocean where, soon afterwards, they came into contact, at least indirectly, with the Portuguese.

A feared race

The Jaga of Angola (also known as the Imbangala) had broken free of the Lunda in the course of the 15th century, under the command of an independent leader known as the *kinguri*. They were feared for their specialist warriors, who inhabited fortified compounds and devoted their lives to battle. Members of the warrior society relinquished family ties. Ritual cannibalism formed part of their initiation. Their leader, who lived at the heart of the compound, was distinguished by a special hairstyle and ritual scars. On tours of inspection, he was accompanied by his wives, who carried quivers for his arrows and dishes of palm wine, the Jagas' favourite beverage.

Neighbouring peoples feared the Jaga in particular for their unpredictability and their propensity to launch surprise attacks. By the 16th century their lands, like the Lundas', stretched to the Atlantic Ocean, where they, too, encountered the Portuguese. After an initial armed confrontation in 1570 when they were driven back by the newcomers' guns, they saw more future in developing a trading relationship and began raiding their African neighbours to supply the Portuguese merchants with slaves.

Royal regalia
So-called 'yet belts' decorated with pendants (above and background) were worn by Luba rulers as part of elaborate costumes designed to proclaim their royal status. This one includes small mussel shells and bags embroidered with glass beads.

North Africa under Ottoman rule

The Ottomans seized control of most of North Africa during the 16th century. To maintain their position, they then had to become a formidable maritime power.

From corsair to admiral
Long feared as a pirate by Europeans in the Mediterranean region, Khair ad-Din was given the nickname 'Barbarossa' for his red beard – which had turned white by the time this portrait was painted shortly before his death in 1546. The son of a former janissary or Ottoman slave-soldier, he was born on the island of Lesbos in the Aegean.

In an eight-year reign, from 1512 to 1520, the Ottoman Sultan Selim I, 'the Grim' made the momentous decision to extend his already great empire into Africa. He was encouraged not just by the fabled riches of Egypt but also by strategic considerations. The battle-hardened Mamelukes, who ruled Syria as well as Egypt at the time and occupied key points on the Red Sea coast, were dangerous rivals for power in the Muslim world. Also, Selim had plans for expansion in Asia and Europe and wanted to secure his southern flank, as the Mameluke domains stretched perilously close to the Ottoman heartland in Asia Minor.

Matters came to a head in 1516, when the Mamelukes allied with Selim's enemy, Persia, and the sultan of Egypt appeared with his army in the Syrian city of Aleppo. Diverting his forces southwards to meet the Egyptian threat, Selim won the Battle of Marj Dabik, fought north of the city. He owed his victory, in large part, to the use of artillery, with which the Mamelukes were poorly provided.

The Ottoman ruler went on to occupy Aleppo and the Syrian capital of Damascus, where he began preparing his forces for an assault on Egypt itself the following year. The decisive encounter was fought on January 23, 1517, at al-Raydaniyya, outside Cairo. Once again, Selim won a crushing victory. The last Mameluke ruler was captured and beheaded. Egypt lay at the sultan's mercy.

The Ottomans' new acquisition brought great riches to the empire. The fertile Nile Delta region produced three, sometimes four, harvests a year. Trade flourished in the cities, and India's wealth flowed in via the Red Sea ports.

The country also had great religious significance. Since 1258, when the last Abbasid caliph had fled from Baghdad to Cairo to escape the invading Mongols, the Mamelukes had been host to the caliphate. Although the caliphs no longer had temporal power, as they had in the early years of Islam, they still laid claim to spiritual leadership of the *umma* – the worldwide Muslim community. The rulers of Egypt also exercised guardianship over the Islamic holy cities of Mecca and Medina. These obligations now fell to the Ottoman sultans, making them the most influential rulers in the Islamic world.

Taking to the sea

The Ottomans found they also had to protect the pilgrims who customarily assembled in Damascus and Cairo before embarking on the *hajj* to Mecca. And they had to ensure that trade routes were kept open at a time when the sea-lanes were coming under increasing threat from Christian Europe. Red Sea traffic was menaced from Portuguese bases in the Indian Ocean, and Spanish naval power was on the rise in the Mediterranean.

As rulers of a land-based empire, the Ottomans struggled to fulfill their new maritime role. Unlike their European rivals, the sultans could not draw on centuries of seafaring experience; at the time of the conquest of Egypt, they hardly possessed a merchant fleet worthy of the name. For personnel and technical know-how, they depended on foreign assistance.

The North African coast at the time was in a state of near-anarchy. The Spanish had seized several important ports from weak, native Islamic dynasties, and in response Muslim adventurers had come to counter the Christian challenge.

Seeking foreign expertise
The Ottomans had no experience in shipbuilding, so they turned to foreigners to help them become a Mediterranean naval power. Christian engineers built them heavily armed vessels such as this galleass, which was powered by oars and sails, and carried 24 cannon. This detail is from a 16th-century Ottoman miniature.

BACKGROUND

The sultan's deputies

In the North African frontier provinces of the Ottoman Empire, the beys were the main regional power brokers. The Turkish word means 'lord', and it served to designate local governors, usually high-ranking civil servants or military officers.

In Egypt, the beys were partly in thrall to the Mamelukes, who had been brought to the region in the Middle Ages as slave-warriors of Caucasian and Circassian descent. After the Ottoman conquest in 1517, they quickly regained their status as a ruling elite, although now nominally in the service of Turkish masters.

In practice, the Mamelukes continued to use their private armies to collect taxes and administer justice, primarily in the countryside. In the Maghreb as well, senior officers ruled almost as independent despots in the Ottoman name.

The most successful of these were two brothers from the island of Lesbos, Aruj and Khair ad-Din; Khair was known as 'Barbarossa' for his red beard.

The two corsairs had first appeared in the western Mediterranean in the early 1500s. The Hafsid rulers of Tunis provided them with a base from which to operate, and from it Aruj conquered Algiers and the port of Tlemcen, arousing the hostility of the Spanish, who already had several well-established bases on the Algerian coast. In 1518 they launched an attack on Tlemcen, and Aruj was killed.

It was to Barbarossa that Selim turned for help in building up Ottoman naval power. Working on the principle that 'my enemy's enemy is my friend', the sultan appointed this scourge of Christian shipping as governor of Algeria, giving him free rein to wage holy war in the Mediterranean. Barbarossa, for his part, was happy enough to acknowledge Ottoman rule in return for the empire's backing.

The Spanish hit back

In the years that followed, Barbarossa inflicted great damage on the Christian lands of the western Mediterranean. He launched raids on southern Italy, pillaged the Balearic Islands and rescued thousands of Muslims from the terrifying clutches of the Spanish Inquisition, ferrying them to safety in North Africa. In 1533, Selim's son, Suleiman the Magnificent, named the corsair Grand Admiral of the Ottoman Fleet in recognition of his services. The next year Barbarossa launched an attack on Tunis, which had been occupied by the Spanish, and raised the green flag of the Prophet in the historic port.

The Holy Roman Emperor, Charles V, sent a fleet of 400 ships to Tunis in 1535 under the command of the Genoese Admiral, Andrea Doria. The Christian armada drove off Barbarossa's smaller naval force, then retook the city with the help of rebel Christian galley slaves, who opened the gates to the attacking force. The victors put the Hafsid sultan, whom Barbarossa had deposed, back in power as a puppet ruler, now more than ever in debt to Spain.

Charles V had less success six years later, when he attempted a similar operation against Algiers. An initial assault on the city by a force of 24,000, including 6000 mercenary German pikemen, was successful, but a violent storm wrecked the Spanish fleet and forced the imperial forces to withdraw with heavy losses. Algiers remained in Ottoman hands.

Port in a storm
In the course of the 16th century the Libyan port of Tripoli was fought over more than once and changed hands three times. The Spanish took it in 1509, then in 1530 Emperor Charles V (ruler of Spain as well as of the central European lands of the Holy Roman Empire) handed control to the Knights of St John, who had been driven out of Rhodes. In 1551 they were forced to cede the city to the Ottomans.

An Ottoman province

Over the following decades, Ottoman forces brought the North African coast as far as independent Morocco under their control. Barbarossa died in 1546, but his equally formidable successor, Dragut, managed to take Tripoli from the Order of the Knights of St John in 1551.

In 1587 Sultan Murad III divided the huge North African territory into three provinces, ruled respectively from Tripoli, Tunis and Algiers. Each was placed under the control of a *bey* or Ottoman governor.

Despite the achievements of Barbarossa and his successors, however, the Ottomans never succeeded in establishing complete control over the Mediterranean sea-lanes. The failed siege of Malta in 1565 and the devastating defeat of the Ottoman fleet at the Battle of Lepanto in 1571 proved the limits of their naval power.

The power of the deys

Ottoman power within the North African possessions was also more tenuous than it seemed. When the sultans encountered resistance to their authority in Egypt, Suleiman decided to integrate much of the old Mameluke military elite into the Ottoman power structure, much as Selim had recruited Barbarossa. The Mamelukes quickly came to control the newly formed

army units, while their leaders continued to dominate Cairo society. In comparison, the Ottoman beys, who were frequently replaced on orders from Istanbul, found their authority increasingly limited. From 1630 on real power was concentrated in the hands of the Mameluke *deys*, the elected military commanders, and from the middle of the century they openly assumed control of the state mechanism, relegating the beys to little more than a ceremonial role.

Similar developments took place in the Maghreb, which was even further from the Ottoman centres of power. In Tripoli, Algeria and Tunisia the deys became the real powers in the land, reducing the beys to relative impotence. The provinces in any case had little enough reason to welcome direct Ottoman rule, marked as it often was by corruption, intrigue and the subordination of local interests to those of the sultans in far-off Turkey.

Meanwhile, in the Red Sea area, Ottoman forces reached a stalemate in their struggle against the Portuguese. The sultans were unable to establish footholds on the coast of the Arabian Peninsula and in Yemen, and their attempts to drive the Portuguese out of their recently won bases in East Africa and the Persian Gulf came to nought.

Knights haven
With Tripoli gone, only Malta remained to the Knights of St John, who turned the island into a fortress. The Ottoman Sultan Suleiman the Magnificent wanted to take it too, but the lengthy and well-planned siege that he launched in 1565 came to nothing.

The battle for the Horn of Africa

With Portuguese help, Christian Ethiopia saved its highland realm from attacks by Muslim forces and from incursions by the warlike Galla people in the south.

Architectural marvel
The fortified palace at Gondar was erected from 1632 on by Emperor Fasiladas. Legend claimed that a buffalo led the ruler to the site, where he found an old hermit who persuaded him to choose the spot as his royal seat.

Over the centuries, the inaccessible highlands of Ethiopia served as a natural bastion from which the nation's Christian rulers had been able to build a powerful empire. Challenged by the rise of Islam, they not only managed to repel attacks launched by Muslim states on the Horn of Africa, but in some cases even went on to conquer their challengers.

From the mid 15th century on, however, the authority of the Ethiopian emperors was on the wane. Local princes governing the nation's provinces had begun to win increasing autonomy at the

expense of the central government, and some even formed alliances with their Muslim neighbours to achieve power.

Charismatic warrior

The balance of power was shifting in the Islamic states. From the beginning of the 16th century, the sultans of Adal had extended their grip over the region from the southern and eastern borders of Ethiopia to the Gulf of Aden. In his new capital of Harar, 200km (125 miles) southeast of modern Djibouti, Ahmad Gran, a charismatic warrior leader, set himself up as supreme ruler, giving himself the title of *imam* to emphasise his claim to spiritual leadership over his people.

Ahmad Gran's origins are shrouded in mystery. Legend has it that he was the child of a relationship between a Muslim woman and an Ethiopian monk, who was slain by his brother monks when they learned of the affair. This tragedy, it was said, lay behind his intense hatred of Christians and his fierce hostility towards Ethiopia. On coming to power in the mid 1520s, he immediately renounced the friendly relations that had hitherto existed between his state and the Christian kingdom and started making preparations for war. This alarmed David II, better known by his birth name of Lebna Dengel, who had ruled Ethiopia since 1508. It was to pre-empt his opponent's military preparations that the Emperor sent his brother-in-law, Ras Degelhan, to confront Ahmad Gran in 1527. After six days of bitter fighting, the heavily depleted Ethiopian forces were forced to withdraw. The battle marked the beginning of a life-or-death struggle between the two states that was to last for more than 30 years and spell the end of Ethiopia's glorious medieval empire. At stake was the kingdom's

very survival as a Christian state isolated in Muslim northeast Africa.

In the wake of Ahmad's victory, Muslim warriors raided Ethiopian border lands, pillaging and burning as they went. There was worse to come: in 1529 Ahmad Gran formally declared a *jihad*, a holy war, calling on all Muslims to join the campaign against Ethiopia, whose Christian tradition stretched back for more than a millennium. Among those who answered his call were tribesmen from the Somali lands, the Danakil Plain and the Red Sea coast, attracted not just by religious zeal but also by the prospect of land and spoils of war.

Clash of faiths

In 1529, a major battle was fought at Shimbra Kure to the southeast of the present-day city of Addis Ababa. Surrounded by his bodyguard, Lebna Dengel personally directed the Ethiopian forces from the ranks. He was unprepared, though, for his opponents' use of firearms, which had never previously been used on an Ethiopian battlefield. The presence of a corps of musketmen swung the day in Ahmad Gran's favour, and eventually Lebna Dengel was forced to concede defeat. Fortunately for him, Ahmad had also lost so many warriors he could not exploit his victory and was forced to return to Adal shortly after the engagement to replenish his forces.

Two years later he was back, and by 1532 Muslim forces had overrun all of the southern and eastern provinces of

Symbol of power
The emperors of Ethiopia showed off their wealth and authority in magnificent crowns. This one is preserved in the treasury at Aksum, an early capital of the country.

Ethiopia. The superiority of the Islamic armies was largely down to renewed supplies of muskets and cannons, provided via the Red Sea by the Ottomans who had conquered Egypt in 1517. The

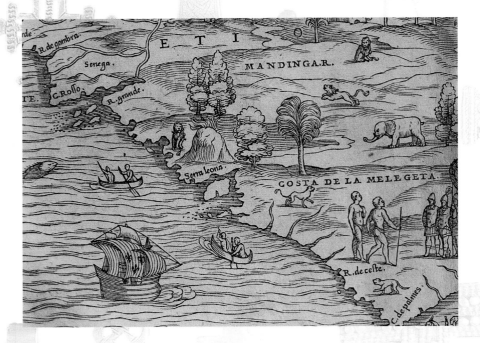

Unknown land
A detail from an early map of Africa which appeared in Giambattista Ramusio's *Of Navigations and Voyages,* a classic compilation of travellers' tales published in Italy in 1556. European notions of Africa were more than a little hazy at the time. Ethiopia is shown sprawling across the centre of the continent, and tales of lions and elephants obviously caught the cartographer's imagination.

firepower of the new weapons was less important than the psychological effect: men used to fighting with swords and lances were terrified and confused by the boom of the cannons and the swirling gunsmoke – and by the dreadful injuries the guns inflicted.

Three years later the Muslims advanced as far as Laste and the Tigre Plateau in the far north of Ethiopia, putting Ahmad Gran in control of two-thirds of the entire kingdom. Lebna Dengel was left defending the central highlands.

Conversion by sword and taxes
The threat to Christian Ethiopia was the greater because Ahmad Gran, unlike all previous Muslim invaders, wanted not just to occupy the nation but also to convert it forcibly to Islam. The inhabitants of conquered provinces were left in no doubt of the evil consequences that awaited them if they failed to adopt the new religion. Two princes who refused to

give up their beliefs were brought before the sultan, who personally threatened them with beheading.

Besides threatening violence, Ahmad Gran's followers tried to win new converts by appealing to people's self-interest, for non-believers were subject to the *jiziya* tax imposed in most Muslim countries on those who did not accept the dominant religion. Most of the population proved happy enough to go along with the conquerors' wishes, until by one account 'barely one in ten' of the native people remained loyal to Ethiopia's traditional Coptic Christianity.

Trail of devastation
Ahmad Gran's campaigns left much of the country destroyed. Churches and monasteries were sacked and burned to the ground. One contemporary chronicle describes the burning of the Church of Makana Sellase in Amhara: 'The imam and several of his followers entered the church and were dazzled by the sight that met their eyes. The interior was rich in gold and silver, adorned with inlaid pearls… The imam instructed his confederates that everyone should take away whatever they could carry, so they set to work with a thousand axes, stripping the gold and the inlays from the walls from afternoon right through to late in the evening. Each individual took as much gold as he wanted, enough to set himself up for life. But almost a third of the gold went up in flames, along with the church itself.'

Many other sanctuaries shared the same fate. The sacking of Atronsa Maryam (the Tabernacle of Mary), another celebrated church in the Amhara region, went on from midday until the following morning, and the looters called on the help of porters and mules to cart off their booty, which included ritual objects of silver and gold along with valuable brocades and manuscripts bound in gold leaf. When the pillaging finally finished, they set the building on fire. Some of the monks were so distraught at the sight that they are reported to have hurled themselves headlong into the flames.

Too weak by this time to confront his enemies in pitched battle, Lebna Dengel could only conduct a guerrilla resistance. In 1537 he lost his eldest son, killed by one of Ahmad Gran's officers. Another son was captured two years later and sent as a prisoner to Yemen. The royal compound at Amba Geshen in the Amhara region was captured in 1540 and its treasury looted.

Seeking foreign aid

In these desperate times Lebna Dengel turned for help to the Portuguese, who had established a powerful presence on Africa's East Coast over the preceding 35 years. Contact with Europeans was nothing new for the kingdom; a 30-strong Ethiopian delegation had visited Rome and various western courts as early as 1306 – then, too, seeking help against the Muslims. European interest had been further stimulated by the legend of Prester John ('Priest John'), a mysterious Christian ruler said to control a vast empire somewhere in the east. A Portuguese delegation had visited Lebna Dengel's court in 1520, but at the time

the young ruler saw no reason to further the alliance. However, one member of the Portuguese mission, a man called João Bermudes, had stayed on at the Ethiopian court. The emperor now dispatched him to Portugal with an urgent plea for help.

Soon afterwards the emperor was killed in battle and was succeeded by his son Galawdewos. The new emperor was already on the throne when a 400-man Portuguese expeditionary force landed at Massawa on the Red Sea coast. The soldiers, equipped with muskets and artillery to match those of their Muslim opponents, were led by Christovão da Gama, son of the famous seafarer Vasco da Gama. Their arrival soon tipped the balance of power in the conflict. At a first encounter, in 1542, Ahmad Gran was wounded and his men forced to withdraw. The imam responded by reinforcing his army with additional artillery and Turkish auxiliaries. In a subsequent engagement da Gama himelf was captured and executed.

Christian symbols
Ethiopian craftsmen produced vast numbers of crosses of different designs (background, far left). Some were carried in processions or used to adorn churches; others, like this one (left), were worn around the neck for personal use.

Guerrilla country
A landscape in the Tigre region of Ethiopia gives an impression of the mountainous terrain that allowed Emperor Lebna Dengel to conduct a prolonged guerrilla campaign, holding out against the Muslim forces of Ahmad Gran even after they had conquered over two-thirds of his country.

Holy crown
A golden that crown adorns the statue of the Virgin Mary in the Church of Our Lady of Zion in the old royal capital of Aksum. The building was the scene of Ethiopian coronations into modern times.

Despite this setback, the fortunes of war now generally favoured the Ethiopians and their European allies. The decisive engagement was fought at Wayna Daga, east of Lake Tana, in 1543. The battle had barely begun when Ahmad Gran was killed by a musket ball fired by a Portuguese infantryman, causing the Muslim forces to take flight. His army fell apart for want of effective leadership. Muslim rule in Ethiopia thus came to an end, but it took Galawdewos several years to drive the last of the occupation forces from his devastated country.

Most of the Christians who had converted to Islam were happy to return to their original faith. Galawdewos was equally happy to welcome them back, pointing out that if instead he had chosen to kill every apostate, he would soon have 'found himself on his own'.

The Portuguese, who had contributed so much to the victory, established a lasting presence in the country and at first were richly rewarded by the emperor. Discord arose, however, when Jesuit missionaries tried to persuade Galawdewos to accept the spiritual authority of the papacy and convert to the Catholic faith. Unwilling to abandon the traditional Coptic allegiance, the emperor responded by restricting the Europeans to territories on the borders of the empire, keeping them at arm's length from his capital.

Renewed conflict

Later in Galawdewos's reign the struggle with the weakened sultanate of Adal was renewed, although on a scale that was less. One of Ahmad Gran's successors took advantage of the emperor's temporary absence, putting down a rising in the north of the country, to launch fresh incursions. Although these were repelled, Galawdewos was killed in a skirmish in 1559. His severed head was impaled on a pike and for three years was displayed above the city gate of the sultanate's capital, Harar. By the end of that time drought and famine were afflicting the region, and superstitious citizens started to blame their misfortunes on the malign influence of the skull. It was duly returned to Ethiopia, where the dead emperor was venerated as a liberator. A prayer of the time begged: 'Return to us, Galawdewos, lord of peace, grant us your people the grace of reconciliation, leave your place of rest so that the Muslim may not deprive us of our inheritance.'

New threats

With Galawdewos's death, hostilities between Adal and Ethiopia came to an end, with neither side having gained a decisive advantage. One reason for the uneasy peace was that both warring parties found themselves menaced by a new threat. The nomadic Oromo people had begun to encroach on the southern borders of both realms from the early 16th century on. The Ethiopians called them the Gallas – 'wanderers'.

Initially the newcomers limited their attacks to border raids, but they soon took advantage of the ongoing conflict between Ethiopia and Adal to increase the scope of their incursions until they seemed more like full-scale invasions. To make matters worse, the raiders, who had originally struck on foot, now acquired horses, considerably increasing the scope of their actions. For much of the 16th and 17th centuries, successive Ethiopian rulers tried unsuccessfully to bring the intruders to heel. In time, the Gallas settled large areas of southern Ethiopia, integrating with the indigenous population.

Another threat to the empire's unity came from provincial princes, who posed a separatist challenge. Then, in 1557, the Ottomans seized control of the Red Sea port of Massawa, cutting the nation's principal link with the outside world.

A Catholic interlude

Meanwhile, the Portuguese had gained fresh influence at court following the death of Galawdewos, and the activities of Jesuit missionaries exposed the state to a fresh danger. At the turn of the 17th century, rival contenders competed for the throne, and more than one agreed, at the priests' urging, to convert to Catholicism, hoping thereby to secure Portuguese military assistance for their claims.

One of these was Susneyos, who eventually took power in 1607. The new emperor not only publicly proclaimed his own Catholic faith but, to his subjects' alarm, took to dressing in European garb. Susneyos was influenced by a priest called Pedro Páez, the more so after the Jesuit interpreted the appearance of a comet in the night sky as a favourable omen for his reign. Under Páez's persuasion, the emperor enacted

measures that were hostile to the traditions of the Coptic Church. These so enraged its followers, widespread revolts broke out that cost thousands of lives. Eventually Susneyos came to see the political folly of his ways, and shortly before his death in 1632 he renounced his conversion and agreed to fully restore the ancient faith.

A new capital

His son and heir, Fasiladas, began his reign by expelling the Jesuits from the country and moving his capital to Gondar, north of Lake Tana. Fasiladas' reign was marked by famines and further Galla invasions, but even so he succeeded, through skilful diplomacy, in laying the foundations for an economic recovery that would bring fresh prosperity to the empire in the century's second half. Over the next 200 years, Gondar grew to be the most populous city in Ethiopia.

Mythical kings
A detail from a 16th-century map of the Mediterranean (below and background), drawn up by Visconte Maggiolo, shows the legendary Christian ruler Prester John in company with other fabled African kings. Even though early explorers failed in their attempts to locate the great oriental empire the legends promised, Europeans continued to invest great hopes in the Coptic rulers of Ethiopia as potential allies against the Muslims.

Morocco's heyday

After winning a memorable victory over a Portuguese invasion force, Morocco experienced a time of stability and unity under the Saadite Sultan al-Mansur.

Muhammud al-Mutawakkil, the sultan of Morocco, was ousted from power by his uncle, who seized the throne in his own name. The deposed ruler hoped, in 1576, to persuade Portugal's young King Sebastian to help him to regain his inheritance.

In fact Sebastian proved only too happy to respond to the appeal. The Portuguese king had grown up wanting to make his mark as a champion of Christendom. He was burning for an opportunity to launch a crusade against the Ottoman Turks, who had taken control of all of the southern Mediterranean lands except Morocco.

Rare remains
Later dynasties almost totally destroyed the magnificently appointed palace of the Sultan al-Mansur in Marrakesh. The few features that do survive, such as this column capital, testify to the skill of the master-builders who constructed it.

Now, the Ottomans were making their presence felt in Morocco as well – it was with their help that al-Mutawakkil's uncle had taken power. More pragmatic self-interest influenced the King's thinking as

well: intervention on behalf of the exiled claimant would bring Morocco safely into Portugal's sphere of influence. If Morocco's Atlantic ports fell into Ottoman hands, he feared what might happen to his country's vital trade routes down the West African coast.

Sebastian also saw an opportunity to steal a march on Portugal's old rival Spain, which might otherwise establish a presence of its own across the Straits of Gibraltar. With such motives in mind, he agreed to help the exiled sultan to win back his throne.

Ironically, the Saadi dynasty to which the deposed sultan belonged had risen to power partly by championing the cause of Islam against Christian incursions. In 1541, al-Mutawakkil's predecessors had driven the Portuguese from their enclave of Agadir on the Atlantic coast. Claiming to be *sharifs* – direct descendants of the Prophet Muhammad – they had gone on to win control over southern Morocco with the help of Muslim *marabouts* (Sufi religious leaders). By 1548, they had the whole country within their grip.

The Battle of the Three Kings

So the stage was set for a clash of cultures when Sebastian agreed to support al-Mutawakkil by launching a full-scale invasion of Morocco. The decision proved to be utterly calamitous. After two years of preparations, Sebastian and his army set sail in the summer of 1578, only to meet with disaster outside Alcazarquivir, now Ksar el Kebir, 100km (60 miles) south of Tangier. In an engagement that would be

The tombs of the Saadi dynasty sultans date from the time of al-Mansur. Splendidly decorated, they can still be seen in Marrakesh today.

Sweet crop (background)
Sugar cane was widely cultivated in Morocco under the Saadi dynasty. The sugar it yielded was one of the country's leading export commodities.

known as the Battle of the Three Kings, both Sebastian and al-Mutawakkil were killed, as were hundreds of leading Portuguese noblemen; many more were taken prisoner and only freed on the payment of large ransoms.

Yet the victorious Moroccan forces also suffered a bitter loss. That very day, before battle was joined, Sultan Abd al-Malik died suddenly and unexpectedly of natural causes. His brother Ahmed stepped into the breach, leading the Saadite forces against the Portuguese and ultimately emerging triumphant. To mark his success, he subsequently adopted the title of al-Mansur, 'the Victorious'.

Spoils of victory

Al-Mansur reigned for the next 25 years as the fifth Saadite sultan of Morocco. In that time he capitalised on his fame as the nation's saviour to impose unity on a fractured country. He also established an international reputation as a powerful ruler, not just in North Africa itself but also in Europe.

To celebrate his victory, he had a magnificent palace, the el-Bedi, built for himself in Marrakesh, and envoys from England, France, Spain and Turkey flocked to pay their respects. When receiving embassies, al-Mansur followed the example of the great Arab caliphs of the past by sitting behind a curtain that protected the royal personage from the gaze of visitors.

Serious political ideas underlay the sultan's diplomacy. To bolster his position, al-Mansur sensibly avoided open conflict with his Ottoman neighbours while continuing to regard them as a dangerous threat. Similarly, he avoided an overt

rupture with Spain, which took over control of Portugal in 1580 in the course of the succession crisis following King Sebastian's death.

The sultan's closest foreign ties, though, were forged with Queen Elizabeth I of England. The two monarchs corresponded personally, and in 1601 al-Mansur even wrote to suggest a joint trans-Atlantic expedition to seize Spain's West Indian colonies, proposing that the two nations should replace the Spanish settlers with citizens of their own nations. Nothing came of the scheme, but the high regard in which Moroccans were viewed in England at the time can be seen in Shakespeare's plays, both in the dignified Prince of Morocco who features briefly in *The Merchant of Venice* and in the tragic figure of Othello, the Moor of Venice. The Barbary Company, founded by London merchants in 1585 to foster trade with Morocco, was another fruit of the alliance.

An expensive army

Al-Mansur was less successful in his domestic policies, finding himself constantly short of sufficient money to sustain his luxurious court and support his large standing army. His military expenditure was the greater because most of his crack troops were Ottoman mercenaries who expected to be well paid for their services. The ranks were also bolstered by the presence of numerous Moriscos – Muslims who had found a new home in Morocco after their expulsion from Spain in 1492. In addition, al-Mansur took care to ensure that his forces were equipped with up-to-date military technology, most notably artillery and muskets.

A sought-after base
Seen here in a mid-17th-century Dutch engraving, the port of Ceuta guarded the southern side of the Straits of Gibraltar and was hotly contested by Morocco, Portugal and Spain. The Portuguese seized it in 1415, but it passed into Spanish hands following the union of the crowns of Spain and Portugal in 1580.

A place to study
The beautifully appointed Ben Yusuf *madrasah* in the old town of Marrakesh. Up to 900 pupils studied Islamic law, theology and the Koran here.

To raise the revenue needed to sustain such a force, the sultan relied on royal monopolies on the sale of essential commodities. At the same time he imposed a growing burden of direct taxes on the population at large.

The invasion of Songhai

Al-Mansur's most ambitious foreign venture was at least partly inspired by the need to raise money. In 1591 he launched an invasion of the wealthy Songhai Empire to the south, which had its capital at Timbuktu. His troops won a decisive victory at the Battle of Tondibi, and the sultan was subsequently able to drawn on the region's extensive supplies of gold,

winning for himself the fresh epithet of al-Dahabi, 'the Golden'. The success of the Songhai campaign was the high-water mark of Saadi rule.

The dynasty did not long survive al-Mansur's death in 1603. His sons dissipated the inheritance he left them in internecine struggles over the succession, and the country fell apart as they fought for power. The unity that al-Mansur had so carefully fostered was shattered, and the nation fragmented into warring statelets. The Saadites themselves managed to cling onto power in Marrakesh and Fes for a further 56 years, but they were finally supplanted in the mid 17th century by the Alawites.

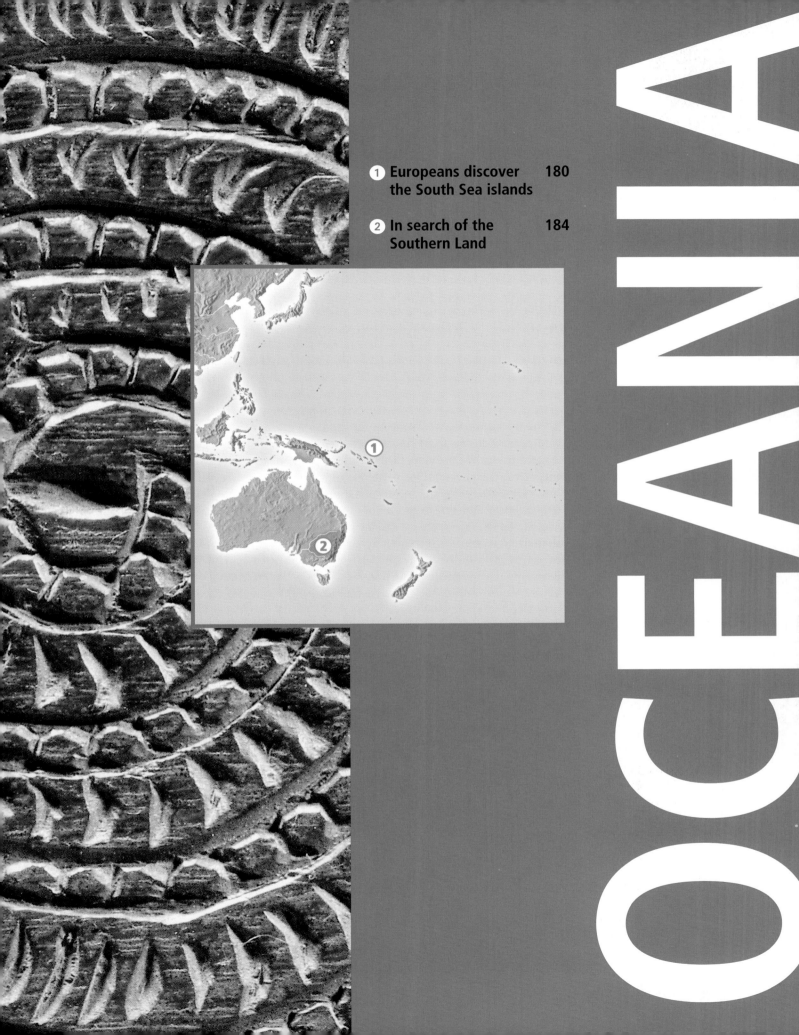

OCEANIA

Europeans discover the South Sea islands

Searching for uncharted territories and unknown riches, Spanish and Portuguese seafarers explored the Pacific Ocean. Magellan led the first European fleet there; one of his ships would make the first circumnavigation of the globe.

The first Europeans to set eyes on the Pacific were on foot. Like most other adventurers at the start of the 16th century, the 38-year-old Spaniard Vasco Núñez de Balboa was hoping to make his fortune. From natives of the Caribbean coast of Darién (a province in today's Panama) he had heard stories of a vast ocean that lay a short way to the west, so he organised an expedition to find it.

For 24 days Balboa and his men battled across the densely forested spine of the Isthmus of Panama. Then, at 11 o'clock on the morning of September 25, 1513, standing on a mountain ridge, they looked out over an endless expanse of blue ocean shimmering in the sunlight. Balboa called the water he had found the 'Southern Sea'; he had no way of knowing that this was the world's largest ocean.

South to the Pacific

Balboa gained little from his discovery – he was executed by a jealous governor six years later, and his head was set on a pole in the main square of the Darién settlement. But news of his find soon attracted other explorers. Back in Europe a Portuguese seafarer named Fernão de Magalhães persuaded the young Spanish King Charles I to fit out an expedition to find a passage to Balboa's Southern Sea. He aimed to sail around the southern tip of the Americas, thus fulfilling Christopher Columbus's dream of finding a westward passage to the Indies. Charles I later became better known as the Holy Roman Emperor Charles V, and Magalhães is remembered by an Anglicised form of his name as Ferdinand Magellan.

After some hesitation, Charles agreed to put five ships at Magellan's disposal. In September 1519 the small fleet set off westward across the Atlantic. They spent the winter months on the coast of Patagonia, then in August 1520 – early

Pathfinder to the Pacific
Although Ferdinand Magellan came from Portugal, he made his epic voyage of exploration under the Spanish flag. Twenty-eight years after Columbus's first voyage west, Magellan proved that the earlier explorer's belief in the existence of a westerly sea passage to Asia was not pie in the sky. Magellan was the first sea captain to sail from the Atlantic to the Pacific and his expedition went on to complete the first circumnavigation of the globe. A 16th-century map (background) by the Flemish cartographer Gerardus Mercator (a Latinisation of Gerhard Kremer) shows the round-the-world route.

spring in the southern hemisphere – set sail once more in search of a passage through to the Southern Sea.

Through the Strait of Magellan

On November 28, Magellan's fleet reached the strait that now bears his name, separating the southern tip of the South American mainland from the island of Tierra del Fuego. It took 38 days to thread a passage through the treacherous 500km (320 mile) channel, and only three vessels reached the other side. There, the open ocean looked so calm that Magellan named it the *Mare Pacificum* (Peaceful Sea).

First appearances were deceptive, however, for Magellan had seriously misjudged the width of the new ocean. He had hoped to reach the Spice Islands, with their lucrative harvest of cloves and nutmegs, within weeks, but three months and twenty days went by before the ships were able to take on fresh provisions. In that time the crews were reduced to surviving on leathery ox hides and worm-eaten biscuits by now soaked in rat's urine. They ate the rats too, when they could catch them. The water in the ship's barrels turned yellow and putrid. Scurvy soon started to take a toll, and the crew became listless and apathetic.

Land at last

Two months into their ordeal the sailors sighted land, but the island – Pukupuka, the most northerly of the Tuamotu group – had no suitable anchorage. Their luck was little better when, 11 days later, they reached land again. This time they tried to replenish their stocks by fishing, but their boats were quickly surrounded

by sharks. The fleet finally made land in early March, when it reached the island of Guam in the Marianas archipelago of Micronesia. Islanders swarmed out in canoes to meet them, and were welcomed aboard. Relations rapidly soured, however, when the visitors helped themselves to everything they could take, including one of the ship's boats, which Magellan could not afford to lose. To reclaim it he led a punitive expedition ashore, setting fire to the huts in the village where he found it.

Sailing on, the fleet soon reached the Philippines archipelago, which they claimed for Spain. At first they were well received by the native inhabitants, and Magellan established cordial relations with the local rulers. To cement the alliance, the admiral even allowed himself to be drawn into an inter-island dispute. It was a fatal mistake, for he was mortally wounded in the encounter, struck down by javelins and spears. He died on April 27, 1521.

The rest of the fleet pressed on, finally reaching the Spice Islands seven months later. By the time they set sail again, only

First ship around the world
After Magellan's death at the hands of hostile natives in the Philippines, his flagship, *Victoria*, sailed on under the command of the Basque Captain Juan Sebastian del Cano to complete the first circumnavigation of the globe. By the time the leaky vessel reached Seville on September 8, 1522, it carried just 17 Europeans and four islanders, plus a cargo of spices. Four more ships that had set out on the voyage were all lost along the way.

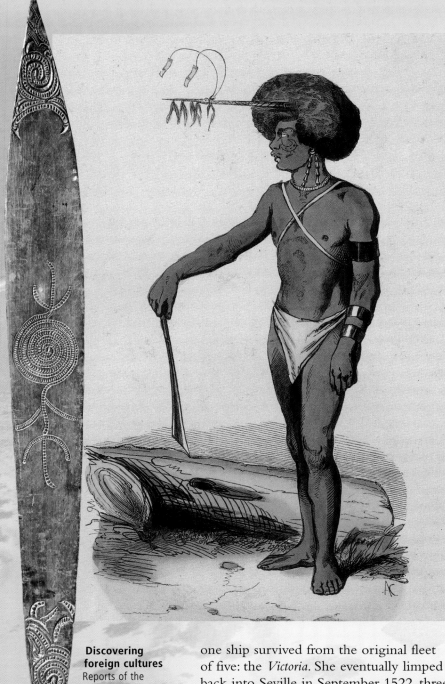

Discovering foreign cultures
Reports of the strange customs of South Sea islanders like this Papuan fascinated Europeans and influenced such literary works as Thomas More's *Utopia* and Shakespeare's *The Tempest*. Above left: a Maori paddle.

in 1529 the Spanish king conceded Portugal's claims to the islands in return for a large cash payment. Yet the voyage had shown that there were other island groups waiting to be discovered – and exploited. Explorers were drawn by the prospect of finding *Terra Incognita Australis*, the unknown southern land said to lie somewhere in the southern seas.

In 1567 the Spanish viceroy of Peru equipped two ships to search for this fabled land, giving command of the expedition to his nephew, Alvaro de Mendaña de Neyra. After 80 days at sea the explorers found an archipelago of inhabited islands. The hostility of the native inhabitants drove them on, but Mendaña's men spread such flattering tales of the discovery on their return to Peru that geographers called them the Solomon Islands, equating them with the Old Testament land of Ophir from which King Solomon acquired gold.

Even so, 26 years passed before Mendaña managed to raise the funds for a second expedition. When he finally did set sail, he took with him 378 prospective settlers in a fleet of four ships. *En route* for the Solomons, he found a nearer group of islands, which he named the Marquesas after his patron, the Marqués de Mendoza, then viceroy of Peru. Pressing on, the fleet missed its intended destination and touched land on the Santa Cruz Islands to the southeast. Mendaña's efforts to found a colony there were thwarted by an outbreak of fever that claimed his own life as well as that of many of the would-be settlers. With Mendaña's helmsman Pedro de Quiros now in command, the survivors set off again and struggled on through great hardship. They finally made port in the Spanish colony of Manila in the Philippines.

one ship survived from the original fleet of five: the *Victoria*. She eventually limped back into Seville in September 1522, three years after setting out, with 21 survivors on board. Even so, they had completed the first circumnavigation of the world.

The unknown southern land

Magellan's expedition did not yield the riches that Spain's King Charles had been hoping for. Even though it had found a westward path to the Spice Islands, the distances involved were too great to make the route commercially viable, and

An unclaimed discovery

Almost 10 years later, in December 1605, Quiros set out again. This time he found a larger island, which he optimistically named *Austrialia del Espíritu Santo*,

Southern Land of the Holy Spirit, thinking that he might have found the unknown continent of legend. In fact he had reached the island now known simply as Espíritu Santo in the Vanuatu group.

Quiros soon gave up the attempt to found a colony there after skirmishes with the islanders. At this point the three ships became separated. Quiros sailed one back to America, but his second in command, Captain Luis Váez de Torres, continued with the other two. They eventually found their way to Manila by way of the dangerous channel along the south coast of New Guinea, becoming the first Europeans to negotiate what would later be named the Torres Strait. Torres must have passed within 100km (60 miles) of the north coast of Australia, but no record of any sighting survives. After Torres' returned to Spain, the authorities hushed up all news of his journey for more than 150 years, wanting to keep any knowledge of the strait from falling into the hands of rival colonial powers. His discoveries only became public after Manila fell to the British in 1762.

A new route to the Pacific

Spain's colonial authorities had good reason to be secretive, for English and Dutch privateers were already creating havoc for them in Pacific waters. Francis Drake had blazed the trail in 1580, when he sailed through the Strait of Magellan on his way to completing the second circumnavigation of the world.

Thirty-five years later, two Dutch navigators, Willem Schouten and Jacob Le Maire, pioneered a new westward route around the tip of South America. Because access to the Magellan Strait was at that time controlled by the Dutch East India Company, rivals of their merchant employer (Jacob's father, Isaac), they sailed further south and found a way around Cape Horn. The passage they discovered lay between the southeastern tip of Tierra del Fuego and the outlying Isla de los Estados. It was longer but simpler than Magellan's route, and is still known as the Strait of Le Maire. By then Pacific navigation was ceasing to be a novelty, but the unknown southern land still waited to be discovered.

Surrounded by sea (background) An aerial view of Saipan, one of the Northern Mariana Islands.

Appropriate architecture Ceremonial halls formed the centrepiece of village life in many Oceanian cultures. The sacred house shown here was sketched on New Guinea by the 19th-century French naval explorer Dumont d'Urville.

In search of the Southern Land

Sailing to and from their bases in the East Indies, Dutch mariners were the first to touch land in Australia, but they did little to exploit the country they discovered by chance.

Willem Janszoon, the Dutch captain of the *Duyfken* (Little Dove) put to sea from Java in 1605 to search for new lands. His employers, the Dutch East India Company, were particularly interested in the 'land called Nova Guinea, which, it is said, is rich in gold'.

Janszoon set a course from the Javanese port of Bantam for the southern coast of New Guinea, which he followed for some 1300km (800 miles). His route took him to the western end of what would later be known as the Torres Strait. Convinced by its shoals and shallows that he was at the mouth of a bay, he turned south and so

missed out on discovering the channel between New Guinea and Australia; five months later the Spanish explorer Luis Váez de Torres navigated it from the east.

Janszoon's route took him to a barren land that he thought was a continuation of the New Guinea coastline. The native inhabitants were not friendly; nine men that he sent ashore to trade were killed. He returned home disheartened, not knowing that he had reached Australia's Cape York Peninsula and that his men had made the first European landfall on an unknown continent.

Hive of activity
From the late 16th century onwards, the Dutch plied a lucrative trade from bases on Java. The centre of commercial activity there was Jakarta, which they renamed Batavia, the Roman name for Holland, early in the 17th century.

South Sea idyll
In 1616 Dirk Hartog, a Dutch sea captain sailing from Holland en route for Java, happened upon the island that now bears his name off the coast of western Australia. He spent three days exploring the site and neighbouring Shark Bay (left) before continuing on his way.

Scholars going back as far as Ptolemy, in the 2nd century AD, had proposed the existence of *Terra Incognita Australis* – an Unknown Southern Land in the southern hemisphere to balance the great Eurasian landmass in the north. The hope of finding this continent was the inspiration for explorers in the South Seas from the mid 16th century onwards.

The Dutch took over the baton of Pacific exploration from the Spanish and Portuguese. Three years before Jaszoon's journey, various Dutch overseas trading companies on the island of Java had merged into one great conglomerate, the Dutch East India Company, with its headquarters on the north coast at Jakarta, later renamed Batavia (modern Jakarta). The company's aims were to exploit the lucrative trade in spices (while excluding Portuguese and English rivals from the region), to explore new markets, and wherever possible to discover better and quicker trade routes. Profit was the dominant motive, so unsuccessful ventures like Janszoon's acted as a strong deterrent to further open-seas exploration.

Chance landfalls

So Dutch exploration of Australasia was desultory, relying as it did on chance landfalls. From 1611 onwards, captains sailing from Holland discovered that they could dramatically reduce their sailing time from the tip of Africa to Batavia by heading due east from the Cape of Good Hope, rather than following Vasco da Gama's original route up the African coast and then across to India.

The new route took them directly towards Australia, and those who failed to turn northwards in time risked being driven by strong westerlies onto its coasts. In this way, Captain Dirk Hartog reached the island that now bears his name off the coast of western Australia on October 25, 1616. To commemorate the event, he engraved an inscription on a flattened pewter platter and nailed it to a tree. This improvised plaque remained there for the next 81 years until a compatriot took it home as a souvenir; it is now in the collections of the Rijksmuseum in Amsterdam.

Pieces of the puzzle
A fragmentary map indicates what was known of Australasia by 1644, in the wake of Abel Tasman's two seminal voyages of discovery.

Later, further chance discoveries persuaded the Dutch authorities of the existence of a substantial landmass in those latitudes, which they patriotically named New Holland. In 1623 a ship called the *Arnhem* was sent to follow the route taken by the *Duyfken* 18 years earlier and ended up tracking a previously unknown area of the north coast that subsequently became known as Arnhem's Land. In 1627 a ship sailing from Europe found its way to the southeastern corner of Australia and followed the continent's southern coastline for 1600km (1000 miles) before turning back.

Audacious seaman
In his lifetime, Abel Tasman got little recognition for his voyages of exploration, sponsored by the Dutch East India Company and its enterprising governor-general in Batavia, Anthony van Diemen. Tasman retired from seafaring at the age of 48, and spent the remaining 11 years of his life in Java as a wealthy landowner.

The accounts that mariners brought back with them of the shores they had sailed around were unremittingly grim. They described a land that was dry and barren, with no fruit trees or anything of obvious value. Some captains sent groups of men ashore to scout the coastal hinterland, but most of these ventures ended in armed confrontations with hostile natives, of whom the explorers had nothing good to say. Commercially motivated company officials could see little gain in following up their discoveries.

That situation changed when a new governor-general arrived in Batavia in 1636. Anthony van Diemen was a man of intense intellectual curiosity who was sure that there was much of value to be discovered in the southern seas. Having undertaken a thorough study of the logs of earlier explorers, he used his powers of persuasion to persuade the company directors to finance a voyage of discovery.

The discovery of Tasmania

The man van Diemen chose to lead the expedition was a 39-year-old sea captain called Abel Tasman. The governor-general provided him with two ships, the *Heemskerk* and the *Zeehaen*, and a crew of 110 men, along with provisions for a year and an assortment of trade goods to barter. On August 14, 1642, Tasman put to sea from Batavia to sail to the island of Mauritius, from where he turned back eastward on a southerly course.

On November 24 his lookouts spotted a mountainous coast, which he mistakenly took for the southern coast of New Holland. Claiming the territory for the Dutch East India Company, he named it Van Diemen's Land. In fact he had found the large offshore island that would later be called Tasmania in his honour.

Dropping anchor, Tasman sent a party of 11 men ashore to reconnoitre the new land. They returned saying that even though they had seen neither people nor signs of habitation, they were sure the land was inhabited; they had noticed smoke rising in the distance, and thought that they had heard voices close by. Before Tasman could himself land to clarify the mystery, adverse winds forced him to sail on, leaving his business there unfinished.

On to New Zealand

Heading due east, Tasman made another important discovery – the South Island of New Zealand. He skirted the east coast of the new land, then went on to make the first European landfalls on Tonga and Fiji, before returning to Java well within the 12-month deadline that had been set. Yet for all the geographical importance of his finds, he did not come back to a hero's welcome. There was no obvious immediate commercial application for any of his discoveries, and in addition he was criticised for not having done more to explore the lands that he had found.

Unfinished quest

Despite such misgivings, Van Diemen was prepared to give Tasman a second chance. In February 1644, he sent him to explore the north coast of New Holland. Like Captain Janszoon before him, Tasman missed discovering the Torres Strait, and so perpetuated the notion that New Guinea and New Holland formed part of a single landmass. But he did succeed in charting Australia's coastline from the Cape York Peninsula to the Northwest Cape.

Gradually, the pieces of the Australian jigsaw puzzle were falling into place. Thanks to the efforts of Tasman and those who had gone before him, the Dutch authorities were forming a picture of

BACKGROUND

From Van Diemen's Land to Tasmania

When Abel Tasman got his first sight of the west coast of what is now Tasmania, on November 24, 1642, he noted in the ship's log: 'This being the first land that we have encountered in the Southern Sea, and it not being claimed by any European nation, we named it Van Diemen's Land in honour of our illustrious patron and governor-general'. The name was changed in the mid 19th century, because 'Van Diemen's Land' was by then associated in people's minds with the brutal penal settlement established there by the British in colonial times. It has been known ever since as Tasmania.

New Holland, albeit an incomplete one, with huge gaps where its east and northeast coasts lay.

Yet with Tasman's second voyage the process of exploration came to an abrupt end. One reason was the death of Van Diemen, chief patron of the exploration, in 1645. Equally important were the views of the East India Company directors in Amsterdam, who let their representatives in Batavia know in no uncertain terms that their patience with unprofitable ventures was exhausted. In their view the company had as much business on its hands as it could handle, and there was little to be gained by opening up new markets that it had neither the money nor the manpower to exploit.

Another century would pass before English mariners took up the challenge that the Dutch had abandoned, finally opening up Australia for European settlement.

Unknown coast
Tasman's mission on his first voyage of 1642–3 was a double one: to find the southern continent and to discover a southerly route from the Indian Ocean to the Pacific and on to Chile. While pursuing these goals he discovered the island of Tasmania (below).

Abbeviations: t = top, c = centre, b = below,
l = left, r = right, T = Timeline, B = background.

AAA = Ancient Art & Architecture Collection
akg = akg-images
BAL = Bridgeman Art Library
RMN = Réunion des Musées nationaux
TAA = The Art Archive

Front cover: Queen Elizabeth I of England – by courtesy of the National Portrait Gallery, London
Back cover, top to bottom: Artothek; Interfoto/Photos12; BPK; RMN/Michele Bellot/BPK; Fotoarchiv, Staatliches Museum für Völkerkunde, Munich

1: RMN/BPK; 2/3: Samana Peninsula, Dominican Republic – Alamy Images © mediacolor's; 4/5: Artothek; 6: TAA/Musee des Beaux Arts Dijon/Dagli Orti; 7 and T: Interfoto/Wilfried Wirth; 8: Interfoto/Aisa; 9 b: Interfoto/Alinari; 9: Interfoto/Bildarchiv Hansmann; 10: TAA/Palazzo Farnese Caprarola/ Dagli Orti; 11 t: TAA/Dagli Orti (A); 12: akg/Erich Lessing; 13 b: TAA/Musee de la Renaissance (Chateau) Ecouen/Dagli Orti; 13: Interfoto/Aisa; 14 and T: akg; 15: Interfoto/Antonius; 16/17t: Interfoto/Zeit Bild; 17: Interfoto/Karl-Heinz Hänel; 18: Interfoto/Toni Schneiders; 19: Interfoto/Aisa; 19 t: Historical Picture Archive/Corbis; 20 Scala/Florence; 20 B: lookGaleria/ Alamy; 21: Interfoto/Aisa; 21 r and T: Interfoto/Photos12; 22: Interfoto/Aisa; 23 l and r: Interfoto/Sammlung Rauch; 23 B and T: Interfoto/Archiv Friedrich; 24: ullstein/Granger Collection; 25 t: Interfoto/Aisa; 25 b: Scala; 26 t: ullstein/ Granger Collection; 26 b: Interfoto/V & A; 27 b and T: Interfoto/AAAC; 27 t: The British Library; 28 b: Interfoto/AAAC; 28: Interfoto/Toni Schneiders; 29 t: Interfoto/ Karger-Decker; 29 b: Interfoto/V & A; 30: Interfoto/Bildarchiv Hansmann; 31 b: DHM Berlin; 31 and T: Interfoto/Victor Radnicky; 32 b: Interfoto/Karl-Heinz Hänel; 32 b: Interfoto/A. Koch; 33/34/35: akg; 36: Interfoto/AAAC; 36 B: TAA/Museo Correr Venice/Dagli Orti; 37: akg; 38: akg/Gerard Degeorge; 38: TAA/Topkapi Museum, Istanbul/Dagli Orti; 39/40: Interfoto/ Aisa; 41: akg; 41 B: Interfoto/V & A; 42: Interfoto/Alinari; 43: akg; 44: Interfoto/Aisa; 44 t: TAA/University Library, Geneva/Dagli Orti; 45: akg/Erich Lessing; 46/48: Interfoto/ Aisa; 49 t: Interfoto/AAAC; 49 b: Markus Bassler/Bildarchiv Monheim; 49: Interfoto/ V & A; 50 b: Interfoto/Photos12; 50 t: Interfoto/V & A; 51 t: Interfoto/Aisa; 51 and T: Interfoto/Mary Evans; 52 b and T: Interfoto/Photos12; 52: Interfoto/Alinari; 53: RMN/ BPK; 54: Interfoto/ Photos12; 54: David A. Barnes/Alamy; 55 Interfoto/Aisa; 56 and T: Interfoto/Aisa; 56: Brand X Pictures/Alamy; 58: TAA/University Library, Geneva/Dagli Orti; 59: BAL; 60: Interfoto/A. Koch; 61 b and T: Interfoto/ Bildarchiv Hansmann; 61: Interfoto/ Toni Schneiders; 62 b: akg/Erich Lessing; 62: Joachim Blauel/Artotek; 62: Interfoto/Hermann Historica OHG; 64 t and br: Dalibor Kusak/Artotek; 64 b: akg/Erich Lessing; 65 t: Interfoto/Aisa; 65: akg; 66 b: Interfoto/ Photos12; 66: akg; 67: Interfoto/Aisa; 67 B: Interfoto/Archiv Friedrich; 68/69 Interfoto/Photos12; 70: Interfoto/Aisa; 71: Courtesy of the Warden and Scholars of New College, Oxford/BAL; 72: Interfoto/Sammlung Rauch; 73: National Maritime Museum; 73 b: Interfoto/ Science & Society; 74: National Maritime Museum; 74 b: National Library of Australia, Canberra/BAL; 74 t and T: akg/Erich Lessing; 75 t: Interfoto/AAAC; 75: Interfoto/ Photos12; 76 tr, tl and T: Interfoto/Aisa; 76: TAA/Album/ Joseph Martin; 77: TAA/Biblioteca Nacional, Madrid/Dagli Orti; 78 b: Interfoto/Photos12; 78 b: TAA/Palazzo Pitti Florence/Dagli Orti (A); 79 t: Interfoto/ Aisa; 79 b: TAA/ Museo Nacional Tiahuanaco, La Paz, Bolivia/Dagli Orti; 80 b: Interfoto/ Aisa; 80: Biblioteca Universidad, Barcelona, Index/BAL; 81: Interfoto/Aisa; 81 t: Interfoto/Bildarchiv Hansmann; 82 ullstein bild; 83: TAA/Biblioteca d'Ajuda, Lisbon/Dagli Orti; 84 b: Interfoto/Aisa; 84 t: Musee Departemental des Antiquites, Rouen, Lauros/BAL; 85: ullstein/Granger Collection; 86: akg; 87 b: picture alliance; 87 t: TAA/National History Museum, Mexico City/Dagli Orti; 88 b: Biblioteca del ICI, Madrid, Index/BAL; 88: Interfoto/Photos12; 89: TAA/Biblioteca Nazionale Marciana, Venice/Dagli Orti; 90 c and T: Interfoto/Bildarchiv Hansmann; 90: akg/Gilles Mermet; 91: akg; 91: Interfoto/Aisa; 92: akg; 93 b and T: Interfoto/Mary Evans; 93: TAA/Plymouth Art

Gallery/Eileen Tweedy; 94 t and T: Privatsammlung, The Stapleton Collection/BAL; 94 b: Scala/Florence; 95: Scala; 95 B: fotofinder; 96 t: New York Public Library/BAL; 96 b: Interfoto/Photos12; 97/98: ullstein/Granger Collection; 99: Interfoto/Aisa; 99 b: TAA/Musee de la Marine Paris/Dagli Orti; 100: Interfoto/ Aisa; 101 b and T: Interfoto/Bildarchiv Hansmann; 10 t: Glenn Harper/Alamy; 102 b: Visions of America, LLC/ Alamy; 102 t: Bettmann/Corbis; 102: Courtesy of Pilgrim Hall Museum, Plymouth, Massachusetts; 103: Interfoto/Aisa; 103 b: North Wind Picture Archives; 105 b: TAA/Museo Navale, Genoa/Dagli Orti (A); 106 bl: BAL; 106 br: Interfoto/AAAC; 106 t: TAA/Bibliotheque Nationale. Paris; 107 bl: British Museum, London, UK, Boltin Picture Library/BAL; 107 tr: Interfoto/Science & Society; 107 br: Interfoto/Aisa; 108: Joel W. Rogers/Corbis; 109: Museo Correr, Venice/Giraudon/BAL; 109 bl: Interfoto/A. Koch; 109 t: akg; 110 b: Interfoto/Bildarchiv Hansmann; 110 t: akg/Erich Lessing; 111: akg; 111 tl: DHM, Berlin; 111 tr: Interfoto/V & A; 112: Interfoto/Sammlung Rauch; 112: Interfoto/Artcolor; 112 b: Interfoto/A. Koch; 113: Interfoto/Karger-Decker; 114/115: BPK; 116: Interfoto/Aisa; 117: ullstein/Granger Collection; 117 l and T: TAA/Laurie Platt Winfrey; 118: akg/Werner Forman; 119: Interfoto/Aisa; 119 B: Interfoto/Alinari; 119: Interfoto/V & A; 120 B: Interfoto/Aisa; 120 and T: akg/Werner Forman; 121/122 tr: Interfoto/Aisa; 122: Interfoto/Alinari; 123: Interfoto/AAAC; 123 B: TAA/British Museum, London/Harper Collins Publishers; 124: Interfoto/AAAC; 124 t and T: TAA/Museu do Caramulo, Portugal/Dagli Orti; 125: Interfoto/Aisa; 126: akg; 127 b: TAA/British Library; 127 t: TAA/Service Historique de la Marine Vincennes/Dagli Orti; 128 and T: ullstein/Granger Collection; 129: Roger Wood/Corbis; 130 and T: Interfoto/Mary Evans; 131 t: BPK; 131 b: Dave Bartruff/Corbis; 132: TAA/British Library; 133 t: Interfoto/Aisa; 133 br: Privatsammlung, Bonhams, London/BAL; 133 bl: RMN/Martine Beck-Coppola/BPK; 133 B: Interfoto/V & A; 134 t: Livrustkammaren (The Royal Armoury), Stockholm/BAL; 134: World Religions Photo Library/Alamy; 135: Scala/Florence; 136 B: Interfoto/Photos12; 136 b: The Trustees of The British Museum; 137 t and b: Scala; 138: akg; 139: RMN/Thierry Ollivier/BPK; 140: Interfoto/Aisa; 140 t: Interfoto/V & A; 141: Klaus Fessel; 142 and T: Interfoto/Mary Evans; 143: RMN/ Thierry Ollivier/ BPK; 143: Michael Freeman/Corbis; 144: Privatsammlung, Dinodia/BAL; 144: Rainer Kiedrowski/Bildarchiv Monheim; 145 t: Interfoto/AAAC; 145: Interfoto/V & A; 146: akg/Gerard Degeorge; 146 and T: Chris George/Alamy; 147: Rainer Kiedrowski/Bildarchiv Monheim; 148: RMN/Herve Lewandowski/BPK; 149 b, B and T: RMN/Thierry Ollivier/BPK; 149 t: KPA; 150: Interfoto/Aisa; 151: Hulton-Deutsch Collection/Corbis; 152: Morandi/Mauritius images; 153 b: akg; 153 t: TAA/Navy Historical Service Vincennes France/Dagli Orti; 154/155: RMN/Michele Bellot/BPK; 156 and T: Robert Harding Picture Library Ltd/Alamy; 157 and T: akg; 158 b: BAL; 158: The Trustees of The British Museum; 159 B: akg/Joseph Martin; 159: TAA/Marine Museum, Lisbon/Dagli Orti; 160 t and T: akg; 160 Danita Delimont/Alamy; 161 b: BAL; 162: RMN/Michele Bellot/BPK; 163: The Minneapolis Institute of Arts/The Eitel Morrison Van Derlip Fund; 164 and T: Christies Images/Corbis; 165: akg/Cameraphoto; 167: Interfoto/Friedel Gierth; 168 and T, 169: Interfoto/Aisa; 170: RMN/BPK; 170: TAA/Biblioteca Nazionale Marciana, Venice/Dagli Orti; 171 b: picture alliance; 172: BAL; 172: David Wall/Alamy; 174: Sandro Vannini/Corbis; 175 and T: Rapho/laif; 176: Interfoto/Aisa; 176 B: ullstein/Granger Collection; 177: mauritius images/Rossenbach; 178/179: Fotoarchiv, Staatliches Museum für Völkerkunde, Munich; 180 tl: Interfoto/Karger-Decker; 180: Interfoto/Aisa; 180: KPA; 181 and T: Interfoto/Sammlung Rauch; 182: TAA/Musee des Arts Decoratifs, Paris/Dagli Orti (A); 182: Kenny Williams/Alamy; 182 l: Fotoarchiv, Staatliches Museum für Völkerkunde, Munich; 183: TAA/Musee de la Marine Paris/Dagli Orti; 184: ullstein/Granger Collection; 185 b and T: Interfoto/Karger-Decker; 185: Sergio Pitamitz/Alamy; Privatsammlung/BAL; 187: TAA/Travelsite/Global.

Maps originated by Kartographic Müller & Richert GbR, Gotha, Germany, and translated into English by Alison Ewington.

The Illustrated History of the World:
DISCOVERY AND RELIGIOUS CRISIS was published by The Reader's Digest Association Ltd, London.

The Reader's Digest Association Ltd
11 Westferry Circus, Canary Wharf, London E14 4HE
www.readersdigest.co.uk

First English edition copyright © 2006

Reader's Digest English Edition
Series editor: Christine Noble
Volume editor/writer: Tony Allan
Translated from German by: Peter Lewis
Designer: Jane McKenna
Copy editor: Jill Steed
Proofreader: Ron Pankhurst
Indexer: Marie Lorimer
Product production manager: Claudette Bramble
Production controller: Katherine Bunn

Reader's Digest, General Books
Editorial director: Julian Browne
Art director: Nick Clark
Prepress account manager: Sandra Fuller

Colour proofing: Colour Systems Ltd, London
Printed and bound by: Arvato Iberia, Europe

We are committed to the quality of our products and the service we provide to our customers. We value your comments, so please feel free to contact us on 08705 113366, or via our website at: **www.readersdigest.co.uk** If you have any comments or suggestions about the content of our books, you can email us at: **gbeditorial@readersdigest.co.uk**

First published as *Reader's Digest Illustrierte Weltgeschichte: ENTDECKUNGEN UND GLAUBENSKRISE* © 2006 Reader's Digest – Deutschland, Schweiz, Österreich Verlag Das Beste GmbH – Stuttgart, Zürich, Vienna

Reader's Digest, German Edition
Writers: Monika Dreykorn, Karin Feuerstein-Praßer, Andrea Groß-Schulte, Marion Jung, Dr. Cornelia Lawrenz, Dr Wolfgang Mayer, Otto Schertler, Karin Schneider-Ferber, Harry D. Schurdel, Dr. Holger Sonnabend, Dr. Roland Weis
Editing and design: MCS Schabert GmbH
Colour separations: Meyle + Müller GmbH + Co., Pforzheim.

CONCEPT CODE: GR 0081/G/S
BOOK CODE: 632-007-1
ISBN (10): 0 276 44123 0
ISBN (13): 978 0 276 44123 3
ORACLE CODE: 351600017H.00.24